Praise for *Dinner with DiMaggio*

"His baseball accomplishments, impressive and historic as they are, do not alone explain why DiMaggio's name still resonates as it does. His importance is connected to a particular place and time in the history of the game and the country. Hemingway referenced DiMaggio. So did Paul Simon. A line from the early '40s song 'Joltin' Joe DiMaggio' by the Les Brown Orchestra goes like this: 'He lives in baseball's Hall of Fame, he got there blow-by-blow, our kids will tell their kids his name, Joltin' Joe DiMaggio.' Turns out that was true."

—Bob Costas

"So many special things about Joe DiMaggio are revealed by this book—his love of children, his contempt of pretense, and his iconic place in American history—all brought forth here by his closest friend in New York, Dr. Rock Positano. Joe was quiet, not silent, about the pivotal events of the twentieth century, and he shared them with Dr. Positano: Marilyn, the Kennedys, Frank Sinatra, and so many fascinating anecdotes add flesh to the bare bones of this iconic American. This is an important book because Joe is the hero we need in these times: Joe, as Dr. Positano shows, did not compromise his principles for political correctness, hurt feelings, or the favor of the crowd. He was a true American original."

—Arianna Huffington

"Joe DiMaggio brought a unique excitement to New York City, his adopted hometown, which extended beyond baseball. Joe's great friend Dr. Rock Positano conveys the excitement of DiMaggio's reign beautifully in this book. It is a thrill to read from cover to cover."

—David N. Dinkins, 106th Mayor, City of New York

"Joe DiMaggio and Rock Positano were fortunate to have found each other, a genuine hero in need of a genuine healer, each an expert in his field. Rock's professional skills are matched by his kindness and generosity of spirit. There will never be another Joe. But we are all fortunate to have the equally singular Rock still exercising his skills as both doctor and friend."

—Frank Langella

"Joe DiMaggio loved and trusted Rock for all the reasons so many of us do: He is a friend who never shies away from *your* battles, but joins them instead. All of us face adversity in life. Having Dr. Positano as a friend is like having a thousand friends. DiMaggio recognized his ability to make people feel secure and safe from the challenges and stress of everyday life. Those of us, like Joe DiMaggio, who have Rock by our sides walk a little steadier, in more ways than one."

—Keith Ablow, MD, Fox News Network

"Dr. Rock Positano is not only a phenomenally gifted doctor, he is a hugely empathetic companion who understands and treats the whole person, not just the injury. Joe DiMaggio found in the good doctor an Italian-American brother and a confidant. The result is this strikingly intimate portrait of a man who has often seemed as private and remote as he is heroic. Paul Simon famously asked, 'Where have you gone, Joe DiMaggio?' We have the answer now: You can find him right here."

—Anthony DeCurtis, contributing editor, *Rolling Stone*

"This book summarizes so many of the vibrant principles I espouse . . . the importance of being you . . . the critical need of sharing your 'authentic self' undiluted by worry or criticism. I am pleased that this very genuine American hero was also a strong believer in being himself . . . Joe DiMaggio . . . without fail . . . and with no worries. . . ."

—Tony Robbins, author of *Unshakeable*

DINNER WITH
DiMAGGIO

Memories of an American Hero

DR. ROCK POSITANO
and JOHN POSITANO

With a Foreword by
Francis Ford Coppola

And an Introduction by
Fay T. Vincent

Simon & Schuster
New York London Toronto Sydney New Delhi

Simon & Schuster
1230 Avenue of the Americas
New York, NY 10020

First Simon & Schuster hardcover edition May 2017

SIMON & SCHUSTER and colophon are registered trademarks of Simon & Schuster, Inc.

For information about special discounts for bulk purchases, please contact Simon & Schuster Special Sales at 1-866-506-1949 or business@simonandschuster.com.

The Simon & Schuster Speakers Bureau can bring authors to your live event. For more information or to book an event, contact the Simon & Schuster Speakers Bureau at 1-866-248-3049 or visit our website at www.simonspeakers.com.

Interior design by Renato Stanisic

Manufactured in the United States of America

10 9 8 7 6 5 4 3 2 1

Library of Congress Cataloging-in-Publication Data

Names: Positano, Rock G., author. | Positano, John, author.
Title: Dinner with Dimaggio : Memories of an American Hero / by Dr. Rock Positano and John Positano ; With a foreword by Francis Ford Coppola.
Description: First Simon & Schuster hardcover edition. | New York : Simon & Schuster, 2017. | Includes index.
Identifiers: LCCN 2016051476| ISBN 9781501156847 (hardback) | ISBN 1501156845 | ISBN 9781501156861 (ebook)
Subjects: LCSH: DiMaggio, Joe, 1914–1999. | Baseball players—United States—Biography. | BISAC: BIOGRAPHY & AUTOBIOGRAPHY / Sports. | SPORTS & RECREATION / Baseball / General. | SPORTS & RECREATION / General.
Classification: LCC GV865.D5 P67 2017 | DDC 796.357092 [B] —dc23 LC record available at https://lccn.loc.gov/2016051476

ISBN 978-1-5011-5684-7
ISBN 978-1-5011-5686-1 (ebook)

This book is dedicated to the team of people who made it possible:

Frances and Rocco Positano
Isabel and Angelo Positano
Antoinette and Daniel Bagnuola
Nonna Ninci and Tino
Rosalia and Giuseppe DiMaggio

Bill and Dolores Gallo
Joseph P. DiMaggio Jr.
Dominic P. DiMaggio
Vincent P. DiMaggio
Positano Clan

Morris Engelberg, Esq.
Marilyn Monroe
Dorothy Arnold
Cathy and Dick Burke
Mario Faustini
Nat Recine
Johnny Arcaro
Paula DiMaggio Hamra
Kathie DiMaggio Stein

Barry Halper
Fay Vincent
George Steinbrenner
Gianni Garavelli
Brotherhood and Sisterhood of
Alpha Phi Delta (APD)
St. Athanasius Parish,
Brooklyn, New York

Contents

Foreword

When I was a boy of seven, I was a passionate baseball fan, a New York Yankees fan, as was my father. He had once met Babe Ruth, and I was so proud of that. My father was a classical flute player, but would volunteer to play piccolo with the band at Yankee Stadium to see the games for free. It was at that time that he met the Babe—the "Bambino," the "Sultan of Swat!"

Two years later, I became a statistic during the infantile paralysis epidemic of 1949 and found myself paralyzed, unable to walk or move any part of the left side of my body. My mother told me that had I died, they would have always wept when they saw a baseball game, because I had always said I wanted to be a baseball player.

My father was the chief musical arranger at Radio City Music Hall during that dark time. The big boss of the Music Hall was Leon Leonidoff, who, as it turned out, was a good friend of Joe DiMaggio. Somehow, the Yankee Clipper learned of my condition, a nine-year-old Yankee fan lying paralyzed at home. He took a new, clean baseball and brought it to each team member of the 1949 World Champs, and each one signed it, along with a prominent DiMaggio signature on the top, and my father brought that ball home to me.

Each signature was in different ink, so I knew the ball was the real thing and not a printed or mass produced signed ball. It meant so much to me that Joe had taken the ball in his hand and went one by one to have all of his teammates sign it, including Yogi Berra, Phil Rizzuto, Stirnweiss, Bobby Brown—all my heroes.

I loved Joe DiMaggio for this kindness shown to a boy he didn't know. Whenever something happened to him, his career, and his marriage, I remembered my feeling of gratitude and appreciation for his kindness to me.

Of course, I still have that baseball. The signatures have faded somewhat due to exposure to light, but I can still make out the names and, most prominently, Joe DiMaggio's beautiful signature.

Francis Ford Coppola
AUGUST 2016

Introduction

L et me be clear at the outset: Joe DiMaggio was my hero as a kid growing up in New Haven. One of the sublime delights of my professional life was the time I spent with the Yankee Clipper, and the opportunity I was afforded to know him as a friend. I got to work with Joe on baseball and personal issues and to enjoy many quiet meals with him and Dr. Rock Positano. This book is the product of their relationship, fueled by robust plates of superb pasta.

There have been many books written about Joe, because he was so gifted at his profession, yet so enigmatic. He remains fascinating. Though his elegant baseball life was public, his insistent demand for privacy keeps him unknown to this day. To describe him as quiet is to concede the inadequacy of the word. He simply did not want others to intrude into those unique places in his psyche where he found motivation to excel and the rewards of being an adulated sports figure.

This book is Dr. Rock's attempt to share with the rest of us the remarkable person the Great Joe Di was. There is a Joe in these pages who will surprise and delight those who never witnessed the shielded side of Joe. Who knew he was so religious, so insecure about being Italian, and so patriotic?

I was fortunate to become a friend—I say this carefully—of Dom, the youngest DiMaggio brother. I knew the enormous respect in which Dom held his older brother. When I asked Dom which pitcher gave him the most trouble, his answer was Bob Feller. I was surprised and reminded him Joe had told me he had little trouble hitting Feller.

Dom's admonition was full of pride.

"Commissioner, my brother could hit everyone, so you cannot go by that."

Dom's allegiance to Joe was rooted in the shared experiences he and Joe endured as Italian kids who knew the sting of discrimination. This book is written by one successful Italian about another one. Joe would be pleased.

In my long baseball-watching life, I consider Joe the best baseball player I ever saw play. Today, the statistical summary of his career is notably glorious. His career BA is .325; he played on nine World Series teams in his thirteen years; he won two batting titles and three MVP awards. He also hit 361 home runs while striking out only 369 times in his entire career. His fifty-six-game hitting streak in 1941 is a record that may never be broken.

These statistics do not tell of the times he saved a game with a superb catch or throw, of the times he stretched a single to a double late in a game in the effort to get a win, or of the times he made a smart play that preserved a victory or prevented a loss. His teammate Dr. Bobby Brown made that point at the memorial service for Joe. Bobby said you had to play with him to know how great he was. Joe DiMaggio was the leader of a team that always seemed to win.

This book is about a man and not simply about a baseball player. Joe was much too complex a person to be forced into a box. This book is about the good Joe. Dr. Positano has shown us the Joe he knew while also letting us see why he so admired and respected Joe as a friend.

Of course, none of us could ever ignore that Joe was the great man at our table when we sat with him. He exuded the aura of royalty that is imbued in the greats who roam among the rest of us. Joe had been burned by the many who wanted something from him. He trusted very few. Wary and hesitant, he felt comfortable only with those who let him define their relationship. He knew only his way.

He surely trusted Dr. Positano. You are about to enjoy this book about a complex and interesting man who also played great center field. This book invites you and me into some surprising corners of the DiMaggio world. I can still see Joe moving under a high fly ball hit to his centerfield, but now I can listen to Joe as he talked to Rock. Joe, the player, rarely spoke. Rock and few others knew the off-field person. This book adds to the legend by opening up the man in some new ways.

In his time, Joe was an enormous public personality. The best thing I can say about this book is that Joe was worthy of the attention he generated. The book demonstrates why that is true.

Fay T. Vincent
COMMISSIONER OF
BASEBALL, 1989-92

DINNER WITH
DiMAGGIO

CHAPTER 1

The Last American Hero

Tuesday, June 15, 1993

Called my grand daughter Paula at 9:15 A.M. — which is 6:15 in California. We finally got to talk. She has been working most the time at Longs drug store at night — the reason we have not connected. Last night, she went to her daughters' stage show, which took place at night. and she did not get home until 11:00 PM. Thats why Paula did not kall — as it was 2:15 PM. here. She told me that Vanessa did a very good job as a "fire bug". She was the lead girl. My one big regret is that I was not there. Paula told me, that Vanessa kept asking for me — as she wanted me to watch her. and frankly I did tell her sometime ago that I would watch for perform. I used to go and watch her at school during her class (Ballet). I forgot it completely. as at least I would have called her to explain, before the show.

I decided to write this memoir on what would have been Joe DiMaggio's hundredth birthday, November 25, 2014. We had become close friends during the last ten years of his life, despite more than forty years' difference in our ages. I had tried to write my memories of Joe with the help of others. The chemistry was never right, and it didn't work. On his centennial, I realized that only I could write this book, with my brother John, because it is so personal. Nobody knows the landscape better than the two of us. I intended to write a memoir of my friendship with Joe DiMaggio, not another baseball book.

I had invited his family for dinner at Campagnola on the Upper East Side to celebrate the memory of "Big Joe," as his great-grandkids called him. His granddaughter Paula and her husband Jim Hamra along with their daughters Vanassa, her new husband, and Valerie joined me for the celebration. I felt privileged to sit at the dinner table with the people whom Joe Di loved and cared for the most in the world. I know Big Joe would have been thrilled that we were having a family dinner to celebrate his birthday. Since the dinner table was sacred to Joe, *Dinner with DiMaggio* seemed the perfect title for this memoir.

As we enjoyed our meal, our conversation was full of the Yankee Clipper, one of the great heroes of the twentieth century. As I recounted stories he had told me, it became evident that they had never heard many of them. It was a revelation to me that Joe Di didn't share many of his stories with his family. When it came to his family, it was all about them. He always put them first. When he was with them, they were the focus, not his legend. For Joe DiMaggio, kids always took precedence, no matter who else was in the room.

I had learned that he compartmentalized his life as a means of self-preservation. Joe's life was a jigsaw puzzle, and only he had all the pieces. He believed that if no one could put it all together, he would have more freedom. Joe was always in control. His insistence on privacy is critical to understanding Joe as an icon and a man.

"Doc, there's a difference—a big difference—between secrecy and privacy," Joe explained to me one day as we drove through the rat maze of Manhattan traffic. "Secrecy is when you hide something, but privacy is when you have information that's privileged, that belongs to nobody except family. That's the reason you never tell anyone about your kids, your family life, or your personal life. They will use it against you if they could. You always need to protect your family."

I have followed his advice to this day.

Joe had a life in Florida, a life in California, and a life in New York. He made sure that no one life ever totally intersected with the others. People in Florida knew certain things that people in New York and California did not, and the same was true of the other places where he spent time. That's probably one of the reasons there have been so many books and such a variety of opinions about Joe, because no one knew him completely. In the end, only he held all the pieces of the puzzle, and he always kept us guessing.

Joe reminded me of a theory I learned in quantum physics at New York University, the Heisenberg uncertainty principle. Simply stated, this theory holds that the position and velocity of an object cannot be measured exactly at the same time. For Joe it was the DiMaggio uncertainty principle regarding who he was.

Joe was inscrutable to journalists and hearsay biographers, because he was closed mouth about personal information. He knew that the less he said, the more control he had over his image. His personal life was a forbidden zone. To his credit, there was never a double standard, because he would not intrude into the privacy of others. People who did not know him well sometimes judged him to be aloof, remote, even shy, which was far from the truth. He often commented that people who had never even sat down with him for a cup of coffee could not write a book about him.

———

MY FRIENDSHIP WITH Joe DiMaggio began with the heel spur in his right foot that had sidelined him for sixty-five games in 1949, one of the physical ailments that forced him to retire in 1951. It led to our meeting thirty-nine years later in 1990.

At thirty-two, I had a fledgling foot-and-ankle practice in Manhattan at the Hospital for Special Surgery. I specialized in nonsurgical treatment of foot and ankle disorders. I credit Joe's famously botched heel-spur surgery and Leonardo da Vinci's anatomical drawings of the foot and ankle as my inspirations for developing nonsurgical programs while I was at Yale Medical School and the New York College of Podiatric Medicine in Harlem. The nonsurgical ethos was considered a unique approach to caring for foot-and-ankle problems.

Bill Gallo, the dean of American sportswriters and a brilliant cartoonist at the *New York Daily News*, introduced me to the Yankee Clipper. As Bill told me, while he was having lunch one day with Joe at a restaurant on West Thirty-fourth Street, the Clipper complained about his still painful right heel, which continued to give him trouble and affect his quality of life. Bill thought I could help Joe, so he mentioned that he had a good friend who had done a lot of work on heel pain and foot disorders at Yale. That was a plus for me, because Joe's son had attended Yale, and Joe had great respect for Ivy League education. Bill offered to see if I could help him with his problem. Gallo also mentioned that I was a guy Joe might like to hang out with. According to Bill, Joe looked skeptical and did not appear terribly enthusiastic.

Joe prized the streetwise virtue of complete discretion. His friendship with a journalist was a departure from the norm for him. Gallo was the exception to the no-journalist rule, because he kept his mouth shut. Dave Anderson of the *New York Times* was another member of this very exclusive club. Charlie Rose, the late Tim Russert, Bob Costas, Al Michaels, and Bryant Gumbel also made the exclusive and coveted DiMaggio safe-zone list. He would have no problem talking in an elevator in front of these journalists. In his eyes, they were all honorable and maintained the highest professional standards and discretion.

"Doc," Joe explained to me later, "When you tell Gallo something is off the record, it is just that. You'll never see it appear somewhere else. That's a trick you see with these newspaper fellows. They'll tell you something is off the record, then trade the information with another one of their buddies. Then it shows up somewhere else. Not Gallo. His word is his word: no tricks, smoke, or mirrors."

Gallo called me and asked me to do him a favor. He wanted me to see a friend of his, who was coincidentally staying in the same building as my office at Sixty-eighth Street and Fifth Avenue.

Whenever he was in town, Joe stayed at the seventh-floor apartment of Atlantic City restaurateur Dick Burke, located on Fifth Avenue. Dick Burke was a Horatio Alger figure, a rags-to-riches former street waif who, as a boy, had sold newspapers to Joe when Joe strolled on the boardwalk in Atlantic City. Dick had gone on to be a big success, and eventually opened the Irish Pub on St. James Place in Atlantic City, where Joe was always a welcome guest. Dick Burke and his wife, Cathy, were family to Joe. Since the Burkes spent little time at their Fifth Avenue place, they gave Joe a key, and 860 Fifth Avenue became Joe's home base in New York. The Burkes were remarkably gracious and generous to Joe, and he returned the favor.

When Bill told me his friend was Joe DiMaggio, all I could say was, "You're kidding me."

After assuring me that he wasn't pulling my leg, Gallo advised me to drop Joe a note.

I was eager to make the connection. I gave the doorman a note, which read, "Hi, I'm Dr. Rock Positano, Bill Gallo's friend, and he asked me to drop you this note."

I didn't expect anything to come of it. At about six forty-five that evening, my assistant, Christine Albano, answered the doorbell, to find two men at the door. One of them was unmistakably Joe DiMaggio, impeccably dressed in an overcoat, blazer, shirt, and tie. She buzzed me and announced, "You're not going to believe who's out here and wants to say hello."

"Who is it?" I asked, near the end of a long day.

"Joe DiMaggio, with his friend, Mr. Burke."

Her answer nearly knocked me off my feet. I couldn't believe he actually had come down to say hello to me the same day I sent him the note.

I raced to the reception area with my hand extended and said, "Mr. DiMaggio, it's an honor to meet you."

Joe, always a consummate gentleman, turned to Dick Burke and said, "Dr. Positano, I would like you to meet my dear friend, Mr. Burke."

"Mr. Burke, it is a pleasure to meet you." I matched his formality.

Then Joe cut in. "I've heard a lot about you, Doc, from our friend Bill Gallo."

"That's great, Mr. DiMaggio," I responded, not knowing how important being a mutual friend was to Joltin' Joe. An introduction from Bill Gallo was golden and never in question. I was very careful about how I addressed him, as he was a gentleman from the old school. I came to know that nothing irritated the Clipper more than someone he didn't know calling him Joe. Impeccable manners were extremely important to DiMaggio. He gave you permission to call him Joe.

"Mr. Gallo suggested that I drop you a line," I explained. I still couldn't believe it, the most famous heel and sports medicine injury in history—even more renowned than that of Achilles—needed my attention.

Both men went into an examination room and took off their coats. When I looked at Joe's foot, I saw that the surgery on his heel, performed in the '40s, had been bungled. The famous heel, the Holy Grail of sports injuries known all around the world and repeatedly mentioned in the Ernest Hemingway classic, *The Old Man and the Sea,* mesmerized me. It was a foot doctor's fantasy and dream. In addition, he had a large arthritic left big toe, which was a consequence of fouling numerous balls off his foot in the batter's box.

"When they did the heel spur incision, they did a Griffith's, which is a fish-mouth incision," I explained. "They not only removed the spur but also the fat pad, so you have been walking on bone with no cushion." I learned later that sharing ill-fitting, hand-me-down shoes from his brothers also contributed to his heel and foot problems. Wearing shoes of the wrong size is a prescription for foot disaster.

I recommended a special orthopedic foot strapping and a prescription orthotic that would calm down the soft tissue inflammation in the area and reduce the force and tension in the tendons and ligaments of the bottom part of his heel. In two weeks, he showed considerable improvement, but just treating Joe was not enough for him or me. I was determined to heal him and allow him to enjoy walking and playing golf.

When I wanted to take X-rays of his foot, which was standard medical procedure, Joe refused to be X-rayed.

He said, "It's not that I don't trust you, Doc, but I don't want this X-ray showing up at one of these memorabilia shows. It could fetch a lot of money."

Clearly, Joe didn't trust me, even though I was a professional trying to help him. I was a little insulted, but decided not to get defensive or to take him on. I had to rely on reports he had his Florida doctors send, which wasn't an ideal way to treat him or to observe the progress he was making. His concern seemed over the top to me, but I didn't know much about him then. Now, it makes perfect sense.

Joe was accustomed to people wanting to exploit his name and legend to make money, and that made him guarded and suspicious. In his book of life, everyone started in the negative column and had to prove himself trustworthy.

About three months after our first meeting, Joe dropped by my office unannounced and alone. "Hey, Doc, you want to grab a cup of coffee?" he asked.

As if I'd refuse.

We went around the corner to the Gardenia Café, an upscale Greek diner on Madison Avenue and East 67th Street. That is how our friendship outside my office began.

I can't recall how many people have asked me, "What do you talk about with Joe DiMaggio?"

My answer was, "Everything."

I became like New York family to him. He was as protective of me as he was of his grandchildren and great-grandchildren. Over time, he let me into his private zone, but, as I learned, not even family or very close associates and friends knew the whole picture. That was by design.

I experienced his tendency to compartmentalize his life. He was brilliant, even strategic, about it. Napoleon would have been proud of the Clipper. Soon after Joe's death, I had a call from a guy named Joe Nachio, who identified himself as one of Joe's oldest friends from Panama. I assumed he was one more fan claiming to be Joe's supposed best friend. I had never heard of him. Nachio told me that he had known Joe since the 1930s. We got to talking. I was surprised by how much he knew about me. Apparently, Joe Di had told him a lot about his young doctor friend in New York, but had never mentioned Nachio to me. I later learned they were so close that Joe had stayed at his friend's house in Panama to escape the furor following the breakup of his marriage to Marilyn Monroe. As I said, no one knew the whole picture when it came to Joe. I was getting a firsthand lesson from the professor himself.

I was initially suspicious of Joe Nachio, because I've run into so many people who claimed to have enjoyed a close relationship with Joe and had dined with him often. There were two litmus tests to the truth of these claims: coffee and garlic. Joe's eating habits were peculiar, especially as to how he liked his coffee. When pretenders would talk about Joe's ordering a cappuccino or gulping down a double espresso with Sambuca, I knew they had never had coffee with Joe. Joe always ordered "a half cup of decaffeinated coffee and, on the side, a small pot of hot water." Joe would mix the little pot of hot water into his decaf like a precision chemist, not one drop over the mark. He never took coffee any other way.

As for the garlic test, though Joe was a true son of Sicily, he avoided garlic. When someone told me he ate at an Italian restaurant with Joe, I'd ask him what Joe had ordered. When the answer was, "He ate rigatoni with garlic, loaded with garlic. He loves garlic," I knew he had never broken bread with Joe. And rigatoni was not Joe's favorite pasta.

Joe might have liked garlic, but I believe he steered clear of it, because he was concerned about smelling like a "dago." Ethnic stereotypes were stronger in Joe's heyday than they are now. Italians and Italian-Americans were judged far more harshly than in these politically correct times.

During his last decade, I became his New York surrogate son and later a buffer and an expediter, a young friend who could read his mind and take care of things to keep him in his comfort zone. When he played with the Yankees at the height of his fame, he was not able to enjoy New York. He had become a prisoner of his fame. Baseball was America's game, and the Clipper was front and center. He was mobbed wherever he went. He was as popular as the pope or the president. When I met him in 1990, he was ready to regain the part of his life he had sacrificed to his celebrity.

At the time we were introduced, he lived quietly in Florida, visited his family in California, and spent ten to fifteen days a month in New York City, where he plugged into a circuit of excitement—an abundance of people, places, and events. He was known to everyone and was a welcome guest everywhere. He was one of the most recognizable figures in town.

Joe always referred to the boys from Westchester during our initial courting stage. He met his friends at Alex & Henry's in Eastchester, New York. They would always fete Joe with bottles of Dom Pérignon. He loved the stuff.

One day, he asked if I would mind their coming down to have dinner with us. He was a gentleman and asked my permission. I was game. We wound up eating at Sant Ambroeus on Madison Avenue. There was instant chemistry. These fellows acted more like my doting uncles than dinner companions. They treated me with the utmost respect and generosity. There was never a check to pay when "the boys" from Westchester were at the dinner table. Joe was happy to marry his two social spheres and appreciated how we all genuinely cared about him and liked one another.

Whenever he came to New York, I escorted Joe around town and became the Manhattan contingent of what I called the "Bat Pack," his pals from Westchester. I thought the name was appropriate and ironic at the same time. Sinatra had his Rat Pack, and now DiMaggio his Bat Pack. The members of his inner circle included Johnny Arcaro, a retired postal worker in his early seventies, and Nat Recine and Mario Faustini, cousins in their fifties, who owned Alex & Henry's Roman Gardens and catering hall in Eastchester, New York.

Joe called Johnny Arcaro, "Johnny Power," because of his lively personality. Johnny loved to dance and kept them laughing. A dapper dresser, Johnny had a full head of silver-gray hair and sported a signature pair of big, black-tinted glasses. Johnny used to carry around one-hundred-dollar bills with Joe's picture in the middle of the bill instead of Ben Franklin's. This was his calling card. If Joe had known about it, he would have been furious.

Nat Recine's father, Henry, and his uncle, Alex, who was Mario Faustini's grandfather, had opened a sandwich shop on Courtlandt Avenue near Yankee Stadium in the Bronx in 1946. Joe used to frequent the place.

In 1975, when the new generation opened an Alex & Henry's in

Westchester, Joe was loyal to the family. When he went to their place, he always sat at a table in front of a mural of weeping willows. He preferred that the cousins meet him in New York. Manhattan was where he wanted to be.

When I first met him, Joe had been meeting this core group of buddies at various restaurants for a couple of years. The Westchester division never asked anything of Joe, but they did compete for his attention. And then I joined the group. I knew people in Manhattan, and Joe was looking for a good time in town, which I knew how to find. Westchester couldn't compete with Rock Positano's New York, and Joe knew it. New York was his elixir of youth and his lifeline to fun. I felt lucky to spend time with him whenever he was in town. It was a *dovere*, an honored duty, to be with Joe.

A newly minted doctor, a couple of hundred-thousand dollars in debt from student loans from Yale School of Medicine, New York College of Podiatric Medicine, and New York University, I was working fourteen or fifteen hours a day, seven days a week, to build my practice. I had no personal life and barely saw my kids.

The kids did extremely well growing up, no thanks to me, but because they have a fabulous mother and grandmother, who were doting and supportive. They had the benefit of a bilingual environment. Their mother and grandma insisted on discipline and hard work.

I didn't have the luxury of playtime or the assistance and support of a wealthy family to help me get started. Joe opened up a new world for me, and served as a tremendous source of inspiration. I couldn't lose with DiMaggio on my team. He was my safety net for the high wire of life.

A street kid from Brooklyn, I grew up in the sixties, long after Joe's baseball career. Though Mickey Mantle was a hero to my brother John and me, my father and uncles considered Joe DiMaggio the greatest Italian ever, and the greatest ballplayer of all time. His name was a constant at our Sunday dinners at our grandparents' cold-water flat in Williamsburg, Brooklyn. To John and me, he was an old man who sold coffee makers. We couldn't begin to understand why the men in our family, who were not easily impressed, venerated him so much. It wasn't until Joe and I became friends that I began to grasp the magnitude of his legend. His success story and his style, dignity, and grace made him a lasting American icon.

I didn't have a bias, because I never saw him play baseball, hit in fifty-six straight games, or win nine World Series. More important, I knew DiMaggio the man, the guy who loved his family, took my clothes to the laundry, and had coffee with me in the morning, not the baseball legend who was married to Marilyn Monroe.

When we met, Joe was seventy-six, and I was thirty-two, fresh out of professional school at Yale. In the course of our friendship, the great American icon revealed to me the man behind the image he so carefully crafted and protected. He didn't put it out there, but he knew I would figure it out. Actions, not words, made me begin to understand his very complex and convoluted personality. My respect for him has only grown since his death eighteen years ago. His influence on me has been immeasurable.

When I started to think about writing a memoir, I reviewed and balanced the good times as well as the rocky ones. Looking back today, it didn't take me long to realize that he was using his experience to smooth the way for me, to make it all easier. I admired Joe despite his shortcomings and, like all of us, he had his own baggage. He scrupulously guarded his good name, the same way he meticulously combed his hair, knotted his tie, shined his shoes, and folded his clothes, because he knew he was a role model to so many people. He took his position in life seriously. I came to realize that Joe's isolation was his heroism.

Whatever he did, Joe DiMaggio gave his all to make sure he never came up short. He wanted to be an example, to show what a hero was like. For Joe, maintaining an immaculate reputation was important for the game he loved and his own legacy. I can imagine my father and uncles shaking their heads and agreeing. "They don't make them like him anymore." When I look at many of today's sports stars, I have to concur.

DINNER WITH DIMAGGIO is an account of our friendship as it evolved over almost a decade. At first, I kowtowed to him but, after two or three years, the relationship flipped. He could relax when he was with me, because he knew I would protect him and allow him to lead the type of life he wanted in New York. He began to rely on me. I never asked for anything, treated him with the respect he deserved, and helped him to enjoy the last ten years of his life in the place that meant the most to him. Once he trusted me, he opened up with all sorts of memories and insights that were not widely known. I had an unprecedented view of the inner life of a great American icon. Knowing him changed me forever.

My memories of our times together are full of rare stories that capture Joe's street smarts, intellectual brilliance, compassion, inflexible code of behavior, and bittersweet recollections. Nothing written here was off limits, as these were conversations Joe shared with his close friends in New York, the Bat Pack, and me.

I feel privileged to have been Joe DiMaggio's friend. Having a regular seat at the dinner table with Joe qualified you as a confidant. Behind his polished reserve, he was a complex man who experienced unparalleled celebrity in his lifetime. He held firm to his principles and never compromised. Joe valued decency above all, and remained self-effacing in spite of his fame.

He was a natural storyteller and an adept listener, so I hope that gift shines through in *Dinner with DiMaggio*. I want readers to feel as if they have pulled up a chair at his table at one of his favorite restaurants, ready for a memorable night with one of the last great American heroes.

By the time we met, I was already in the habit of taking medical notes after seeing each patient. After our patient–doctor relationship ended with the eradication of his foot pain, our meetings became social. I made notes every time I saw DiMaggio. Keeping notes on our times together seemed important. To me, he was part of history, like Julius Caesar, George Washington, the Wright Brothers, or Neil Armstrong. I wanted to have a record of our conversations and Joe's stories. I took on the role of his New York historian. I never expected to use or share these notes with others. I have relied on these notes to reconstruct our many exchanges found in these pages.

In addition, I have handwritten pages from Joe DiMaggio's diaries. Excerpts from the diary pages are reproduced at the start of every chapter. He refers often to people, situations, and concerns that I have chronicled in this book. His own diaries support my memory and my notes of our meetings.

Not until I celebrated his centennial birthday with his family did I appreciate that I had a front row view of a legendary figure that has never been made public. Since so many negative things have been written about Joe DiMaggio, I want to add my unique point of view to fill out and balance the portrait. I had to write this book to keep Joe DiMaggio's legacy alive for the youngest generation. I didn't want the memory of this great man to fade. Ten-year-old boys and girls in Little League today have to be aware that Joe DiMaggio was an important figure in our history.

He was my teacher. I became his protector, and then his teacher. The connection we made was profound. He remains an inspiration to me eighteen years after his death. My goal is to bring Joe DiMaggio to life with this flesh-and-blood portrait. We could all use some heroes to look up to, especially during these crazy and challenging times.

Welcome to the dinner table and your seat next to Joe DiMaggio.

CHAPTER 2

An Unlikely Friendship

Friday - June 4, 1993

After some soup at Gordon's restaurant we left at 2:00 P.M. for Alex and Harrys to say hello to Nat Theatre.

We went to their restaurant to have dinner at 7:30 P.M. Dr. Rock Positano was there.

Had a rough night requiring autographs for a number of bowlers — who made reservations there for dinner and dancing.

Saturday - June 12, 1993

Up at 8 A.M. — Rocky Positano called at ten A.M. to meet him at his office at 10:30 to have another treatment to my ankle. Swelling seems to be subsiding, but, for how long? Will continue the treatments as long as I'm in New York at least until this coming week — and watch the results.

My routine seems to be making me feel better the last couple of days. Have ignored my walks, etc. as I have been feeling tired. So, I've been pushing myself.

O*nce Joe's foot improved, he* loved to walk around the city. He followed the Italian custom of the *passeggiata*, the stroll every villager makes usually after work in the early evening. I would pick him up from Burke's apartment on East 68th Street and Fifth Avenue, bordering on the Museum Mile. I had moved my office around the corner to 12 East 68th between Fifth and Madison. Joe and I often used the service entrance to avoid prying eyes.

Joe favored East 68th Street, because Elle MacPherson, the Australian supermodel, lived there. She was a patient and neighbor of mine. One day, walking back to my office from Madison with Joe, we bumped into Elle. Though he didn't show it when I introduced them, Joe was absolutely captivated by this fetching beauty. He developed a late-life crush on her. The *parafulmine*, Italian for lightning bolt, hit him hard.

His bearing would become more regal, and a smile would cross his face as we passed her place. His usual rapid pace slowed down to a crawl. Every time we approached her building, he would turn to me and ask, "You think Ellie will be coming down anytime soon?"

Joe's conversations as we walked to and from Madison Avenue were fixated on Elle. He would insist that we go out of our way and linger in front of her residence, just in case she happened to emerge. His puppy love was becoming hard to tolerate. I determined to do something about it.

"Listen, Joe," I said one day, "why don't I try to set up a dinner for you and Elle? She's a very sweet girl, and she knows you are respectable . . . why not?"

"What would a gorgeous, young model like that see in a guy like me?" Joe lamented. "I'm not even going to think about it, Doc."

I didn't press it, and Joe's crush did not abate. I finally resolved to do something about it.

The Westchester crew planned to meet at Coco Pazzo to celebrate Joe's birthday. When Joe and I were seated with the Bat Pack, the maître d's, Tom Piscitello and John Fanning, came to the table.

"Mr. DiMaggio, we have a fax for you," the maître d's announced.

"A fax? A fax from who?" Joe asked, surprised.

They handed him a folded piece of paper that contained a handwritten cartoon from Elle with a note that read,

Mr. DiMaggio—
Happy, happy birthday to you. Sorry I can't be with you, but I am here filming a movie. I hope this card will keep you warm.

Elle

Joe got a kick out of his birthday greeting, as did the rest of us.

On our many walks, he continued to ask how Elle was doing. I finally had to break the bad news that Elle was involved with someone else, which put an end to his infatuation. But we still walked on East 68th Street.

After Elle's building, we would head toward Madison Avenue. Billy Martin's Western Wear store was on the corner. Joe sometimes reminisced about Martin, who was one of the few Yankees he actually liked. He thought that Martin was one of the most spirited players, but that he didn't have the best baseball skills. Joe believed Martin's heart and determination made him a good player and, eventually, a great manager. Billy Martin was one of the few ballplayers who could mess with Joe and get away with it, which was unusual, because, when it came to baseball, Joe was all business.

David Halberstam, the writer and a social acquaintance, told me that the friendship between Martin and DiMaggio began when Martin violated the most sacred rule of Yankee etiquette. He had the presumption to ask DiMaggio out for dinner. The invitation was so startling that his teammates long remembered the brazen gesture. Joe was amused, accepted the invitation, and the two became friends. Having dinner with Joe was not to be taken lightly, and his Yankee teammates knew it very well.

Once Joe and I hit Madison on our walk, it was fair game. Buses would stop, and the drivers would open their windows and yell, "Hey, Joe!" Joe always acknowledged his fans with his famous salutelike wave. Bus riders would stick their heads out their windows and wave to get his attention. It didn't matter that the Clipper had not put on a uniform for more than forty years. He remained one of the most recognizable celebrities in the city. People would trip over themselves, walk into doors, and miss curbs at seeing Joe DiMaggio. I called it "The DiMaggio Effect." It didn't matter if you were a famous star, a billionaire, or the guy next door. The "Effect" would hit everyone in the same way.

When Joe walked into the most star-studded restaurant, the room went dead silent. Celebrities, athletes, singers, rock and roll stars, it didn't matter who, would stop in their tracks, cease talking, and stare at an American icon.

I also noticed that Joe had a diuretic effect on many males in the dining room. Other diners would watch our table, and the minute Joe rose to go to the men's room, a flurry of men left their tables and followed him.

I can remember one night at Campagna, a hot entertainment spot. A line extended almost a hundred feet from our usual table, second on the left, to the entrance with people waiting to say hello to Joe and shake his hand. That night, Joe was focusing on our waitress, Robin Beattie, who always treated Joe well. He always left her a big tip, which he rarely did otherwise. When Robin told us the date of her birthday, Joe went a little quiet. After Robin left, Joe mentioned that she had the same birthday as Marilyn. He stared straight ahead.

Joe looked to the end of the line and said, "Hey, Doc! That looks like Tony Bennett waiting in line." It was. Tony, a true gentleman, didn't want to buck the line. He waited a good fifteen minutes to reach

Joe. Joe was thrilled to see Tony. They commented about how great each other looked. I couldn't disagree with that. Later on in the evening the chef and co-owner, Mark Strausman, pulled me over and said, "Rock, the biggest celebs and sport stars come into this restaurant and nobody stops the room like DiMaggio. Everyone goes dead silent. I have never seen anything like this."

Another night, music lawyer honcho, Allen Grubman, was seated at a nearby table with a group of music executives. All were watching Joe, visibly in awe of him. When Joe left the table to use the men's room, Grubman and his people abruptly left the table and made a bee-line in Joe's direction to have a close-up glimpse. I later introduced Joe to Grubman and his pals. Joe remarked to me, "That guy has one hell of a head of hair."

Well into his seventies, Joe had the gait of a twenty-year-old. No huffing and puffing. If I didn't keep pace, he would just keep walking and leave me in the dust. He loved to pass the Dominican Academy, a Catholic girls' school on East 68th Street, run by nuns. He waved to the girls. He admonished the smoking teenage girls, puffing away out of sight of the nuns, that smoking was bad for their health. They responded to him with respect and reverence, even if they didn't have a clue who he was in the sports world.

When we walked, he always checked for change on the sidewalks, but not because he needed the money. Joe, like many athletes, was very superstitious. He would pick up a coin only if it were heads up. He wouldn't leave home without a tiny shell and a small polished stone his great-granddaughter, Vanassa, had brought back from the beach and given to him. On a few occasions, we had to return to the apartment to pick up these items when he had left them behind. He never did explain why the shell and stone went with him everywhere.

He liked things to be simple and consistent. "Nothing I hate more than surprises," he would always say. I realized that his being a consistent man in inconsistent times added to his appeal.

We had a regular reserved table at the Gardenia Café, where we would stop when Joe was hungry. Backed by a wall, the table was in a small corner to the left of the cash register. Joe sat facing the wall, so that he wouldn't have to make eye contact with the patrons who came in and out and paid their tab at the register. Peter Katsichtis, the owner, was very protective and did his best to keep his star-struck customers from bothering Joe when he was eating.

Patrons would always try to get the Clipper's attention. After many futile attempts to have Joe smile at her, one woman pulled one of the funniest moves ever. When Joe had his head turned, she came up to the table and stole the only remaining potato on Joe's dish. She surely got his attention. He was flabbergasted.

"Can you imagine, Doc, the balls on that gal stealing the last potato from my plate?" I was amused to see that she was able to rattle him. She definitely got his attention.

The waitstaff knew what to bring Joe: a half cup of decaffeinated coffee with a half cup of hot water on the side, never with sugar. He would pour the hot water precisely into the half-cup of decaf, never spilling a drop. He loved plain pound cake, toasted on the topside. He would cut the piece in half and share it with me. Joe liked Yankee bean or chicken-noodle soup in a cup, not a bowl. His sandwich of choice was turkey white meat, freshly roasted, not processed, on whole-wheat toast with no mayonnaise. He would only ask for half a sandwich.

Joe had an interesting way of eating Italian delicacies such as salami and prosciutto, which I observed countless times. Meticulously cutting the fat off a piece of prosciutto, he would not leave a single remnant of the white perimeter. He did it with a precision that would have made any *salumeria* owner proud.

Joe always covered the tab at the start of our friendship. He would take out a wad of cash that was held together by a rubber band. Early on, I was fascinated by his quirks. When I asked him why he used a rubber band instead of a wallet, he said it was more difficult for a pickpocket to steal your cash, because the rubber band would get caught on the fabric of the pocket. A wallet would slide out with ease. Joe had it all figured out. To this day, I use the rubber band as well. The Clipper was right.

ONE DAY, JOE surprised me with a question that I didn't know how to answer. He had just taken a sip of coffee and was still holding his cup when he said, "You never talk baseball with me."

I knew better than to bring up the subject before he initiated a conversation about his sport.

Then, he asked, "Who's your all-time favorite baseball player?"

Of course, Joe expected me to name him. I knew I couldn't insult him, but I was sure Joe would see through any attempt at flattery. I didn't want to offend him before our friendship even got off the ground. I had to rely on my Bensonhurst street savvy. I knew it was important for me to be honest.

"Well, Joe, it was—errrr . . . uh—Mickey Mantle." I told the truth and looked Joe straight in the eye.

Joe was quiet. I couldn't read his expression. He could not have been pleased. I went on to explain my position in hopes of calming him down.

I couldn't tell him that in our P.S. 226 schoolyard on Bay Parkway and 60th Street, there was never a mention of Joe DiMaggio. We used to flip baseball cards, a game which seems like a prehistoric hobby now. Every professional team had each player's photograph on the front of the card with a unique colored border and team name banner. The back of the card listed the player's statistics. The cards came five to a pack. As an extra bonus, a stale piece of bubble gum was in the package along with the cards. I never knew anyone to sample the gum.

Players took turns flipping cards. If you flipped your card, and it matched the color of the last card, you got the whole stack underneath the cards just played.

Since he was retired by then, we never saw a Joe DiMaggio baseball trading card, which, of course, consigned Joe DiMaggio to the black hole of unknown sports players. John and I would try to fool other kids into giving up a Mickey Mantle, a Willie Mays, or a Roger Maris, but we would have refused a Joe DiMaggio, even if one somehow ended up on the dead pile. It would have been worthless, like the gum.

This is one childhood story that would not amuse Joe. I scrambled to find the right words.

"Yeah, Joe, Mickey Mantle," I confessed. "After all, you were retired before I could even watch television. I was born in the late fifties, and you retired in 1951. I never watched you play, I wasn't even born yet. My brother and I knew you as Mr. Coffee and the guy with perfectly coiffed silver hair who sang off-key in the Bowery Savings Bank commercials."

"Doc, wrong answer." Staring straight ahead, Joe seemed hurt, but he soon rallied.

"No question about it—Mickey was there to replace me in center field, and I knew it."

I couldn't believe what he was telling me.

"What made it even worse is that management at the time, including Casey Stengel, asked me to make Mantle a great fielder. Now I wasn't too crazy about training my replacement, but I did what they asked me to."

"So, what was your advice?" I had to ask.

"Well, Doc, I told him if he could stay away from the broads, booze, and carousing all night, he might be a great player.

"Doc, I also told him that if he did not listen to this advice, he would be all washed up." Joe returned to his coffee with a cryptic smile on his face.

As we know now, Mickey Mantle never lived up to his potential. Mantle lived a dissolute life. He caroused with Billy Martin and drank before and after games. According to Joe, Mantle became all washed up. I did remind Joe that despite all of Mickey Mantle's distractions, he was still one of the greatest Yankees ever.

"LET'S GET OUT of here," Joe said as he reached for the check.

I thought about Joe's reaction to my naming Mickey Mantle as my favorite ballplayer. I realized that one of the reasons Joe was comfortable with me was precisely because I didn't know him as an iconic baseball legend. He started in the negative column with me as I did with him. It was an interesting dynamic. No one had the advantage, except that I always respected my elders. I often deferred to him and was protective, as I would be for any elder. As our friendship developed, I grew to respect and admire Joe DiMaggio the man quite apart from Joe DiMaggio the iconic baseball player.

OUR CONVERSATIONS WOULD usually turn to my childhood in Brooklyn, my family, and our shared working-class Italian heritage and street values. Joe wanted to know my story, and it was refreshing for him to hear about someone else's life for a change. The Clipper always respected the fact that though I came from the wrong side of the elevated subway tracks, my upbringing kept me out of trouble. He valued education, professionalism, discretion, benign self-promotion. In his eyes, I excelled in the first three.

I had two Master's degrees and a health degree from an Ivy League school and the oldest college of podiatric medicine in the country. My practice was growing quickly. I was at the number-one orthopedic hospital in the world, the Hospital for Special Surgery, and I made it my business to expand my growing network of contacts. I also did not get much R and R.

He was intrigued to know how a young doctor started from scratch to build a thriving foot and ankle practice. I explained my decision about where to set up my practice after I graduated from professional school. An outer borough or a suburban town was not for me. I was driven to make it in Manhattan. My biggest fear in life was to be ordinary. I figured there was no sense in starting small. I began to network on the Upper East Side, the most fashionable part of town at the time. I developed a reputation as a very reliable doctor, who combined a streetwise edge with medical acumen. I was available around the clock. I managed to build a distinguished cadre of patients, who became friends and referred their friends and friends of their friends to me.

Joe was encouraging. He identified with aiming high and going for it.

"If you build it, they will come." The theme of *Field of Dreams* was my mantra. I needed a hook. After I became familiar with Joe's heel situation and the disastrous outcome of his surgery—they used maggots to remove the infected skin—I appreciated even more how important feet are to a person's quality of life. I was determined to start a different protocol that recognized problems in the foot and ankle at an early stage, then did everything possible to stabilize the foot and make it work better without resorting to surgery.

I was determined to build it and to watch people come to benefit from this level of nonsurgical care. As for my practice, my hook became, "Don't butcher people, and they will talk. And if it doesn't need fixing, don't fix it." I knew word of mouth from my happy patients would build my practice. I also realized that in the medical arts profession, no matter how hard you try, you can't always make everybody happy.

JOE'S FAMOUS HEEL suffering and underlying heel injury triggered a new way of treating muscular-skeletal injuries. He inspired me, and other medical professionals, to treat such injuries differently with nonsurgical procedures. His experience was the driving force behind an orthopedic textbook on heel disorders titled *Disorders of the Heel, Rearfoot, and Ankle,* for which I served as co-author and editor with my mentor and colleague Dr. Chitranjan S. Ranawat.

Thousands of patients have been helped due to the work he has inspired, and they owe a real debt to Joe DiMaggio. Joe taught the world that though such injuries are not life threatening, they are very much lifestyle threatening. Joe's injuries, in fact, robbed Joe of years of his career. In this powerful way Joe has left a legacy that rivals his sports record. He had an impact on people's quality of life, which not too many professional athletes have accomplished.

Joe was unbelievably supportive of my approach, because he was a victim of a foot surgery gone bad and later experienced the positive results of a nonsurgical solution. The Joe DiMaggio Sports Foot and Ankle Center was established at the Hospital for Special Surgery, in conjunction with the Primary Sports Care division and Sports Medicine Service, to deliver this quality and standard of non-surgical foot and ankle care.

The Yale School of Public Health established a scholarship in my name, solely with the intent of training doctors from all over the world to manage musculoskeletal injuries without surgery, and to develop new treatment strategies that promise nonsurgical care, which is supported by many grateful patients who have benefited from this standard of care.

EVEN WITH THE gap in our ages, Joe knew I understood his way of life and thinking. Those customs and values go deep. Joe, the son of a San Francisco fisherman who barely spoke English, grew up with his seven siblings in North Beach, an Italian neighborhood in San Francisco. His parents, Giuseppe and Rosalia, were Sicilian immigrants.

My father, Rocco, was a big-band musician during the '30s and '40s who later designed windows for B. Altman and Saks. My brother and I were raised in the Bensonhurst section of Brooklyn, where DiMaggio was a god who walked on water. I was a tough, rough, and rugged latchkey street kid. I could spin and turn it. I was used to living by my wits. I traded in street fights and punch ball for studying classical piano with Sister Margaret DeLourdes and later Vincent Gaudioso.

From the age of eleven, my hairline started to recede. Street punks in the neighborhood taunted me. I was forced to develop a hard shell and fighting skills. Pick on a Positano and the whole family came down on you, from my uncles and cousins to my big brother, John. Joe approved. It wasn't easy walking around Brooklyn with visible hair loss, because the borough was known for its male hair styles.

I wanted to come out of the neighborhood. I was ambitious, played rock-and-roll and classical piano, and worked my way to an Ivy League medical specialty degree. I think Joe respected that. He knew all about the journey. From humble beginnings, we had both worked hard to excel and achieve our goals.

We each had big, extended families. Joe remembered fondly the huge meals—giant portions of gravy meat, swirling plates of spaghetti, freshly caught fish, crusty loaves of bread, washed down by rough red wine—served by his mother, and presided over by his father when he and his siblings were growing up in the Bay Area. These Sunday afternoon dinners continued after Joe made it big and was spending time with the wealthy and powerful in upscale restaurants.

Aside from our similar backgrounds, I was also in the right place at the right time to get to know Joe. My Jewish friends would call it *mazel*. Meeting the Yankee Clipper at a point when he was looking back and ready to talk about what mattered to him gave me unprecedented access to what made him tick. I had a monopoly on his time whenever he was in New York. He was ready to let his guard down. He recognized me as another stand-up guy, a legacy from our pasts. He knew I would not betray him. That was the essence of a stand-up guy, who was loyal, close-mouthed, and ready for a fight. Joe and I were stand-up guys separated by a generation.

We shared an admiration for the institution of the stoop. In Brooklyn, the stoop is more than the landing or steps to an apartment house entrance. A stoop served as a gathering and networking place. On warmer nights, all year 'round, we did two things from stoops. We mocked neighbors or played stoopball with a Spaldeen.

Joe DiMaggio knew something about stoops, as he told me. "We had stoops when I was a kid. We'd hang out on the stoops and watch the world from those steps." He looked wistful as he brought himself back to those times.

"We'd hang out for hours on the stoop." I remembered what we had seen. "There wasn't anything we missed from that vantage point. If a man had a mistress, we'd note it. If a woman had a lover, we'd note it. If a couple was always fighting, we knew. We knew the blowhards on the block. We identified the men who lorded it over the neighbors, because they had money, a lucrative trade, a successful store, and a place in the mob or the unions, which was almost the same thing. We didn't miss a thing.

The stoop was also a place to hear confessions and console our neighbors during the sad times, like when I comforted my childhood crush when her brother was tragically killed in a hazing accident at college.

I told Joe about the Good Humor cyclist. He had a wooden box on top of his bicycle frame with dry ice inside and ice cream. He'd cycle around for a sale. If my father had just gotten paid, we'd get an ice cream.

Joe understood the phrase "if Dad had just gotten paid."

"My old man was the same way," he said. "He had no head for business, but he would treat us if he could afford it."

"And, Joe, stoops were our air-conditioning in summer. We stayed out until we could fall asleep and dream about a better life one day." Gazing at the full moon and stars from the stoop was our reward and was more than enough to make us happy.

"Life was so simple then," Joe reflected. "People would just enjoy little things. Now, they want everything. That's why people have more and are less happy than their parents and grandparents."

Joe understood doing without. Forced consumerism, conspicuous consumption, and wasteful spending were foreign to him, as they were to me. In this intergenerational way, we understood each other as only working-class boys could.

I told Joe the story of the teenage romance that changed my life. I was involved in a friendship with the daughter of a prominent and highly acclaimed Bay Ridge, Brooklyn, doctor. He was a wonderful and gifted healer. Our relationship sparked class warfare between some members of my friend's family and me. Her mom insisted that her daughter attend one of the Seven Sisters colleges, the equivalent of the then all-male Ivy League, to better separate us. I was planning to take my first step out of Brooklyn to attend New York University.

I overheard her mother say, "I am not going to spend thousands of dollars a year on a prestigious college for you to marry a Rock Positano."

Nothing fueled my ambition to succeed more than those cruel words. I was hell bent on becoming an A-list doctor in Manhattan. There was no better launch pad than Brooklyn, and I was going to bring all my street education across the bridge.

I can now understand how the mother felt and even agree with her logic at the time. I was from the other side of the tracks and had yet to prove myself. All parents want the best for their children.

I was given a stay of execution when her parents found out that I could play a mean piano and entertain guests at their dinner parties. I even learned the favorite songs of their guests, such as "From the Vine Came the Grape." I became very popular and was enjoying my newfound success among the group that had been trying to jettison me back to the asphalt schoolyard.

My friend assured me that I was going to be a successful and worldly man one day. She continued to edit my letters for grammar and punctuation, for which I would be forever grateful.

Joe got a kick out of my story. "Bet that mother wouldn't say that now," he said. "That's their loss. I bet she's kickin' herself in the keister now. I've been there, too, Doc."

AT NEW YORK University, I was a member of an Italian-based fraternity called Alpha Phi Delta (APD), the Theta Beta chapter. It is one of the oldest fraternities in the country. Though primarily Italian, the fraternity did not reflect the Italian stereotypes of the 1970s. Academics were front and center. The vowel at the end of our names could not compete with the priority of education. We were a group of street kids who wanted an excellent formal education to make us doubly lethal when we hit the business world.

Joe had a very unbending sense of right and wrong, and you did not want to get on his wrong side. It didn't take long for me to learn that hanging out with Joe was both an honor and a minefield. He often shut out a friend who transgressed his unwritten rules. One wrong move, and you were out.

Punctuality was of utmost importance. Being late was a sure way to get exiled. Once, a fellow named Ed Liberatore was supposed to meet Joe at a hotel. Neither was aware that there were a few hotels with the same name. Liberatore showed up on time, as did Joe, but at different hotels. Joe cut him off, which I called being sent to Siberia.

I learned there were other rules with Joe. I knew to never bring up baseball unless the great one did first; to never, never mention Marilyn Monroe, DiMaggio's wife of only nine months; and to add

Frank Sinatra and the Kennedys to the forbidden list. I learned that I was not to ask any questions, but when he felt like it, he often volunteered information that would leave me with my mouth hanging open. The minute Joe knew you were actually listening to him speak, he would shut up like a clam. If I wanted to hear the story in its entirety, especially if it was of a personal nature, I knew not to make eye contact.

IN THE EARLY days of our friendship, I catalogued his quirks and habits in an effort to understand and appreciate him. Joe seemed to enjoy exposing me to more sophisticated things and introducing me to his many friends and acquaintances. He knew everyone, and I soaked it up. He once said to me, "I show you once, and you get it."

I became Joe's social vehicle about town, and driving with him was not fun and games, to put it mildly. He always sat in the front seat. Riding shotgun, he acted as if he had a second steering wheel and brake pedal in front of him. I felt as if I were in a driver's ed car.

If he saw a traffic light two blocks away, he would say, "Watch, that light is going to turn, be careful."

One of my favorite driving lines from him was, "Hey, Doc, I don't like how that guy is driving. Go over to the right and avoid him."

I found it amusing. When we were doing highway driving to Atlantic City, he would often nod off. If his head was drooping and his eyes were closed, I would step on the gas. The minute I sensed he was waking up, I would return to the speed limit. Somehow Joe had a knack, even when he was sleeping, to know if I exceeded the speed limit.

"Doc, you were going a little too fast there," he would say as he woke up.

"How do you know? You were sleeping," I tried to dismiss his accusation.

"Oh, it's just a feeling I have," he explained before commanding, "Slow down."

As a passenger Joe directed traffic as well as the driver. If I hadn't been able to laugh about it, Joe's backseat driving could have driven me crazy.

HE TOOK GREAT interest in my day-to-day life. Not one to mince words, he was as quick to scold as he was to praise me. Joe always gave me spot-on advice based on the highest standards. He had a lot to teach me and passed on his street savvy, as well as his considerable wisdom at every opportunity. I was inspired by Joe and felt lucky to have him in my corner. He was remarkably generous to me with his time and advice.

During my first week on staff at the Hospital for Special Surgery in 1991, Joe showed up unexpectedly. "Let's take a walk around the hospital," he suggested, knowing full well what he was doing.

He attracted a crowd of medical professionals of all ages, who were eager to meet him and shake the hand of a living legend. Though entertainment executives were waiting to honor Joe at the Friars Club, he took the time to meet my colleagues and went out of his way to praise my work to the head of my department. He said, "If I had known Dr. Positano fifty years ago, I would have had five more years playing ball."

An endorsement like that is hard to beat.

Joe could be remarkably helpful. He was capable of being a regular guy, not a stuffed shirt. There was no task that was beneath Joe. For an afternoon, Joe became my medical assistant. He thought nothing of answering my phones in the office, speaking with patients, and greeting them at the door. Once I overheard a patient say, "Are you Joe DiMaggio?"

He replied, "No, but people say I look and sound just like him."

I was beaming with pride when I rented my medical office in a landmark building around the corner from where Joe stayed. I had barely signed the lease when I decided to tell Joe about my new space. I boasted about it when he visited me at the hospital. I invited him to inspect the suite, and Joe accepted with great satisfaction, a reaction I had not anticipated. Joe was not easily impressed, but he seemed to be so when he saw the offices.

"This is swell, Doc. I'm proud of you." He was sincerely enthusiastic.

Soon after, I was busy at the hospital and had arranged for my mother to wait for the desks, stationery, machinery, and all the equipment needed for my practice. I was going to leave the offices unattended until she arrived.

I told Joe, "I'm waiting for my mother to call. She's coming in from Brooklyn to sit and wait for the furniture to be delivered and for the phone guys to wire us up."

Joe shook his silver head. "Don't bother your mother, Doc. I have nothing important to do all day. Call her right now and tell her not to come. I'll stay at the office and wait for those guys."

"Thanks, but I couldn't ask you to do that," I replied. "Besides, I don't know when they are coming."

"You didn't ask me—I offered." Joe wouldn't budge. "I've got a lot to read here." He pointed to a small stack of newspapers he was carrying with him that day. "My *New York Times, Wall Street Journal, New York Post,* and *Daily News.*"

We arrived at the new office. A plastic milk crate was the only thing in the place. Joe seized it as soon as he saw it.

"This is fine. I have my seat, my papers. Doc, go to the hospital now and take care of all the sick people who need you."

I thanked him and left, still reluctant. Five long hours passed before I was able to pry myself away from my rounds and return to my new offices. I found Joe camped out on the milk crate without furniture or phone lines.

"Damn! I can't believe they haven't delivered the furniture yet. I'm so sorry, Joe."

Joe was unfazed. "Don't worry, Doc. I've been sitting here all day entertaining myself by looking at how much money I made on the stock market."

I would not have imagined his patience. I started to apologize again when the sound of the office doorbell echoed through the empty space.

I tried to race to the door, but Joe was there first.

"Let me take care of this," he said.

I couldn't help feeling sorry for the poor bastard on the other side of the door, who was going to receive a reception he would never forget.

A shabbily dressed young man in his thirties, wearing a New York Yankees cap, was too busy shifting through the furniture delivery papers to even look up when Joe answered the door.

"Delivery for Dr. Positano. Please sign here," he mumbled, eyes focused on his paperwork. When he finally looked up, he was shocked. "Holy Christ, you're Joe DiMaggio," the stunned deliveryman exclaimed.

"Many people have told me I look just like him. Though you are observant and very bright, as I look at my Joe DiMaggio wrist watch, I see that you are about four hours late."

The delivery guy was dejected.

"How can you expect the doctor to help sick people if he is sitting here waiting for you?" Joe asked him in a sharp tone.

"But, but . . . you're my idol," he said.

"This is a helluva way to impress your idol," Joe shot back. "C'mon, get that stuff in here before it depreciates." Joe didn't let him off the hook. "You know, I was never late for a game, even when I had a cause. It was just the right thing to do. Punctuality is the courtesy of kings."

The deliveryman looked even more chagrined, but Joe continued anyway.

"If more people like you took their jobs seriously, life would be a lot easier." Joe began to lecture. "Look, no matter what your job is do your best at it. Impress yourself, even if your boss or your customers are unappreciative. Be your own boss!"

The deliveryman smiled.

"Martin Luther King, Jr., taught us to do the best at what we do, even if it's sweeping the floors. Take these habits from job to job."

In his rush to deliver the furniture and impress his idol, the deliveryman began lifting with his back. Joe winced.

"Hey, buddy, watch your back there. Lift with your legs. I know what it's like to miss a season on account of injury."

Joe proceeded to inspect and direct the placement of every stick of furniture delivered—Joe DiMaggio, interior decorator. The furniture stayed that way for years, because I couldn't bear to move it. I thought it would be bad luck to change a thing.

When he was satisfied, Joe called the man over.

"Okay, you've earned your tip," he said with a smile. "Give me that invoice. I'll sign it, and it'll be worth something one day."

Joe signed the invoice for the grateful deliveryman,

Best wishes, and don't ever be late again.

Joe DiMaggio

Later that night, after nine o'clock, as my able-bodied moving assistant, Joe DiMaggio, and I were setting up my office, the doorbell rang. It was my mom and her companion, Pat Auletta. They arrived unannounced to congratulate and encourage the new tenant. I have to give you some backstory here.

My mother, Frances, was made a young widow with the sudden and unexpected death of my father at a family wedding. Italians called it a *morto di lusso*, a luxury death, because the deceased barely suffered and did not linger in pain over months and years as so many do. But this was no luxury death for the family left behind.

My mom felt her life was over in that Old World way, but many years later she met a kind gentleman, Pat Auletta, who was the informal mayor of Coney Island. Pat had been married to a wonderful woman, formerly Nettie Tennenbaum, whom he lost to cancer. They lived in one of the buildings owned by Fred Trump, President Trump's father. Pat owned food concessions at various city facilities. Both Pat and Mom Positano held their deceased in high regard.

I invited them in. When Pat saw who was opening my boxes in the middle of my waiting room, he was speechless. He was a crazy admirer of Joe DiMaggio. Pat didn't know what to say, but Joe did. I had spoken glowingly of Pat to Joe.

Joe could not have been nicer to Pat. They talked about baseball, their own kids playing sports, and, of course, their old neighborhoods as if they had known each other for years. Chemistry is chemistry, and Joe and Pat were clearly not oil and vinegar.

Mom was pleased to see them hit it off. She made one of those statements that only a proud mother would say, "Joe, did you know Rocky was a great baseball player?"

I had played for the sandlot St. Athanasius Little League on Bay Parkway. I played left field. They called me Pocket Rocket Positano, because I had a great arm and could throw runners out at the plate from left field without a bounce, but I wasn't about to tell Joe about it.

I was so mortified I almost sank to the floor. Pat winked, and Joe shot me a "You gotta be kidding me," expression.

Further adding to my embarrassment, Joe said with a wink, "Doc, I never knew you were a great baseball player."

When Joe excused himself for a moment, I turned to my mother and said, "Mom, how can you tell Joe DiMaggio that I was a great baseball player? Do you have any idea who he is?"

Pat Auletta guffawed.

On Joe's return, Pat was able to pull off something most people would face the DiMaggio firing squad for. Oblivious to the situation he could be setting up, Pat said, "Joe, I have a great son named Ken. He is a writer and has done very well. He is a huge baseball fan and a left-hander at that. If I may, could I impose upon you to sign a baseball for him?"

I stood there frozen. I had no idea how the great DiMaggio would respond. You see, Joe rarely signed anything for anyone. His closest confidant and lawyer in Florida, Morris Engelberg, had told him years before that signing a picture or a baseball was the same as taking money and throwing it out the window. He learned very well from Morris. Even I was afraid to ask Joe for a picture. Making such a request was a sure way to be exiled to Siberia.

Without hesitation, Joe said, "Sure." He turned to me and asked me to remind him to do it.

The Clipper was all about chemistry, and he could spot a good man from a mile away and an asshole from a light year away. Pat Auletta was good people, and Joe knew it.

Pat was thrilled. He knew how much a signed ball from Joe Di would mean to his son.

A few weeks later, Joe and I were watching television when he turned to me and said, "Hey, Doc, I never signed that baseball for that nice man's son. Let's do it now so we don't forget and make us both look bad." Joe signed the ball to Ken with his Sharpie and carefully wrapped the ball in tissue paper with precision and finesse so that the autograph would not smudge. Unfortunately, that ball's delivery was delayed by years.

We lost Pat from the cancer that had claimed his wife, Nettie. It was an extremely sad time for all of us. I had completely forgotten that I had the signed ball. I came upon it one day. I wanted to be certain that I kept my promise to Pat and Joe. I found Ken's address and sent him the baseball with a note explaining that his dad personally asked the Clipper to sign it some years before, but I had lost track of the ball.

Ken was overwhelmed with emotion when he received that package.

He said it was one helluva gift from his dad, and that he had cried when he received the ball. The timing of the gift's delivery could not have been better. It was the baseball from heaven.

Over the years, I witnessed so many instances of Joe DiMaggio's generosity and sensitivity. He had a way of touching the lives of friends and strangers wherever he was.

CHAPTER 3

Dinner with DiMaggio

Saturday - June 19, 1993

John Arcaro - will be here at 6:30 P.m. as well as Dr. Positano. I have too many dinner appointments and appearances. Cancelled but Arcaro. Positano and I went to an Italian restaurant down by the village and had some good pasta.

I *soon found out that the* honor of having dinner with Joe DiMaggio was not to be underestimated. I had left Joe behind in my office reading his papers while I ran errands one afternoon. Walking along Madison toward Billy Martin's Western Apparel store, I saw a familiar face. It was Yankee Phil "Scooter" Rizzuto, whom I had already met through Joe. Joe was always proud to tell people that he introduced Phil to his wife, Cora, many years earlier.

I called out to him, "Mr. Rizzuto, how are you?"

Rizzuto seemed pleasantly surprised as he greeted me, "Great to see you, Rock."

I asked him what he was doing in this neck of the woods.

"I'm waiting for Cora. She's inside Billy Martin's place buying stuff for the kids. How is Joe doing?"

"I just left him in my office up the block. I'm going to meet up with him later for dinner." I had a bright idea. "Hey, why don't you join us? I'm sure he'd love to see you."

The Scooter was apologetic, but firmly negative and timid at the same time. "That's very nice of you, but I would never feel comfortable eating with him," Joe's former teammate explained. "I am still in awe of him fifty years after playing on the same team. That's how much I still respect and fear him. I never ate with him when we were playing together. It wouldn't feel right."

"I can't believe you still feel this way," I responded.

"I can't explain it to you. It's very kind of you to want to include me. I don't think you realize what a big deal it is to eat dinner with Joe, have coffee with Joe, to be a friend. He sees something very special in you. People would kill to be as close to him as you are."

I was taking in what Scooter said.

"Rock, I gotta go. I see Cora paying the bill. Please send my best to Joe." He noticed my bewildered expression and stayed long enough to explain Joe's hold on his fellow athletes. "Playing on the same team with Joe was amazing. I always knew, whatever the score when we were losing, just looking back and seeing Joe in center field gave me faith that we still had a chance of winning the game. He was that powerful a figure."

That exchange gave me a new understanding not only of the power of Joe's leadership and legend but also of how significant sharing a meal was to my friend. Dinner was a sacrament to Joe, a meal you shared with people you cared about.

I learned how important it was to him when I broke one of his cardinal rules. Having dinner with Joe or socializing with him in any way meant never inviting anyone—even family—along, regardless of wealth or social position, before Joe vetted the would-be guest. He had to know everything about the person brought to the table: family, friends, what he did for a living. As he often told me, he didn't like surprises.

In my honeymoon period, at the beginning of our friendship, I broke this important rule and paid for it. I had invited Dr. John Hunter, a prominent and gifted plastic surgeon in Manhattan, to join us for dinner one night. Hunter had recommended a very good Italian restaurant on Third Avenue, Due.

John was a close personal friend, but Joe viewed him as an interloper. The three of us sat quietly until Hunter excused himself for a minute.

"You didn't have the courtesy to ask my permission for him to come along and eat with us." Joe was coldly angry. "What makes you think you can invite a total stranger to break bread with me?"

"Joe, he's a friend of mine," I sputtered, surprised by the intensity of his reaction. "I've known him for years, and he has been very helpful to me in my career."

"Doc, I don't care how long you've known him or what kind of friend he is. You didn't clear it with me first."

I was hurt and baffled at the same time. I thought by seating Hunter next to Joe, the two would find it easy to talk. Boy, was I wrong.

There was no eye contact between Joe and Hunter. Instead, Joe menaced me with cold, mean stares. There were two tracks of conversations. Joe faced forward to answer Hunter's questions without acknowledging his existence. The other sight line was between Joe and me.

When we finished the meal, Joe got stranger still. We dropped Joe at his apartment, and he left the car without a good night. Hunter apologized to Joe in case he had offended him. Joe simply slammed the door.

I got Joe's message. I'd never do that again.

Almost always polite, Joe sent an autographed baseball to Hunter a week later as a form of apology. He felt bad about his behavior.

Another intruder fared far better. Joe and I were to meet for lunch at Three Guys Diner. When I arrived, he greeted me by saying, "I ordered lunch for you, because someone who cares about you and your diet is helping you to lose that spare tire I'm looking at. What the hell type of diet are you on anyway?"

All I could say was, "I lose this argument no matter what."

I looked around the place trying to cut the conversation off. At the door, I noticed a friend, Dr. Larry Rosenthal, one of the city's leading cosmetic dentists, who was entering the diner. Larry waved. I just smiled back, because I didn't want to warn Joe that we had company.

Larry hesitated. It was clear that he didn't know how to approach the table to meet one of his idols. Larry, who is creative and innovative, thought quickly about how to best approach the table without putting his life in danger. He spotted a five-foot-tall bowling trophy in the window. He lifted it to the amusement of other diners. Joe's back was to Larry, so he didn't see him heading toward the table. The patrons in the diner were chuckling.

"Oh, my God, what's that crazy bastard doing?" I whispered to Joe.

"What are you mumbling about, Doc?" Joe asked with irritation.

Larry staggered over with the trophy. I swear it was the biggest trophy I've ever seen. Larry carried the trophy like the True Cross to Joe, who sat there stunned.

Larry started his presentation. "Mr. DiMaggio, on behalf of New York City, congratulations on winning this trophy!"

I had no idea how Joe would react.

Joe burst into laughter, along with the customers, the staff, and me.

"Well, thank you, young man. There's no way I'm gonna get mad at you for interrupting my lunch when you bring over a trophy this size!" Joe seemed touched.

"I gotta give you credit," he continued. "In all my years, this is one of the more ingenious ways of coming over to say hello to me at a table." He was still laughing.

"Joe, may I call you Joe?" Larry asked with proper respect.

Joe nodded.

"It's a pleasure, Joe. I loved watching the look of panic on Rock's face. If you ever need those teeth fixed, Rock knows where to find me."

"Thanks. Hope to see you around real soon." Joe was cordial.

Larry walked off happy, but he left the gigantic trophy at the table.

Joe pointed to it and said, "Okay, Doc. Now you put this trophy back in the window."

The patrons all laughed at the fool's errand.

"God bless Rosenthal. He gets the laugh, and I get laughed at," I complained.

My friend managed to break one of Joe's cardinal rules and got away with it.

THE TRUTH IS that if Joe didn't protect himself, he would never get through a meal without thoughtless interruptions from fans wanting his autograph or taking pictures. That is why he tended to eat at places where the owners treated him with respect and knew his rules and habits. His tables of choice were often in out of the way places, such as near the kitchen or in a remote corner, so that he might enjoy a meal unnoticed.

Though Joe never once had a problem with picking up the tab at dinner, restaurateurs often refused to let him pay. He was great for business. The problem was that some restaurant owners did not respect his currency.

Dinner was inviolable to him in an Old World way, but being comped almost always came with a price. Many restaurant owners sent a steady stream of their favorite customers to the table and expected the Yankee Clipper to sign autographs and pose for pictures. It drove him nuts, but he was rarely rude to a fan.

For Joe, an autograph was a form of currency and no different from dropping the check at the end of a meal. Joe was aware that every time he signed anything it was the equivalent of money flying out of his pocket. That image stuck with the Clipper.

He had no problem signing and posing for a few pictures when he had finished eating. After all, the owner had shown him respect with a good meal, compliments of the house, and did want to show his appreciation.

He once said to me, after one too many fans approached our table, "I have no problem paying the tab, but giving me a meal on the arm and interrupting our dinner is not treating me and my friends with respect. It's not right."

Nothing infuriated Joe more than an owner sending over customers, then not picking up the tab. If such an intrusion happened, that restaurant would never see Joe DiMaggio again.

WHEN JOE FLEW up from Florida, I often picked him up at the airport. On the way into town, we had a tradition of stopping in Brooklyn at Bamonte's on Withers Street, not too far from the roar of the

Brooklyn-Queens Expressway. My mother came from Greenpoint, just over the divider from the restaurant. At the time, Greenpoint was a sprawl of industrial buildings and three-story wood-frame houses.

Joe loved good food. He understood that the local mobsters had high standards when it came to Italian food and would never eat at a restaurant that served bad food. The "boys" were regulars at Bamonte's, along with business executives, entertainment and sports stars, and neighborhood people. Just as in medicine, you can't discriminate in whom you treat or in this case to whom you serve dinner. Joe knew all about mobsters, because sports means gambling, and where there is gambling there are gangsters. He also ran into the mob in Hollywood, where the unions and some producers were known to mix with gangsters. It was inevitable that, at some point, he would find himself eating in the company of Mafiosi at Bamonte's.

The Yankee Clipper was not intimidated by the mob, but he was respectful. In his view, they were businessmen—illegitimate businessmen. Joe referred to them with the classic Italian gesture, pressing one side of his nose with his finger and pushing it up, making a pug nose. Even though he was Sicilian, he would never make the gesture to their faces. He avoided getting the pug noses of mobbed-up guys out of joint.

I shared his take on gangsters. Growing up Italian, I saw there was a career path to the mob that most don't take. You ended up owing too much for a favor, and they never failed to show up to collect with interest. Even so, I considered the Mafia to be businessmen who solved their mergers and conflicts outside the courts. From an early age, my brother and I knew local made men in Bensonhurst.

Time has shown that politicians, judges, and businessmen are often not much different. Hoods don't start unnecessary wars, pyramid your life savings away on Wall Street, or post photos of their private parts on YouTube. Mobsters don't point fingers or pretend to be superior. They don't presume to be untouchable pillars of the community. There is nothing phony about a gangster, and there was nothing phony about

Joe DiMaggio. Joe would never disrespect a member of the Mafia, and mobsters adored Joe, but not the other way around, as I was soon to find out.

On our way to our regular table at Bamonte's that night, we passed by tables of locals and heard respectful murmurs about Mr. DiMaggio. For privacy, we sat off the main aisle at the very back of the restaurant, to the far right next to a refrigerator case, laden with cannoli, ricotta cheesecake, and creamy desserts. We were looking forward to a satisfying meal. Joe faced the room, which provided him with a vantage point of diners who might approach to seek his autograph and disrupt our dinner.

The local *caporegime*, a label usually shortened to *capo*, which refers to a high-ranking made member of a crime family who heads a group of soldiers, happened to be at Bamonte's that night with his crew. I won't name him here. He is a courtly, if sometimes vicious, mobster, who loves the veal specialty at Bamonte's. We learned that he was making a circuit of the local so-called firehouses of organized crime in northern Brooklyn, the social clubs in which things sometimes aren't so social. Needless to say, no one ever turned him down for a table.

The gangster spotted us.

When he and his wrecking crew began digging into a huge bowl of pasta, Joe turned to me and said, "I don't feel right being here tonight. There's a tableful of pug noses over there," he said as he made the traditional gesture.

I hoped no one at that table noticed.

"It looks like a mobbed-up night. We shouldn't be seen here tonight. It's not good for my image." Joe gazed over at the gathering of thugs and made eye contact with the hardened men.

I was squirming and felt the need to keep us both out of cement shoes. Trying to be diplomatic, I said, "Relax, Joe, you've watched too many movies. Anthony Bamonte can't discriminate. The food is good here, and these boys always pay the bill and know the best places to eat."

"Hey, those aren't Eagle Scouts over there," Joe responded. "They're looking over here. They recognize me.

"And one's coming over," Joe said in alarm.

The *capo* had removed his napkin from his lap, had gotten up, and was headed for our table.

"Quick, Doc, get rid of those two empty chairs at our table, just in case they have any ideas about sitting down with us."

But the mobster reached our table before I could make a move. I turned to Joe and said quietly, "Joe, this one is Tony X—a hard case if you ever saw one."

Tony X reportedly threatened a federal judge before his sentencing in Foley Square a year earlier. He was now on probation, so his threats must have worked. Tony was reputed to be able to fieldstrip any weapon blindfolded and knew every prescribed way to dissolve a body. He was a dark and ominous man, with a narrow nose and an indecipherable grin.

Beginning with a nod, he comported himself with exaggerated deference. I was sure he used the same manner to disarm his victims.

"You must excuse me, sirs. Mr. DiMaggio, I am a great admirer of yours. May I talk with you before dinner?"

Joe gave a small nod and said, "You may talk to me standing up. You can't break bread with me. I don't break bread with . . . uh . . ." Joe couldn't find the right word, such as plumbing contractor, electrician, or olive-oil importer to substitute for mobster to avoid being stuffed in the back of a Cadillac sedan trunk found floating in Jamaica Bay.

To my relief, he got away with the slight.

"No words need to be said. I understand." Tony went on to explain, "We would all like to meet you, if that is fine with you, of course, Signore DiMaggio."

It was certainly fine with me. I hoped Joe felt the same way.

"Who's we?" Joe asked.

The old hoodlum responded in a fatherly, benign fashion, "My friends and I. May we come over here? They really want to shake your hand."

I knew Joe had real reservations. He feared being photographed with Mafiosi.

"Well, I guess a fan is a fan, but no pictures—okay. I really want us to get to dinner soon." Joe was wise enough to cave in.

Visibly pleased, the *capo* waved to his table. His dinner companions were men who would make J. Edgar Hoover quail. None of them were south of six-foot-three and 300 well-fed pounds. I assumed they were hit men or enforcers, dressed in Armani and Brioni. Tony X lined them up like second-graders on a field trip. As they took their places, they straightened out their silk ties, pressed their suits with their hands, and ran their fingers through their hair. Tony brought and introduced each member of the crew in turn.

Joe was amused as each giant stepped forward to shake his hand. I used all my brainpower to will him not to slight the mobsters.

Tony X dipped his head and said, "Thank you, Mr. DiMaggio. The dinner, please, is on us."

Joe shook his head no. "That's okay, Mr. X, but I pay for my own meals. Thank you, anyway."

Tony X seemed to understand and did not insist. He returned to the hoods at their table with a schoolboy bounce in his step. The DiMaggio Effect strikes again.

"I guess he was the den mother of those scouts, huh?" Joe asked grinning. "That last guy. He looked familiar."

I was happy to fill him in. "Joe, supposedly that last one bit the ear off an Arizona policeman five years ago—and it was a routine traffic stop."

"Glad he already had some pasta tonight," Joe joked, then moved in with a lesson. "Always make sure that fellows like this owe you, not the other way around. The Old Guard had class. These young bucks don't have a clue about honor or class. These mobsters are like flashy sports cars—all showoffs. They don't remember honor or respect. Ever notice how many of them end up as rats? They turn on their own family."

Having owned a restaurant himself, Joe was a tough critic of food, atmosphere, and service, and Bamonte's was one of his favorites.

Bamonte's homemade *stracciatella*, an Italian egg drop soup, and the *pastina in brodo* tasted the way Joe's mother made them. Joe idolized his mother. He was a typical Italian-American *mammalucia*, the apple of his mother's eye. He loved Bamonte's *pastina in brodo*, but it was a salty soup.

"Maybe you should lay off the *pastina*," I warned Joe one night as the soup was brought steaming from the kitchen soon after we had dug into the antipasto. Anthony Bamonte knew how to keep Joe happy.

Joe gave me a lecture on restaurant etiquette. "Never tell a restaurant owner that the food doesn't taste good. Best to eat and shut up, because you don't want to offend him."

Joe proceeded to eat the *pastina in brodo* and woke up the next morning with his ankles swollen to twice their normal size. Though his legs looked like the Michelin tire man, he would rather suffer the physical consequences of eating a highly salted soup than offend the owner. His behavior was also dictated by another one of his guiding principles: don't let anyone ever know you are afraid, weak, or suffering. Even well into his seventies, Joe was not willing to seem vulnerable.

At another memorable evening at Bamonte's, I watched Joe help himself to olives served just for him. Joe loved his olives—oil cured, green, spicy, parsley encrusted, you name it. And let's not forget the celery sticks served standing in ice water.

When the owner, Anthony Bamonte, saw us, he came over beaming. Bamonte, like his fellow restaurateurs, knew Joe was good for business. Joe knew good food and could eat anywhere. If he chose your restaurant, the endorsement was worth more than any four-star review in the *New York Times* or *Zagat*'s. When Joe was dining out, word spread like wildfire through the neighborhood in which the restaurant was located. Half the neighborhood would show up to eat when they heard Joltin' Joe was enjoying a meal in a local restaurant.

"Hey, Joe, do you mind if I join you?" the owner asked. "Doc, okay by you?"

We nodded, and Joe gestured toward a chair.

"Anthony, I always love seeing you and your wonderful family here at the restaurant. You all go out of the way to make me and the Doc feel at home."

"Joe, it's our pleasure and honor. I just want you to enjoy yourself and relax when you come here. Then I'm happy."

Anthony turned to me and said, "Doc, you been busy? The guys at the bar saw you on television last week. You looked great. It's hard to believe you grew up around here.

"The guys were saying that they remember you when you gave those three punks a beating at McCarren Park when you were a kid. You grated their faces against the fence."

I remembered, alright. It was my residency in Brooklyn social theory.

"Yeah, I do," I muttered, not exactly comfortable that this blast from the past had come up.

"They never came back again after that." Anthony chuckled.

Joe chimed in. "Tell Anthony about the time you defended the rabbi."

"Ah, come on," I protested.

"No, really, it's a good story," Joe insisted.

I couldn't refuse a command performance from Joe.

"My brother John and I sort of adopted the world's poorest shul as kids, and they adopted us. It was on the outskirts of the wealthiest Jewish community in the world. We became Shabbos goys and made money doing things for the shul's members that they were forbidden to do on the Sabbath, such as opening letters, turning on lights, and other everyday rituals. We were the only Catholic school kids who liked Chanukah better than Christmas, because of the gelt we received from our satisfied neighbors and customers. We preferred this over the holiday Italian lemon cookies from the local bakeshops. We sang 'Dreidel Bells' not 'Jingle Bells' at the holiday parties.

"Anyway, the shul was a walk-in shul, not the granite temples you see in Manhattan. This was a world away. The members were mostly old folks.

"The neighborhood toughs took to interrupting services with catcalls, smoke bombs, and firecrackers during the warm months and snowballs in the winter. Until they tried it in front of us."

"What happened?" Anthony asked as Joe smiled in approval.

"One day, we cuffed some imbecile for throwing a snowball at the tall, black hat of the rabbi, even though we admired the shot from across 65th Street."

"Dank you, boys," the rabbi said as he readjusted his fur hat on his head after retrieving it from the street.

"Our grandmother always told us to be good to the Jews . . . they have friends in high places."

"I'll second that," Joe agreed. "But you were probably just bruising for a fight."

"Not true—the rabbi needed our help."

"I know, I know. You were a stand-up guy even then," Joe laughed.

"Besides, we were bigger than the other kids, and no one bothered us. We didn't have to fight."

Joe was so relaxed that night I decided it was a perfect opportunity to tell him a funny story.

"Anthony, I love my roots," I said as I winked at the restaurateur. "I used to walk around these streets with my grandpa Danny, the gravedigger, and my Uncle Joe. Whenever they heard hoofbeats from the horses pulling wagons, mobile shops filled with produce or fish on ice, they would send my brother and me out with a pail to pick up the horseshit. They had two shovels that they kinda borrowed from the Parks Department to pick up the manure."

"Now wait a minute, Doc. Why would they . . . ?" Joe started to ask a question.

Anthony and I laughed. Anthony continued with an old neighborhood story we both knew well. "Joe, here's why. With all the tomato and victory gardens around here, people needed horseshit. They used a lot for planting, for fertilizer, you know.

"Anyway, manure was at a premium. I remember all the old guys running into the streets and fighting over who was going to get the prized horseshit for their gardens. The 'Mustache Petes,' the old Italians from the other side, the old timers said that horseshit made the tomatoes and the eggplant grow larger. In this neighborhood, people would have fights over who had the biggest tomatoes and eggplants. It was just as important as who had the biggest dick in Greenpoint. Really," Anthony concluded.

Joe was incredulous. "Horseshit for tomatoes and eggplant? That's a new one."

Anthony continued the narrative. "Yeah, Joe, there are a lot of uses for horseshit. The doctor in the neighborhood used it for patients."

Joe was outright dismissive. "C'mon Anthony, you guys are pulling my leg."

"No, Joe, it's true," Anthony responded. "A family doctor around here used to put the horse manure on open wounds. It supposedly brought the infection out. Horseshit was an antibiotic in the old days o' Brooklyn . . . Greenpoint antibiotic."

Joe bought it. "Imagine—horseshit," was his only comment.

Anthony turned to me. "But, Doc, there was one really bad result. A guy named Whitey had a terrible gash in his leg. So, Whitey limped his way up to old Dr. Barricini, who packed the gash with horseshit from the street. Dr. Barricini told Whitey to go home, get rest, and stay off the leg."

"I've never heard anything like it," I said. "What happened, Anthony?"

"Later that night, Whitey was bangin' on Dr. Barricini's door at three in the morning screaming with pain. He was drunk as a skunk and in horrible pain.

"The neighbors stuck their heads out their windows to see what all the screaming was about. There was Whitey screamin' for help. He was screaming, 'That horseshit is killing me!' "

I could barely keep a straight face, but Joe was riveted.

"What happened to Whitey? Did he . . . ?" Joe was really concerned.

"Here's what happened." Anthony loved telling this story about the old neighborhood. "Barricini looked at the leg, which was swollen to three times its normal size. Barricini delivered his diagnosis, 'No, it's no good.' He told Whitey that he had to go to the hospital immediately. The leg had to be opened to drain all the pus."

Joe paled. "Anthony, what happened?"

"Dr. Barricini told Whitey that the horse where the manure was from must have been a sick horse."

It dawned on Joe that we were having a little fun with him.

"What? Oh, c'mon. Doc? Anthony?"

"This is a true story, Joe. I wouldn't lie. I mean it." Anthony would not back down.

"Sounds like the good doctor was a horse's ass," Joe said.

Anthony maintained his straight face for a beat, then burst out laughing, and we joined him. Joe was a good sport and could take a joke.

Joe changed tack. "Anthony, can I ask you a question?"

"Sure, Joe, anything."

"I noticed on my way in here that the picture of my mother and me—the one that I had signed for you—is now over the men's room door."

I hadn't noticed. Joe would consider this sacrilege and an insult to his mother. We had been having such a great evening. I braced myself for what might well follow.

"You know, Anthony, that's one picture I never sign at autograph shows. Only special friends get my signature on anything personal like that. Can you maybe put it in a nicer place?"

I was relieved that Joe was respectful but let it be known that he was not pleased.

"Joe, no offense was meant," Anthony explained, aware that the situation was dicey. "There's a good reason why the photo's over the men's room door. Diesel, you know, the bartender here, and I, were afraid that someone was going to walk off with that rare picture of you and your mother. People around here know the value of that photo, especially since you signed it."

Joe was open but still not satisfied. "Okay . . ."

Anthony continued. "We thought the best place to put it would be over the bathroom door so that Diesel can always keep an eye on it from the bar. And if someone was going to try to lift it, he'd have to get up on a chair to get it. We hung it there to protect it."

Joe accepted the explanation. His mother's honor was satisfied.

"Okay, Anthony, I get it," Joe said with a twinkle in his eye. "But I do have to commend you for the place you put Mantle's picture—over the men's urinal in the bathroom. The perfect spot for that jerk." Joltin' Joe did not have much respect for my childhood baseball hero.

"Thanks for not putting that picture of me in the shithouse!"

"You're very welcome, Joe. Very welcome." Anthony's relief was apparent.

The three of us had a good laugh. Dinner with DiMaggio was almost always a great time.

CHAPTER 4

In the Melting Pot

Saturday - June 19, 1993

Have met
gone over my future appearance that I have to make shortly,
and he has not lived up to his word about going over
my talk, — but, this is a practice he goes through
ninety % of the time. He does have my papers that give
me an idea of what I want to say. I always trust
people, when things are done. So being my philosophy —
I have it all worked out what I will say during my acceptance.

The path of the Positano family intersected with Joe DiMaggio's at an Italian fundraiser years before I met the Yankee Clipper. A long-lost Positano family heirloom captured the legendary Joe DiMaggio with my uncle and father at a charity event. The cherished photograph was a framed, table-wide shot of Father John Positano, my brother's namesake, at a communion breakfast with Joe DiMaggio. Father John, an Augustinian priest who was a legend in his own right, raised a parish from the tomato fields of Vineland, New Jersey, with donations of food and money from the Progresso Soup Company but without support from his bishop.

Father John Positano was a master at fundraising, using his great talent with the clarinet. Our Lady of Pompeii Church and St. Mary's school in Vineland, New Jersey, were his pride and joy. The Order of St. Augustine priests ran the show. His flock included Fabian, Frankie Avalon, Joey Bishop, and Ted Mack, to name a few. He came to our house in Brooklyn with baskets of peppers and eggplant from the Progresso Soup farm. We jammed with my dad on the piano, my brother on the guitar, and me on the trumpet. But he would always take my sheet music, which I had saved up to buy. I got smart and started to hide the music before he got to the house.

In the photo, Joe was sitting in the center of a long table of dignitaries, all sipping coffee and eating powdered eggs. Father John was front and center with Joe. At the back, leaning forward, was our father, Rocco, who gazed reverently at Joe. Though Pop was a decorated combat veteran of the Pacific and a crack shot with a rifle, he was clearly enthralled as he leaned toward his idol. I can only imagine what Pop would have said if he had lived to see his son hanging out with Joe DiMaggio in the glittering world of Manhattan.

My father played USO baseball with Phil Rizzuto and Chuck

Connors, the television legend of *The Rifleman*. He played ball for informal, Minor League teams in Bensonhurst and Sunset Park, Brooklyn. Dad never fully accepted the fact that he wasn't cut out to be a Major League ballplayer, so he tried to make up for it with John and me. We played ball on the same fields as Dad, Connors, and Sandy Koufax at Erasmus High School. Dad would line us up against a green wood plank fence and pitch balls for us to hit. We had to compete with the deafening sounds of the F-train el that was adjacent to the field. Many a foul ball landed in the Jewish cemetery located across McDonald Avenue. Nobody ever wanted to retrieve the ball from the resting place.

The press and biographers always focused on Joe's immigrant roots and how wonderful it was that this poor Italian boy became an American icon. He made a point of attending Italian-American events and wanted to be a shining example of his people for all people.

Joe DiMaggio's America wasn't a melting pot. Neither was mine, growing up in Bensonhurst. When I was a child and when Joe began to play ball, Italians were at the bottom rung of the social ladder.

Though Joe made no public announcements about any bias and prejudice he suffered, he told a different story in private. Early in his career, Joe was stung by sports articles that reported he rubbed his hair with olive oil and combed it so-called dago style. There's no question in my mind that insults like these contributed to his fastidiousness, which was so often interpreted as vanity.

Joe embodied the immigrant work ethic. A good Italian-American son, he wanted to please his parents. He felt he had a responsibility to the family and wanted to pull his weight. As a young man, he was grounded in living Italian-American style, which combined shared hardship and the joys of family life.

His father wanted all five of his sons to join the family fishing business. Joe didn't like working on his father's boat, because he got seasick. The smell of dead fish made him sicker. Giuseppe was furious that Joe wouldn't help.

"My father knew that I didn't want to be a fisherman, that's for sure," Joe told me. "I hated the very smell of fish, old fish the worst. So Pop wrote me off for the family business, such as it was."

Joe knew early in his teens that he had a gift for playing baseball. He was actually "late" to the game and had preferred other sports to baseball. He knew he could excel in this sport. Joe was driven to go where he had the strongest chance of being the best and of making good money. Predictably, his immigrant father took a dim view of playing a game for a living.

"My father wanted me to be a bookkeeper," Joe revealed, still dismayed by the thought. "He thought I was *lagnuso*, lazy, not a go-getter. He figured that bookkeepers sat down all day. My father thought I needed a job with very little exertion required, so bookkeeper came to mind."

"Why did he think you were lazy?" I asked.

"There were two jobs in the family business," Joe explained. "The first was actually fishing—bringing in the haul in nets. The other job was cleaning the bottom of the boat. That was less work, but very unpleasant. It made me queasy and seasick." Joe grimaced at the memory. "Let's just say that I had enthusiasm for neither job, and I didn't hide my opinion from my father."

Joe went on to tell me that his father was convinced that Joe's siblings would make it big before he would. Joe had been a disappointment, rejected by his father at a young age. He made the cut only after he was a star and a financial success. Joe's role model for fatherhood had little to do with unconditional love and acceptance, which appears to have played out in the next generation, possibly contributing to Joe's estrangement from his own son.

Sports were a meal ticket to Joe. It was a chance to escape doing ship-shank knots in nets, to avoid cutting off fish heads, and to flee the bottom of his father's old boat. He viewed his pursuit of sports as a pathway to getting the trappings of education without the seat time.

Joe had a rigorous mind and a sharp wit, but his lack of schooling was a source of insecurity. Joe's memory was terrific. He used this attribute brilliantly in his baseball career, and it served him well after he retired. As he once explained to me, what made him an iconic baseball player had as much to do with his memory and intellect as with his physical prowess.

DiMaggio was intellectually brilliant. His knowledge of the game and how it should be played was the equivalent of a Yale or Harvard education. He called his brother Dom "the professor," but Joe was the real deal and a full professor in all areas of the game. He could predict the pitch a pitcher would throw by remembering what that pitcher threw to him in the past. He used his mind. He waited in the batter's box, knowing that a curve ball or a fastball down the middle was coming, and would rocket the ball over the fence.

The strength of his memory was often evident when he was asked to sign an autograph. Someone could approach him with a picture or a baseball, and the Clipper would say, "Hey, wait a minute. Didn't I sign a ball for this same guy a couple of years ago?" People would be flabbergasted that he had remembered and would walk away in disbelief.

It was nearly impossible to fool Joe. It is never a good idea to try to pull the wool over a Sicilian's eyes, but this is especially true of a Sicilian with an elephant's memory like Joe's. I learned not to try. Never forgetting Joe's Sicilian heritage was essential to knowing him.

To get away from fishing, Joe, his older brother Vince, and younger brother Dominic took to the neighborhood sandlots. Baseball was the big game of the time, and the boys had athletic skill.

Joe dropped out of high school when he was sixteen. He did a variety of odd jobs, and developed a growing reputation as a semi-pro baseball player. Late in the 1932 season, he joined Vince, who had signed earlier in the year, to play for the San Francisco Seals of the Pacific Coast League (PCL). The PCL was a highly regarded independent league, just a half step below the Major Leagues.

Baseball was, and still is, a sport in which immigrants could make a name for themselves and ease their assimilation into the culture. Joe's father and others of his generation knew nothing about baseball, because sports were a pastime for wealthy men. Joe's father considered baseball to be trivial, neither respectable nor careerworthy. He had no enthusiasm for the game until his three sons began to bring home big baseball contracts. Then Giuseppe caught the fever.

"My father could predict my hitting average every year," Joe told me with pride. "He could be accurate to the hit—how about that?"

I was impressed that a man who couldn't spell baseball in Italian or English and had learned the game in middle age in a foreign country, had developed this remarkable ability. But I should not have been surprised. I had watched Joe Di predict with unerring accuracy the outcome of any game he watched, often against the odds. It was probably genetic—like father, like son.

I wanted to know about the prejudice he and his family experienced. In the hope that he would talk about how he reacted to anti-Italian slurs, I told him some family stories about the slights the Positanos suffered and how my grandfather had to change his name to find work.

I proceeded to narrate some dramatic Positano history. When our paternal grandparents came from Italy, the only jobs available were coal mining and sand hogging. Descended from *carabinieri*, Italian military police, and a tall, well-built man, my grandfather became a watchman at the coalmines in Freeland, Pennsylvania. Since the coalmines did not often hire foreigners and his English was not very good, he used a neighbor's name when he applied to the mine. He changed our name from Positano to Foster. My father's name was Rocky Foster, not Rocky Positano. They stopped using the Italian last name. It gave me a better understanding and empathy for what my Jewish friends and their families had to endure when they took the name of towns in Italy as their surname.

Joe related to the problem. "I was always happy with my real name," Joe said after my lead-in to the story. "People sometimes mentioned that I should go Anglo, but I never would, never could. I knew that there was a price to pay, but I was willing to do so.

"My father didn't think of becoming an American citizen," he went on. "He was old country and only spoke a little English. It didn't bother him, and no one cared about it until Pearl Harbor." Joe started a slow boil as he talked.

The United States government had reached a solution for the 600,000 or so Italians who were not citizens in the opening months of World War II. They were called "enemy aliens," and their movements were restricted. Giuseppe DiMaggio became an enemy alien. Joe told me what had happened.

"The government passed all sorts of laws saying that people like my father—a harmless guy—was an enemy alien. Imagine the balls of that, Doc!" Joe still found it incredible after all this time. "They passed a law that he couldn't go fishing, couldn't own a gun, couldn't even own a flashlight. He lost his livelihood." Joe shook his head. "He wasn't allowed to fish, because San Francisco and Oakland were big ports, shipping out military convoys.

"A few years earlier, I had made enough money from baseball, and I knew that my father always wanted to own a restaurant. So I bundled together some money and went into business with him as a partner. We called the restaurant on Fisherman's Wharf DiMaggio's Seafood Restaurant—for the draw, right? The place was right off the pier. You can't get fresher fish than that!"

"Sounds great," I said.

Joe continued his story. "The war broke out. Italians, like the Japanese and Germans, were foreign enemies. Japanese, Italians, and Germans already in the United States were getting investigated. The Japanese were put into camps, imprisoned for their nationality."

"Not a great moment in American history," I remarked.

"My old man wasn't sent to a camp like the Japanese—that wasn't in the cards. But California was the front line."

"So, what happened?" I had never heard about this before.

"Some stupid bastards passed a rule that Italians, whether fish-ermen, boat owners, even restaurant owners, couldn't be anywhere within a mile of the harbor. The thinking was that they could be sabo-teurs, planning to blow up facilities and boats."

"Oh, no." I got the picture. "They saw DiMaggio's restaurant down the street from the piers where the ships are loaded . . ."

"Yep, they knew the DiMaggio was me, and I was American born. It didn't matter. My father was a partner and managed the place. So a Fed came to me one day and told me that Dad was a foreign national and was banned from managing or even visiting DiMaggio's Seafood Restaurant. But he said we could relocate the restaurant several miles inland."

"I can't believe they put you through that."

Joe shrugged his shoulders. "Eventually, we ironed things out with the government. In the meantime, Dad was prohibited from entering his own restaurant. He couldn't understand why he was banned from a restaurant named for him."

He went on, "Here I was, playing my part in the war, traveling the whole Pacific in the Army and entertaining the troops, and my father was not allowed to even stop by his restaurant for a glass of wine and a few pieces of bread. I had nothing to say in the matter. I just shut up and did my tour."

"Do you think your being the Yankee Clipper had anything to do with the government's finally giving your father fewer restrictions?" I was curious.

"I'll never know," he responded. "A million Italian-Americans served in the war, and more than half that number had to worry about owning a flashlight and carrying an Enemy Alien card. It makes me angry to this day."

———————

JOE HATED THAT war. I heard about it at a dinner one night with Mario Faustini. Three Marines on leave were sitting nearby. The leathernecks recognized Joe in the crowd and nodded to him. Joe grinned and nodded back.

"You know, you've never mentioned your time in the service," Mario commented.

"I'd like to say I was a hero, Mario," Joe responded, "but that would be stretching things a bit too far."

I could tell Joe wanted to change the subject, but I was curious about this time in his life. "Joe, why don't you tell Mario the story about the baseball game you almost didn't play?"

"Doc, why don't you shut up?" Joe shot back. "That's not a story that I'm particularly proud of." Joe had come close to apologizing for his outburst.

"C'mon, Joe, it's only us here." Sensing a great story, Mario persisted.

Joe nodded. "I was in the USO . . . that's the entertainment command of the armed forces. I was in the entertainment end of the war."

I have since read that FDR and General George Marshall, chief of the armed services in World War Two, did not want Joe shipped overseas to a combat command. They were concerned that if an enemy sniper blew off his head, it would severely damage the morale of an army of Joe Di fans in uniform. So Joe played ball.

"A bunch of professional ball players—Rizzuto, Williams—were getting set to play an exhibition game at a makeshift stadium at one of the bases," Joe continued with his story. "The brass decided it was good for the soldiers' morale to watch baseball games."

"You mean Ted Williams . . . of the Red Sox, Joe?" Mario asked.

"Yeah . . . that Ted Williams," Joe said. "Let me tell you something about Ted Williams. He and I were never the best of friends on or off the field, but he was a real war hero, a flyboy. He was a crack pilot, a fighting ace, who locked wings with a fella called John

Glenn." He looked up to see if we got it. "Yeah, that John Glenn . . . the astronaut."

I was surprised to hear Joe extol his archrival Williams while he minimized his own role in the war. I had to ask, "What made Williams such an ace?"

"Simple, real simple, he had great eyes," Joe said as he pointed to his own eyes. "Like an eagle, I tell ya. He could make out the eyes of an enemy pilot as well as he could see the seams on a baseball." Joe's admiration was not grudging.

"Doc," he continued, "he could pick out the silvery speck of an enemy plane from miles out and get the jump on the enemy pilot, but . . ." Joe decided not to go overboard. "Uh, enough of that hero."

He got back on track. "On the morning before the exhibition game, I heard that soldiers were taking bets on who was going to win." His expression darkened.

"It infuriated me. I mean, it was against every one of my principles," Joe explained. "I played the game to win, but I played the game for its own sake, war or no war. I would never have my name associated with gambling—morale boosting or not."

Mario asked, "So, what did you do?"

"I got hold of the commanding officer, a captain, and told him that I wasn't going to play that game no matter what. He almost had a fit, because he was flying in a general to see the game." Joe paused for effect. "He got on the horn and rounded up the divisional platoon of military police. These big, red-neck Southern boys broke up the gambling on the base."

"And?" Mario wanted to hear the rest of the story.

"I played the game, and we won. The captain got another bar for his shoulders. Man, was he happy!" Joe concluded.

Joe went on to arrange for night games. He prompted the Army to use its Corps of Engineers to install lights at the makeshift stadiums.

I was curious about how Joe handled the uniform. It was hard to imagine him in standard Army issue. "What kind of uniform did you wear during the war?"

He grinned. "Oh, Doc . . . I was the sight, I tell ya. I had a good Italian tailor fit me. My uniform was custom tailored and fit like a glove. My pants—not like yours, Doc—were perfectly creased, like in the army reg. The knot in my tie was right out of the manual. You could see the reflection of your face on my polished shoes.

"But I hated that war. There was no glory in it for me. It robbed me out of three seasons of my prime. I was so young. I never did recover those seasons or get my form back. There I was, left to play with mediocre wartime players. I felt more like a circus clown entertaining the troops."

The memories brought a scowl to Joe's face.

"Doc, think about the number of World Series championships and pennants I could have won in those three seasons."

It was time to cheer him up.

"But your enemies at the time, the Japs," Mario said, "they go crazy for you even until this day."

Joe smiled.

"Yes, they were baseball nuts even then. The Japanese called me 'Banzai Joe' after the war. I would go to their exhibition games in Japan and kill their pitchers. Even today, I can't walk down the street in Japan without getting mobbed and followed by fans, but, hey, the war's over!"

Joe served in the Army for his country. He traded his substantial $43,750 salary from the Yankees for $50 a month as an army enlisted man. When he joined the Army, DiMaggio was a twenty-eight-year-old superstar at the height of his athletic powers. By the time he was discharged from the service, he was nearly thirty-one, divorced, underweight, malnourished, and bitter. Those three years, 1943 to 1945, created a gap in his playing career that cut his career totals significantly. Few would disagree with this assessment.

One of my favorites of Joe's melting-pot stories was his account of the famous force play from hell, one of the dumbest errors in baseball history, which involved the label *dago*. The derogatory term, originally used to describe Italians right off the boat, was in wide use in less politically correct days. When Joe was playing ball, Hispanics as well as Italians were called dagos. This story of one of the legendary errors in baseball has been told before, but I heard this version directly from Joe's mouth.

"We were playing at Yankee Stadium one Sunday. Lefty Gomez was pitching."

Joe made a melting-pot observation. "Lefty's political views had nothing to do with his nickname. He was called Lefty, because he pitched left-handed, to distinguish him from another Gomez, who pitched right-handed. Hispanic-Americans were easily confused for one another in those days.

"I was in center field, Tony Lazzeri at second base, and Frankie Crosetti was playing shortstop. A batter bunted toward the pitcher's mound. Gomez fumbled around for it.

"The coaches were screaming furiously, because a runner was going from first base to second, and he had to be thrown out.

"Well, Gomez finally grabbed the ball, and the coaches were yelling directions to him.

"A coach ordered, 'Throw the ball to the dago!'

"Cradling the ball, Gomez had a choice of dagos. There was DiMaggio, Crosetti, and Lazzeri to choose from. Lefty stood there baffled. The coaches yelled in unison, 'Throw the ball to the dago!'

"Gomez didn't know where to throw the ball. I was the Italian prime dago. There was Tony on second, and Frankie ready to tag out the runner. Gomez was a good Yankee and wanted to follow the vague directions.

"Lefty figured that I was the dago of choice and threw the ball all the way out to me in center, which made no sense. Center field was nowhere near the runner, who could not believe his luck.

"'What the hell is he doing?' everyone asked.

"I fielded the ball from Gomez and called 'Time!' The runner was safe at second.

"I ran to the infield to discuss what had happened. I hadn't heard the directions about throwing balls to dagos. I was collected when I spoke to Gomez. 'Lefty, can I ask you why—with a man on first base and running to second—why would you throw the ball out to me in center field?'

"'I got so confused,' Lefty responded, 'when they were screaming to throw the ball to the dago, I threw the ball to you, Joe, not Tony or Frankie.'

"'Okay,' I said to him, 'that explains it.'

"I didn't take it personally. I just walked back to center field laughing."

Joe got a kick out of telling this story, but the truth is that the Yankees might have lost the game because one dago looked like another to the enlightened coaches. I'm glad to say that things certainly have changed.

One day, over breakfast, Joe reminisced about the Yankees of his time. Joe often spoke about Tony Lazzeri, for whom he had a soft spot, especially with regard to his post baseball career. Lazzeri suffered from epilepsy, a seizure disorder. Joe was sorry to hear that Lazzeri had fallen down a flight of stairs after suffering a seizure, which contributed to his ultimate demise.

———

JOE HAD AN uncanny knack for attracting and keeping admirers. That's why going out with him in New York City was so exciting. He was recognized wherever he went and always knew someone in the room when we were out on the town. Sometimes, I forgot the extent of his fame or underestimated his celebrity, and he did, too. But then something would happen to demonstrate to me that he was still a hero to a lot of people. Take the time he decided to attend Sunday Mass at St. Patrick's Cathedral on Fifth Avenue. Of course, I was dragged along.

Few people realized what a devout Catholic Joe was. I called him a 4-C, which stands for a closet card-carrying Catholic. He wanted to impress upon me that a little religion was good for the soul, which was akin to his belief that even the best players needed a little coaching. I was flattered that he was trying to save my soul, so I went along for the ride.

I was horrified that he had chosen the Cathedral. There are multiple entrances, and knots of tourists, not there to pray, gathered by the doors. Tourists were always prowling from wall to wall and pew to pew, many dropping coins in the well-positioned collection boxes at the entrances and in the chapels, each dedicated to a saint. Since it was a Sunday, it would be a heavy tourist day, because crowds came to see the Cardinal perform Mass.

"Joe, I can take you to any church you like," I said. "It could be St. Joe's Hole in the Wall in Canarsie."

It had fallen on me to take care of him and to guide him away from a potentially chaotic situation. I tried to convince him to go to another church that day, but he would hear none of it. I was annoyed that he didn't trust my judgment.

"No, Doc. I have a secret weapon to fool the tourists and autograph hounds . . . sunglasses." He whipped out a pair from his jacket pocket. "They won't recognize me with these. I'm just gonna walk down the aisle, and you'll see. No fuss, no bother, no autographs. Wait and see."

"Joe, you've got to be out of your friggin' mind," I responded with eloquence. "Sunglasses, silver hair, classic profile. Joe, it won't work."

He turned to me and said, "Doc, I want to go to the Cardinal's Mass at St. Patrick's. I am not going to let my religion suffer because people recognize me. I want a normal life, to receive communion."

"Normal life, all right. You'll be embarrassed by the coverage. Get ready for a *New York Post* spread, complete with a bad picture."

Joe shook his head with Old Testament fervor. "You'll see, Mr. Yale Man. The sunglasses will work. You walk the point, and I'll follow."

I led the way for the ambush ahead through the East 51st Street entrance of the Cathedral, muttering, "This is gonna be interesting."

We weaved our way through the tourists, who recognized Joe immediately. The buzz and head turning was a dead giveaway. If someone didn't recognize Joe, a neighbor in the crowd would fill him in. Almost all the tourists identified Joe trying to sneak into a pew during the homily, the speech given by the priest celebrating the Mass following a scripture reading.

Not far away was the celebrant of the Mass, His Eminence John Cardinal O'Connor, who smiled when he noticed Joe DiMaggio sitting before him, attempting to be invisible.

Looking straight ahead, Joe did his best to ignore the hubbub his presence had created.

"Yeah, we really fooled them, Joe," I whispered to him out of the side of my mouth. "Master of disguise, do you have any books to sign? How about eight-by-ten glossies? This might get ugly."

And then the Cardinal spoke from the pulpit, "My dear parishioners, I am delighted and honored to have in our presence celebrating Mass today . . ." A showman, Cardinal O'Connor paused for effect. "A truly great American—Mr. Joe DiMaggio," the Cardinal announced to the crowd, which numbered about two thousand. The Cathedral erupted with applause.

"Hey, Joe, that disguise really worked, you really fooled them," I commented on his invisible camouflage.

Joe just stared forward.

During the service, a hefty tourist in an "I ❤ New York" tee-shirt approached the pew where we were seated. He wasn't there to exchange the "peace of Christ be with you" handshake with Joe. Instead, the guy pulled out a glossy photograph of the pope, thrust it into Joe's solar plexus, and asked Joe to sign the photograph.

The clueless tourist said something that made me wince. "I'm goin' to put this next to my picture of Marilyn Monroe."

Joe's blank expression changed into a dark scowl.

"I don't think that the pope would like me signing my autograph across the front of his head," Joe growled.

As the tourist retreated without an autograph, I couldn't keep myself from teasing my friend. "Bucking for pope, Joe," I said. "It's about time. Did you know the pope is a baseball fan? Tommy Lasorda told me he manages a whole team of Cardinals at the Vatican."

Joe groaned. "Very funny, Doc. Let's get out of here. I can't even pray in peace."

As we were leaving our pew, the tourists and starstruck Catholics began to seize the religious literature about penance, good works, and proper living, which is available in racks near the entrances and in the side chapels, in the hope that Joe would sign them. No doubt, most would be sold. A Joe DiMaggio inscribed prayer book had to be worth something.

The press of maddened supplicants was threatening to both of us. Prayer books and missals became objects of terror, pressed against us for value enhancement. Frightened for our physical safety, I ran out and enlisted the aid of some New York City patrolmen stationed outside the Cathedral to rescue Joe from the mob. We made it out in one piece. It was Joe's version of the Stations of the Cross leading up to the crucifixion.

Though he wouldn't admit it, Joe was shaken. He must have known that I had been trying to protect him when I tried to get him to go to Mass anywhere but the Cathedral. I think that this incident made him begin to realize that he could rely on me to keep him out of difficult situations without being overbearing about it, even when he didn't listen to me.

THE BIGGEST EVENT of the year for Italian-American New Yorkers is the Columbus Day parade. Held every October, the parade rivals the older St. Patrick's Day Parade. The Italian-American population of the New York area celebrates their heritage and their place in American history with a grand parade up Manhattan's Fifth Avenue that consists of hundreds of floats, bands, marchers, and, of course, politicians and other luminaries who wanted to be Italian for a day.

On October 14, 1991, early in our friendship, Joseph Paul DiMaggio was the grand marshal of the Columbus Day Parade. Joe had been thrilled to the marrow when told of the decision to make him grand marshal. I was soon to learn that his enthusiasm did not mean he was willing to go along with the arrangements as they unfolded. Although the Columbus Day Parade was a beast to orchestrate, Joe was temperamental and demanding when things didn't go his way, especially when it involved a public outing.

Following protocol, the esteemed New York State Judge Eugene Nardelli and his brother Vito had made the offer to Joe, and I was asked to make sure Joe was aware of the invitation. Judge Nardelli guaranteed that I would be by Joe's side to keep him comfortable and to make sure that all went smoothly.

The forecast for that Columbus Day was for warm, sunny weather. A police car picked us up at 860 Fifth Avenue and headed south toward St. Patrick's Cathedral with lights flashing and sirens blasting. When Joe got out of the car, a gathering of more than one hundred photographers snapped away. The sound of cameras clicking was new to me and overwhelming. I'd never seen or heard anything like it. The commotion didn't faze the Clipper. It was nothing new to him.

He noticed that I was a little spooked and tried to make me laugh.

"Doc, these people are all here to take your picture," he joked.

This was one of those defining moments that made me realize Joe wasn't just "Big Joe," who would answer my phones in the office or pick up my pants from the cleaners. The scene was a powerful reminder that I was hanging out with an iconic American legend.

Joe had made it clear to the committee that he wanted to be seated next to me at the kickoff Mass at St. Patrick's Cathedral. The problem was that the grand marshal traditionally was seated between the governor of the State of New York and the mayor of the City of New York in the front row of the Cathedral. In 1991, that meant Governor Mario Cuomo and Mayor David Dinkins. Joe had never agreed to follow the tradition and had no intention of doing so. He was inflexible on the point.

From out of nowhere, one of the Columbus Day organizers, a venerable New York judge who Joe thought was a dead ringer for one of the Super Mario brothers, noticed Joe and me sitting together in the front row. He picked his way through the crowd before Mass and came up to me.

"Listen, pal," the judge was ready to make a ruling, "you can't sit here. These seats are reserved for the mayor and governor."

I didn't have to object, because I knew that Joe would do that for me.

Joe turned to me in the front row of the Cathedral right before Mass with the judge standing there and blasted away, "Doc, who the fuck does this guy think he is? Making me curse like this in a church?"

The people who were within hearing range were open-mouthed.

"This guy has some balls," Joe stage whispered in front of the altar.

Judges and politicians did not intimidate Joe.

"Listen, Doc," Joe proclaimed. "If you're not sitting next to me, I'm not staying. I'll get out of this church faster than the Holy Ghost." Joe was eyeing a side door that opened onto East 51st Street.

I knew that Joltin' Joe would become Boltin' Joe and abandon the two highest elected officials of the Empire State to the hungry media, who would capture their humiliation for posterity.

I tried to convince Joe to go along with it.

Joe was irate. A promise was a promise. "Doc, these are the ground rules. You sit next to me. I don't want to sit next to Dinkins or Cuomo unless you are right here next to me!"

Joe did not have a problem with either of these well-known figures. He liked them as people and respected their position in government, but he knew that he and the politicians were being used as chess pieces on the St. Patrick's Cathedral chessboard. The goal was to create a photo op for the front pages of newspapers the following day.

It was time to call in the church and divine intervention. I figured it was their party, their building. I got the attention of Monsignor Anthony Dalla Villa, the Bronx-raised, street-smart rector of the cathedral.

I spoke sotto voce to my fellow Italian.

"Listen, Father Anthony," I explained to the prelate. "We have a problem here. This judge wants me to move, and Joe doesn't want me to move. Joe will bolt from this cathedral if he doesn't get what he was promised."

The prelate thought it over.

"He'll think nothing of leaving the Mass," I added.

The Monsignor knew Joe from other functions and understood that this was a promise of trouble from a man who always lived up to his promises.

Dalla Villa looked to the heavens.

"Oh, my God, do I need this today?" The prelate seemed to be praying out loud. "With all of this confusion . . . this guy has pissed off Joe, who will take a walk."

"I guarantee he'll walk right out of Mass, and the Cardinal wouldn't be happy about that."

Joe then repeated his threats, in a voice louder than a stage whisper.

"Joe, can we compromise?" I asked in a final attempt to solve the problem. "Would you mind if I sat right behind you. I won't go anywhere."

I was becoming Joe's security blanket in crowds. As famous as he was and as accustomed to having 55,000 people screaming his name in adoration throughout his career, he still feared the unknown. He preferred for me to go with him to functions. He had begun to trust me to read the room, spot trouble before it happened, and pick out the asshole in the vicinity. He also knew I wasn't tied up in the moment. Most people would be starstruck in his company and forget why they were there in the first place. Joe knew I wasn't going to get distracted, which made him feel safe. As he so often said, "One thing's for sure, Doc doesn't take his eye off the ball."

Joe was adamant about not sitting with the politicians. And vocal.

"Doc, I don't want to sit next to those guys," Joe continued. "I asked that you sit here."

"Well, Joe, that's not the way it's going to be today." I was firm. "I'll sit directly behind you. Please, do this for me. I have to deal with these people when you leave town."

"Doc, you can sit behind me," Joe decided. "But I am going to stare straight ahead through the whole service. I won't even look at those two guys."

"Joe, do whatever you have to do," I said with relief.

And Joe was a man of his word. He always delivered on his promises, good or bad. He fulfilled this one.

Governor Cuomo and Mayor Dinkins reached their hands out to Joe, who regarded each extended hand with displeasure before giving them a mechanical shake. This was all about the judge disrespecting me and not about any dislike for Dinkins and Cuomo. Joe was extremely protective, and he was also worried that my feelings had been hurt.

There was no small talk. Joe kept his gaze forward.

At one point, he turned around and said to me, "Doc, if these guys think that they're going to get any good pictures with me today, they're in for a surprise. I'm not going to acknowledge that they are even here."

There was no way the governor and the mayor did not hear what Joe had said. I was mortified, because I was a fan of both.

I assumed that once the Mass was over, the drama would end. I was mistaken. Traditionally, the Cardinal and the grand marshal meet and greet the luminaries attending the Mass. Still miffed about the musical pews incident in the church, Joe complied in his own way. Cardinal O'Connor asked Joe to stand next to him. In turn, Joe asked me to stand next to him. No one protested my privileged post in the greeting line for fear that the Clipper would head for the door. So I had a prominent place in the receiving line. Not bad for a kid from Bensonhurst.

I overheard someone who had just shook my hand say, "I know the Cardinal and DiMaggio, but who is the other fellow I congratulated and shook hands with?"

I loved it. Things were going smoothly at last, and I was enjoying myself. But I saw trouble ahead when Joe's face turned red as a well-dressed guest approached the Cardinal. Their greetings were very cordial. The fellow turned to Joe and extended his hand sincerely.

"Put that hand away," Joe said through gritted teeth. "There's no way I am going to shake it."

The vitriol in Joe's voice made the Cardinal and me want to take refuge in the nearest confessional box.

Bill Fugazy, the limousine king, and a close friend of George Steinbrenner, had evoked Joe's hostility.

But Joe wasn't done. "Stop making that nice sister of yours, the nun, do all your dirty work."

Sister Irene, Bill's sister, always tried to make the peace between Joe and her brother. Joe liked and respected her.

In all fairness to Mr. Fugazy, he had done nothing wrong. There had been a misunderstanding about an appearance as well as a small transgression involving a spat between Joe and George Steinbrenner. Fugazy tried to make peace between them. Fugazy's attempt at a truce was a bust, because he blindsided and surprised Joe with a phone call from Steinbrenner. Fugazy hoped they would make amends if they heard each other's voice. Wrong! DiMaggio hated surprises and did not welcome this one. Joe was just as angry at Fugazy for his honorable and noble attempt as he had been with Steinbrenner. When there was a bad taste in the Clipper's mouth, it could last for a long time. He didn't care where he was or who was with him when he showed his displeasure. Fugazy did a lot for the fabric and culture of New York City during the '70s and '80s and deserved better than that.

None of us knew what to say. Fugazy was a gentleman and walked past Joe, but he did stop to shake my hand and rolled his eyes in disbelief.

Later, I expressed my opinion to Joe and recommended that he should let it go. I don't think Joe was proud of the way he treated Fugazy, and I let him have it good, because I was displeased and embarrassed by his behavior.

At parade time, Joe let it be known that he would not march in lockstep with the governor and the mayor. They avoided him and took a different route. Smart move. I received no resistance from their advance people. If anything, they were relieved. Joe marched right up front. He basked in the pride of the day and enjoyed himself greatly.

Joe didn't like the idea of walking up Fifth Avenue without his own entourage. He asked Johnny Power, one of the Bat Pack, to join. Joe had me recruit private eye Richard "Bo" Dietl to walk within earshot of him, just in case things got rough. Dietl did a great job, and Joe relaxed. He asked me to give his grand marshal sash to Bo as a thank-you.

He was annoyed that the vice grand marshal, Gina Lollobrigida, wanted to be in all the pictures taken along the parade route. Joe asked me to create a big space between the Italian movie star and himself. He didn't want anyone to even entertain the thought that there was something going on between them of a personal nature.

Johnny Power to the rescue. The dapper, elegant Johnny Power jumped all over the opportunity to walk next to Gina, and it did the trick.

Though Joe was proud of representing his people, it had to be on his own terms. This was not the last time I had to assume the role of Joe's negotiator-in-chief. I often found myself protecting Joe from himself. For someone who was so concerned about appearances, he could be self-righteous and rigid in very public situations. I think he grew to appreciate my being a fixer when he got himself into trouble. This sort of behavior certainly contributed to his reputation as a difficult, nasty man, in other words, a pain in the ass. He counted on me to patch things up and to let him know when he had stepped over the line. It was a real shift in our relationship.

He acted this way primarily when people did not honor agreements or something happened that wasn't part of the plan. He had his idiosyncrasies, but I still think he had earned the right to special treatment.

CHAPTER 5

La Bella Figura

Wednesday
~~Tuesday~~ May 12, 1993

John Arcaro called to tell me that Mancini Tailor from Scarsdale, will have my jacket ready to be picked up at 3:00 P.M.

Friday Jun 11, 1993

Laundry came in this afternoon
And the shirts came on a hanger—
I had told them to Box them, because
it's hard to iron sometimes.

Tuesday, June 15, 1993

Took a walk

After my treatment to the ankle —to the Hilton hotel to get a haircut. A trim & shape — my barber is beginning to squint when cuts. He gave me a good haircut.

M any critics considered *Joe DiMaggio* vain and obsessed by his public image. As I grew to know him, I interpreted his behavior differently. I saw him as the embodiment of the Italian tradition of *la bella figura*. At its core, *la bella figura*, which roughly translates to "cutting a beautiful figure," is about presentation: how you look, how you comport yourself, how you make the best possible impression in all things, how you act and respond in the face of adversity. It not only means having a flawless appearance, but also involves presenting yourself well in thought, word, and deed as a matter of personal dignity. It means being gracious in interactions with others in social and public situations and always exhibiting good manners. If you are not familiar with this centuries-old philosophy that rules the lives of Italians, you cannot understand Joe DiMaggio. He was a perfectionist about everything he did and expected others to behave the same way. He would not accept or settle for anything less.

Not merely a gentleman, Joe was very dignified. He had a volcanic temper, but seldom resorted to profanity unless he was really provoked. Joe believed that cursing diluted a point being made rather than emphasized it. He did not need to use obscenities to let it be known that he was angry. He felt that using obscenities showed a lack of intelligence and an inability to communicate effectively.

Though foul language is common in sports, Joe watched what he said. According to Italian credo, cursing out a man, his wife, or his kids could get you into real trouble. In Sicily, letting a stranger know that something is bothering you is not wise. That sort of restraint is a rare commodity today.

Joe possessed an Old World deference to women and was very courtly. He adored, and feared, his mother, and I believe his devotion to her shaped the way he treated all women. He wouldn't tolerate vulgar talk about the opposite sex from his friends. I never saw Joe leer at a woman, but he did show interest in them. They all showed interest back. Women seemed to pick up on his earnest, gentlemanly behavior, and it appealed to them. I watched this elderly man attract women of all ages, races, ethnicities, incomes, and education levels, even though most had never seen him play ball and had only a vague idea of who he was. His charisma was incomparable.

Joe was pickiest about his appearance. He was deeply concerned about how he looked to his fans. He would stand before the mirror at his tailor's shop, bothered by his slight shoulder drop. "Take it in," he ordered, "it won't photograph well."

Joe's tailor was a saint. Joe was a terror to tailors, impossible to please. I had watched tailors duck petrified behind fitting-room curtains when they saw him coming, and I reminded him of it.

Joe protested. "Doc, I like Mukrim. I signed that baseball for him and his kid," he said, referring to this pinch-hit tailor. His usual tailor from Westchester, Al Mancini, was on vacation. Lucky for him.

"Yeah, Joe. It was a devil's bargain for Mukrim. I told him that if you signed that ball for him, you would own him. And you did. He begged me to get you to sign it, but he begged me even more to give it back to you."

Joe laughed. "That's how it is, Doc. I go back five, six times to a tailor if there's so much as an eighth of an inch difference in my pants' length."

"Who's going to notice?" I asked.

"Doc, I would notice! That's my style. My shoulder drop makes a custom fit hard, but I insist on the best fit. I always do. Take my custom Pierre Cardin tuxedo . . . that's a beauty. But I drove them nuts."

His shirts had to be laundered with no starch and folded in a box. The crease in his pants had to be sharp, without a wrinkle, and his tie had to have a perfect knot. His wing-tip shoes were so highly polished that you could actually see your reflection in them, his heels never worn down. His suits had to be French pressed at the Potisman cleaners on York Avenue, because their press was full length and the entire jacket could be pressed uniformly at one time.

Joe was a perfect physical specimen, even as he aged. He was deeply concerned with how he looked to his public. When his body changed, he made the decision sometime in the mid-nineties never to wear the Yankee uniform again. He kept to his word.

He was especially fastidious about his hair, which was enviably thick at his age. It had to be a certain length. His forehead was the critical part, because he considered his widow's peak a trademark. If his hair was one millimeter longer or a little too close to the ear, he immediately went to see Nick the barber across the park at the old Hilton Hotel.

Nick was the one and only barber for Joe in New York. I would often walk with him through midtown to the Hilton Hotel on Sixth Avenue. Nick greeted us in Italian, which never failed to put Joe in a good mood. Joe was proud that I spoke Italian fluently, a skill I had picked up in high school and college. Nick wanted Joe to know that his barbershop visits boosted tourism and business in his shop, which I passed on to Joe.

Joe spent a lot of time in that chair, where he tuned out the world and relaxed. His nails were buffed and clear-polished to perfection. Of course, I didn't spend much time in a barber chair as Joe noted many times, referring to my baldness. I once asked him why his haircut ritual was so important to him.

"Doc, you never know when a photographer is going to be around to take your picture."

Joe went on to explain to me that when he was out in public, he had to maintain certain standards, which applied to the Bat Pack, and me as well. He valued doing things right, and that included looking and acting a certain way.

Though I tried to comply with his exacting standards, I blew it one night. I received a page to answer my phone late one afternoon. Joe had called.

"Doc, what are you doing tonight?" Joe asked when I returned his call.

I was busy, of course, but I always made an exception for Joe.

"Well, I wasn't planning on anything, Joe. What's up?"

"My granddaughters' plans fell through for tonight," Joe explained. "I thought you might join us at the 'Crazy Chef'. . . you know the place I'm talking about—Coco Pazzo."

I had a full work schedule, but Joe was obviously expecting company. "Okay, Joe. I'll finish up here around seven-thirty. I'll call up Danny and Carlos to see if they can get us a table."

"Thanks, Doc." Joe did sound grateful. "It means a lot to me that I show these girls a good time. You know all the hot spots and places to go. If anyone can get us into the Coco Pazzo, you can."

It took some doing. The place was very popular, and tables were scarce. I double-timed my workload at the hospital and squared things away with my patients. I scrambled from the office and arrived at the restaurant on time. Dressed in a jacket and shirt, I hurried past the greetings of the staff and went straight to Joe's table.

His granddaughters gave me a big hello hug. Joe was silent and ominous.

"Uh oh," I thought, "I've got trouble here."

Seeing the expression on their grandfather's face, the young women excused themselves and headed to the restroom.

Joe turned to me and said, "Where's your tie?"

"I don't have to wear a tie at this restaurant," I replied.

"Didn't anyone ever teach you about how to dress in the company of ladies," Joe asked with an edge. "Women—especially my granddaughters—deserve more respect."

I couldn't stifle a sarcastic response. "Well, Joe, I wouldn't say that wearing a cashmere jacket and a silk shirt is dressing down."

"Do you own a tie, Doc? Jacket and tie when you are going out with my granddaughters and me." Joe continued his attack. "All you need is a fur hat. Your outfit would be complete."

I couldn't believe that Joe was saying I looked like a cheap pimp. I can't say I have ever before or since been compared to a Cadillac alley pimp. It definitely wasn't my day. "I can't believe you, Joe . . ."

He wouldn't let me continue. "What's going to happen in the next two minutes is that your beeper is going to go off. You will have to leave this table immediately." Joe had it all worked out. "When the girls come back, I'll tell them that you had an emergency and had to leave but will return shortly."

"I can't believe you're going to make me do this," I protested.

Joe was unmoved. "Go on now, Doc. Get outta here."

He sent me back to my office for a wardrobe change. Fortunately, my office was around the corner.

As I grew to know Joe better, I understood why he was so protective of his granddaughters, Paula and Kathie. Joe explained that the girls had been adopted, and had already felt the pain of not being with their biological parents. Joe Jr., his son, was not capable of taking care of them and showing them the right way. Joe felt bad that the girls did not have the benefit of a strong male role model in their lives, so he stepped in. He felt that they had been abandoned twice, and he was going to make sure it never happened again. He was that honorable and concerned about the welfare of his granddaughters.

Paula especially could drive him crazy, because he cared about her deeply. His favorite great-grandkid was Paula's daughter Vanassa, a little spitfire who had Joe wrapped around her finger. Anything Vanassa wanted from Big Joe, she received.

Paula always marveled at my ability to short-circuit a DiMaggio temper tantrum. I knew precisely how to calm him down and return him back to his sweet and kind self. It was a skill that I learned in the streets. It is always better to defuse a potentially nasty situation and restore reason and fairness.

Joe was also aware of how they dressed. He made fashion suggestions, because he knew women's fashion as well as men's. But back to my wardrobe change.

When the girls returned from the ladies room, they asked Big Joe where I had gone. Joe explained that I had been paged and had to run back to the hospital.

Twenty-five minutes later, I returned wearing a blazer and tie. Everyone, including the staff, noticed that just a few minutes before I was wearing an entirely different outfit.

Joe's granddaughters laughed.

Joe grinned and said, "Say, now that the doc is dressed properly, he can sit down and have dinner with us."

But that wasn't the end of it.

"By the way," Joe added, "that tie doesn't match the jacket, and the knot is not square enough."

He was relentless. Everyone else at the table laughed. But I never went to dinner with Joe DiMaggio without a tie and jacket again.

La bella figura involved a lot more than grooming and manners. Joe believed he had a responsibility to be an example to others. He took his role as a hero seriously.

WHENEVER JOE ARRIVED in New York, I'd meet him at the gate—remember those days?—at the American Airlines terminal at LaGuardia. Joe was a man of habit, and he had a ritual he invariably performed during the ride. Thinking about it today makes me tear up. His behavior seems so innocent, so revealing.

Joe kept a well-worn copy of Ernest Hemingway's *The Old Man and the Sea* in my glove compartment. The book automatically opened to the dog-eared pages that mentioned his name. Now, Joe was not a literary man. He was a shrewd businessman and student of human nature, but I never saw him interested in any other piece of fiction.

The plot of the novella is simple enough. Santiago, the hero, is an old Cuban fisherman who is failing in luck and in health. The Old Man had not caught a fish for eighty-four days. Other fishermen in the village avoided him, because they thought his bad luck would affect their own catch. Every day the Old Man rowed out alone into the Cuban surf. His admiration for Joe DiMaggio kept him going. The Old Man finally has a marlin on the line and begins an epic struggle with the fish. He refused to let his old age and his pains force him to give up.

On many trips from the airport, Joe would read the passages from the book in which Hemingway had used him as an example to be emulated.

"The Old Man thinks, 'I must have confidence, and I must be worthy of the great DiMaggio, who does all things perfectly even with the pain of the bone spur in his heel. What is a bone spur?' he asked himself, 'We do not have them.'"

"Do you believe the great DiMaggio would stay with a fish as long as I will stay with this one," the old man wonders. "I am sure he would and more since he is young and strong. Also his father was a fisherman. But would the bone spur hurt him too much? I do not know," the fisherman said aloud. "I never had a bone spur."

The Old Man catches the marlin, but knows the sharks will surround his little boat to steal his catch. Though the sharks eat most of the gigantic marlin, enough of the carcass is left to claim a record catch. The Old Man has restored his dignity and self-respect as well as the admiration of a young fishing apprentice and his village.

Hemingway extolled the same values of manly persistence in the face of pain, age, and the threat of sharks that mattered to Joe. At the same time, the Old Man drew strength from Joe DiMaggio and honored him for his pain. I believe Joe read and reread passages from *The Old Man and the Sea* as a reminder of the power of his example to influence and inspire others.

I was honored he felt comfortable enough with me not to be self-conscious about my witnessing this ritual. It became clear to me that his repeated reading of the Hemingway passages that related to him underscored the importance of his legacy and the image he worked so hard to maintain. He felt he had a responsibility to be a role model and to embody the traditional values of *la bella figura*.

OUTSIDE JOE'S INNER circle and regular restaurants, Joe had a very big stage to play on. Projecting the right image was of supreme importance to him. He was protective of his reputation. He was extremely careful. Many thought he was hypersensitive about it. An incident which I have called "the Mapplethorpe transfer" illustrates the extremes he would go to to avoid situations that had the potential to embarrass him and put him in a bad light.

Robert Mapplethorpe was an important artist who photographed nude men. His black-and-white erotic nudes now sell for hundreds of thousands of dollars.

At the time, I was woefully unsophisticated about art. Bensonhurst was far from the epicenter of the art world. I was familiar with only two contemporary artists: Norman Rockwell, from his mail-order art school, and Walt Disney, from *The Wonderful World of Color*, which aired on Sunday nights. Mapplethorpe was something else entirely and unknown to me.

A good friend asked me to pick up a parcel from a customer's home on the Upper West Side of Manhattan and to hand deliver it to the Neikrug Gallery on East 68th Street, near my office. I had no idea about Mapplethorpe's work and couldn't imagine it would interfere in any way with picking up Joe for dinner.

When a staff worker at the home handed me the photograph, I was shocked. I looked wide-eyed at a huge black-and-white close-up photograph of a black man's penis. I didn't want to appear to be a prude or homophobic, but I knew that having Joe in my car along with this photograph could be a volatile situation.

I asked for some sort of covering for the photograph. I said it was a valuable piece and had to be transported carefully. That wasn't happening. Luckily, I had a sheet in the trunk of my car that just barely covered the framed photograph. I balanced it against the back seat.

When I picked Joe up, he was game for the night.

"Hey, Doc, it's great to see you. Let's go have some coffee and a bite to eat," Joe greeted me.

I kept my mouth shut and pulled away from the curb.

About ten blocks later, as we neared 59th Street, Joe caught a glimpse of the covered parcel in the back seat. "Doc, what do you have back there?"

I was horrified. I thought the sheet had fallen, and the straightest, dullest, whitest man in New York was being treated to the sight of a giant black dick. I looked back and was relieved that the photo remained covered.

"It's just some art I'm bringing over to the Neikrug Gallery. I didn't think you'd mind if we dropped it off," I explained.

Joe got enthusiastic. "A picture! I love pictures. What kind is it?"

I had to think fast. "Uh, it's just a picture. I haven't had a chance to look at it."

Curious, Joe asked, "Why is it covered?"

"Because it is a very expensive picture—worth twenty-five grand."

Joe's eyebrows arched at the price tag.

"It's fragile, and I don't want to damage it," I said.

Normally, that would have been the end of it, but Joe remained intrigued by the mystery parcel.

"Pull over to the curb. I want to have a look," he demanded.

I did what he said. Mimicking one of Joe's favorite mannerisms, I stared straight ahead. Joe lunged for the photo. Leaning over the seat, he pulled off the sheet. His face inches away from the photograph, he stared at a gigantic penis.

Joe reddened and then exploded. "Doc! What type of art is this?"

I didn't have an answer for him.

"This is pornography. If we get stopped by a cop, they are going to think that I am into pornography. How could you put me in this position?"

I knew that cops often pulled Joe and me over on some pretext like a broken taillight just to say hello to the Clipper. I knew he was imagining the *New York Post* headline: "JOLTIN' JOE CAUGHT HOLDING BIG, BLACK PENIS IN TRAFFIC STOP."

Joe ordered me to put the photo in the trunk. We drove off and made it without further incident.

Joe never wanted to be associated with anything he considered off color. He believed he had an obligation to be squeaky clean as an example to one and all.

Joe actually did have an appreciation for art. He often went to the Neikrug to view the exhibitions. A stunning black-and-white photo of Marilyn Monroe hung in the restroom—not a good idea when Joe was visiting. He was protective of her to his dying day.

The curator had a solution. I called ahead to let him know when Joe was on his way to the gallery. The gallery took down the photo of Marilyn and replaced it with a photo of Salvador Dalí, waxed mustache and all. It became a joke at the gallery. The people who worked there knew Joe was coming when they found Salvador Dalí leering at them from the restroom wall, and Marilyn Monroe's picture had vanished.

JOE WAS SELF-CONSCIOUS and uncomfortable about his lack of formal education. A high school dropout and a fisherman's son, he hobnobbed with the wealthy and famous and never wanted to seem out of his element, to be viewed as "the dago." He made it a point to read the *New York Times* and *Wall Street Journal* cover to cover on a daily basis as part of his information ritual. He read the *New York Post* and the *New York Daily News* for their sports coverage.

"My father only spoke broken English," Joe said one night over supper. "He never really learned proper English. Frankly, Doc, we were a little embarrassed by him. He could have learned English better."

Joe was often asked to give speeches, and he wanted them to mean something. A high-school dropout who reached iconic stature because of baseball might not have been a charismatic speaker. But athletes are performers at heart. Give Joe a script, and he could be brilliant. Joe could command the attention of the room or a stadium. When he spoke, people listened.

Joe was afraid to make speeches, because he dreaded coming off like a sandlot baseball player and a person of little education. He avoided publicly embarrassing himself by getting me to write his New York speeches. I became his mouthpiece and had to draft speeches that gave him the voice he wanted. It wasn't easy to sound like a legend more than twice my age, who wanted to deliver words of wisdom for the ages. He would say to me, "Hey, Doc, let's put that Yale education to work."

He hounded me for months before any event. He was relentless about one particularly important speech. The July 27, 1991, event was a celebration of the fiftieth anniversary of Joe's fifty-six-game hitting streak as well as the annual Old Timers' Game. Joe was going to be honored by Yankee fans, the owner, and the veterans, who were still alive. He would be speaking to forty to fifty news outlets and 56,000 fans in the stadium. Joe's one special requirement was: "Doc, make sure that I don't sound like a ballplayer."

I didn't know what he was talking about. He didn't want to sound like a ballplayer in Yankee Stadium where he was being honored as one of the greatest ballplayers of all time? Babe Ruth may have built Yankee Stadium, but the place enshrined Joe DiMaggio. I had my work cut out for me. I often wondered how I ever got pulled into this supposed honor.

As the elder statesman of the Yankees, he always began his speeches by thanking his teammates, like Lefty Gomez, Tommy Henrich, and Phil "the Scooter" Rizzuto, and whoever else was likely to show up. Every speech I wrote for Joe had the same basic themes: the value of dignity and distinction and the need to do the right thing. Doing good, doing it well, and doing it when everyone could see you doing both was how Joe tried to live his life. He accepted the responsibility that came with his iconic status and felt it imperative to be an example for others.

It goes without saying that Joe was a perfectionist when it came to crafting a speech. I worked on draft after draft, sometimes as many as twenty, as Joe supervised. Sometimes, he stood hovering over my shoulder, and sometimes he pulled up a chair next to me. It makes me tense to think about it to this day. He always found fault with what was on the page. He recited every line repeatedly to get his delivery right. I had to hear the same speech over and over again.

"Remember, Doc, it has to sound like something that only I would say, not you," he said repeatedly.

What had begun as a work of love and appreciation became an ordeal. What made me persevere was that I understood Joe's yearning to be the standard-bearer, to set the bar high for athletes as well as fans. This compulsion made him difficult and lonely, but it is also what made him great. I just shut up, grateful for the opportunity to help Joe maintain his iconic image.

Joe DiMaggio was sorely aware of his place not only as an icon but also as a part of history. It was important to Joe that what he did would hold up to scrutiny, that history would be kind to him. He lived his life by playing to future generations of fans and historians. He knew he represented more than what he achieved as an athlete. He longed to be one for the ages, and achieved his goal by living what he believed in, doing the right thing. I appreciated my role as the person responsible for making sure the New York DiMaggio legacy and level of excellence was intact and preserved.

The downside to his way of life was that he expected others to behave as he did. He could be harsh in his judgment of others. Though I sometimes bore the brunt of his disapproval, he made every effort to instruct me on the DiMaggio rules of engagement, which was an honor for me and an education I could never have received in the streets of Brooklyn or the Ivy League halls of Yale.

CHAPTER 6

A Stand-Up Guy

May 7, 1994

My trip to New York is for receiving an Honorary Degree from N.Y.R. on the 12th during the Students graduation. I will be shopping for a rental tuxedo as I did'nt realize I had to dress black tie for the dinner the night before. Dr. Positano, will also make arrangements to get one too.

Friday June 11, 1993

Up at 7.30 A.M. — Got cleaned and left to see Dr. Positano at 8:30 A.M. He gave me a treatment on my ankle and also get some information on why the leg might be swollen. No carbonation, liquids and watch my diet — as I have in the past — and will have to get back in gear.

Went to the Gardenia restaurant to have a half of turkey sandwich — with a cup of soup.

J oe DiMaggio *evaluated everyone through* the code of honor expressed in being a stand-up guy. He tried to live by the code himself.

Made mobsters coined the term. Men in the neighborhood, who were loyal, who would not rat, who kept their mouths shut, were stand-up guys. It didn't necessarily mean they were good guys.

In truth, it was usually safer to be a stand-up guy than a rat, because the life expectancy of a rat was severely reduced, at least where I grew up on the mean streets of Bensonhurst. Being a stand-up guy means doing the right thing by a friend under perilous circumstances and doing so without a glimmer of fear, or expecting a return favor or payback. There is honor on the streets.

I aimed to be a stand-up guy when I was ten or eleven, a story that Joe enjoyed. Back in the old neighborhood, we lived in a two-story brick apartment building with stores on the ground floor and apartments on the top floor. One of the stores was an old-time luncheonette, which served sandwiches, hand-packed ice cream, lots of nickel candy, and gum with baseball cards. The owners were a Jewish Romanian woman named Sonia and her husband, Milton. Both in their fifties, they showed up to work wearing starched white shirts and pants. Sonia was a grandmotherly figure, who wore her hair in a bun. In addition to dispensing the best tuna salad on Kaiser rolls anywhere, and making the best chopped liver in New York, Sonia had a sideline. This adorable, sweet lady with an accent was a bookie who helped run numbers out of her candy store.

Joe listened with great interest as I set the scene. Stories from the old neighborhood brought it all back to him. He knew all about bookies, because gamblers, bookies, and mobsters tried to get him to cooperate with them. They badgered him to lose or win by a certain score or hold back on hitting.

"I never took a bribe," Joe told me. "I never threw a game. I can't say the same for other players."

One day, I got dressed in my white tee-shirt, blue-jean shorts, and Keds, and headed out to the corner of 65th Street and 24th Avenue. As I rounded the corner on busy 65th Street, I noticed a Chrysler sedan with black wall tires and two shoddily dressed men inside, double parked alongside a hydrant, which would earn anyone except a plain-clothes cop a hefty parking summons. I was a streetwise kid. They were obviously cops on a stakeout. The black-wall tires were the give-away. The city was too cheap to get the white-wall tires popular at the time. So much for being undercover.

Joe was amused. "You knew this at thirteen?"

"Oh, yeah," I replied. "But that's not all. There was a pile of cigarette butts alongside the sedan. I put it all together. A Chrysler sedan beside a hydrant with two characters inside meant a gambling stakeout."

"So, how did you act on this tip?" he asked.

"I liked to hang out at the luncheonette. I bought my trading cards there and my tuna salad sandwiches with chocolate egg creams. I knew the old men who were regulars. They spent their time marking down numbers or names of horses, races, and dates. I had figured out that Sonia made a living by charging the gamblers and bookies a vig."

Joe shook his head, impressed by my early street savvy.

"I walked into the store bouncing a Spaldeen punch ball," I continued. "I bellied up to the counter. Sonia smiled and asked what I wanted. I told her I wanted to let her know that she was about to have company and uninvited guests. I explained that the place was being watched by two men in a car parked in front of her store."

"How did she react?" Joe was hooked.

"She didn't say much, Joe," I replied. "Everyone in the luncheonette went on autopilot. The old men flushed the numbers slips down the toilet and put cash into their wallets. She chased them away."

"Then what happened?" Joe asked with a grin. After all, he was a streetwise kid who grew to be a streetwise man.

"Two minutes later a bunch of blue coats busted into the place. They scattered and searched, but found nothing. The top blue coat went up to Sonia, who was mixing me a Brooklyn special egg cream. The Irishman sneered at Sonia."

"He must have been pissed off," Joe observed with glee.

"You bet he was. He said he knew she was running the numbers from the store. Sonia managed to look shocked. 'I don't run numbers,' she said calmly. 'I wouldn't have that in my store. I have nice clientele. I don't break the law.'

"I sat there sipping my egg cream right in front of Sonia and the cops.

"The big blue coat looked me over, and said, 'I saw the little dago kid'—he meant me—'walk into your store a few minutes before the raid, and every rat scattered. I can put one and one together.' I finished my egg cream without responding and walked nonchalantly past the cops and out the door. I had done my bit for the neighborhood."

Joe laughed. My neighborhood code was identical to his. Rats were the lowest of the low. "Doc, you did the right thing," he said. "We had the same type of cop in San Francisco when I was growing up. I was a dago, too. I was even called dago by the sportswriters. It just rolled off their tongues. Things were different then."

We both were thrown back to a lost era and the tradition of the stand-up guy. Joe had a visceral hatred of big mouths. Southern Italians tend to have a genetic dislike of gossipers. He trusted me, because he realized that friend or foe, close or estranged, I would never talk to a reporter.

One night at dinner, out of the blue, Joe said to me, "Doc, I know you're a good friend."

I was immediately apprehensive. He had never said anything that personal to me.

"What brings up that observation?" I asked.

"You aren't a snitch. You don't pry into matters. That was your upbringing, I guess," he observed.

"Joe, I grew up in a neighborhood that was known for being discreet—though it wasn't called being discreet in Bensonhurst. Even when we got out of Bensonhurst, we did have the sense to keep our mouths shut with the baggage."

"I can tell you that my San Francisco neighborhood was the same. We didn't rat on each other," Joe agreed.

"That's even when you were no longer friends?" I asked.

"Especially so. What use would that be, Doc—if you could keep a secret only if you liked someone? Then you'd be blackmailed," he added.

"I could not agree with you more, Joe. That's what we believed in the old neighborhood. Friends come and go, but confidences stayed," I summed it up.

"God, I know a lot." Joe hinted at all the secrets he kept.

I was certain that was the understatement of the century. Joe's sources were authoritative, legitimate, far-reaching, and accurate. Let's put it this way, Joe knew as much about the real story behind historic events and people as he did about baseball.

Before I could continue the conversation, Joe changed the subject and gestured to the waiter. "Let's check out the menu. Something with vegetables. Yeah, vegetables."

For Joe, turning rat was the lowest thing a man could do. Hoods didn't charm Joe, but they didn't repel him either. In his estimation, they were no better and no worse than other men who bullied their way to bigger bucks. The Mob sold drugs, bootlegged booze, ran whores, and broke the legs of debtors. Joe did not stigmatize them nor did he view them differently from the likes of the Rockefellers and Kennedys.

The courage of a stand-up guy was often a topic of conversation between us. A story from Joe's Hollywood days in the late '40s and '50s was particularly vivid. Everyone was ratting on everybody else about being a member of the Communist Party. Senator Joe McCarthy's public lynchings were becoming notorious. Hollywood studios were blacklisting anyone believed to be a Communist or fellow traveler. Colleagues were ratting each other out anonymously. They were often coerced and motivated by the fear of being blacklisted themselves. Guilt by association was common. People in the entertainment industry steered clear of anyone who was on the list, fearing that they would never work again. It was a time when few people had any courage.

"Lemme tell you a story," Joe offered during a conversation we were having about the political scandal of the day while we were eating at Vivolo on the Upper East Side. "One night back in the forties, I was in the Stork Club having dinner with Marlene Dietrich, Lauren Bacall, Douglas Fairbanks Jr., and Humphrey Bogart. Those Hollywood big shots were all baseball fans. But they loved to talk about themselves more. I was along for the ride, so I had to sit there and listen to them talk about how great they were. I was the best dressed at the table."

"That's a helluva table," I said, "legendary."

Joe dismissed my remark with a wave of his hand. Their fame was not the point nor was he even interested in that aspect.

"Out of the corner of my eye I spotted someone slowly and deliberately heading toward our table. He looked familiar to me, but I didn't realize who he was until he was about five feet away."

"Who was it, Joe?"

"He said, 'Excuse me, Mr. DiMaggio, my name is Charlie Chaplin. I wanted to let you know how much I've admired you over the years. I just wanted to shake your hand.'"

Now, I loved Charlie Chaplin. "Jesus, Joe," I said in awe. "Charlie Chaplin was a fan of yours? He was . . ."

Before I could finish the thought, Joe interrupted. "You've heard only half the story. Here's the rest. Something you probably don't know about. I was pleased to meet him. I didn't know that he was being blackballed by the entertainment industry and not welcome in Tinseltown. Some jerk thought that Charlie Chaplin was a Commie. Can you imagine?"

"Someone thought Chaplin was subversive," I explained. "That was typical of the times. Blacklists, Joe McCarthy, the House Un-American Activities Committee . . . it was a big witch hunt. The fools even thought that Commies were in the White House, that Truman was sympathetic to Russia."

"Right you are. Those were bad times. I tell you, Chaplin wouldn't even look at my dinner companions or acknowledge their presence. My companions and their huge egos were flabbergasted that he had ignored them but made a point to say hello to me. It occurred to me later that they didn't want to be associated with him and the reputation around him, and he knew it."

"They were snubbed by a genius, before they could give him the cold shoulder. They probably rubbed elbows with him for years . . . rat bastards," I commented. "I'm surprised it wasn't in the papers. It was at the Stork Club after all, and we're not talking about minor celebrities."

"Walter Winchell never got hold of that one, because our movie friends didn't want to be shown up by a dago baseball player or associated with Charlie Chaplin."

For all their fame, those Hollywood swags were in DiMaggio lingo "just rats." They wouldn't even stand up for Charlie Chaplin, one of the genius filmmakers of all time.

I became a big time stand-up guy in Joe's book by doing him a favor about three years after we met. Helping him out was a turning point in our relationship.

We were at Bravo Gianni, one of our regular places for dinner. Gianni's place was a unique restaurant in many ways. The food was phenomenal. Gianni Garavelli was one of the best restaurant men in the city. What made the place special was the mix of clients who were members of this exclusive dining club and how people from very different backgrounds could all dine there at the same time without incident. Joe would sometimes answer the restaurant's phone, "Good evening, Bravo Gianni's," in his distinctive voice, to the delight and entertainment of the other regulars seated at their designated tables. He was great at taking reservations. As he once pointed out to me, "Ya know, Doc, I used to have a restaurant in the Bay Area . . ."

I remember one night former President Bill Clinton was dining with his secretary of defense, William Cohen, across the room. There were three Secret Service tables on either side of them. In the middle of the room were three tables occupied by some of the top made men in the mob. Only in Bravo Gianni could this happen without problems. Everyone knew who everyone else was in that restaurant but, for that moment, it didn't matter and everyone minded his own business. All rules and regulations were suspended in that dining room.

As we sat down to dinner that night, I noticed that Joe was off—a little too quiet—so I asked, "The usual tonight, Joe, the farfalle di Maggio . . . tomato sauce, thin link sausage, bowtie pasta?"

Joe was distracted. "Order anything. I've got no appetite tonight . . ."

Joe liked his food. I was concerned.

"Joe, what's the matter? What's troubling you?"

"Oh, it's nothing, Doc, I don't want to bother you with it." Joe looked down at his hands, which were folded in his lap, like a crestfallen schoolboy.

"What's up?" I asked. "You're not looking me in the eye. That's just not like you."

"Doc, I gotta little problem," he began, reluctant to continue.

"Out with it," I said.

"I'm a little scared about something. It's not that I'm asking you for a favor . . . but . . . but . . ."

Now I was really worried. "Is your health okay? Are you feeling okay?" I asked automatically, always the doctor. "I know the best physicians. . . ."

"It's got nothing to do with my health, Doc," he interrupted me, looking even more uncomfortable. "I have a big problem."

"So, what is it?"

"There's a bad guy in San Francisco who's trying to blackmail me about something that happened over fifty years ago."

"What are you talking about?" I was alarmed. "What could have happened fifty years ago that surfaces now?"

"It's something that happened after the war. This guy has information about a special bank account that had been set up for me by some of the club owners. Back then, I used to make appearances at the clubs in New York and out in San Francisco. Nobody paid me for it. I just did it as a favor, because these people were friends. They deposited money in a special account for me."

"Well, what's the problem with that," I asked. "Is this about taxes? Did you claim the money?"

"It was an innocent thing." Joe was in agony. "You know, it was the same deal as here in New York at places like Toots Shor's and Jack Dempsey's. I'd stroll in and make myself known. Guys would see me hanging out at a table, eating, and drinking. After a while, they'd start buying rounds and picking up the tab. Soon, they'd spend a mountain of cash. It was good for business if I hung out at a bar or restaurant. I mean, Toots was making serious money here—serious money. In New York, there was no problem with guys like Toots and Dempsey. They were on the level. Out on the coast, it was a different story."

I was mystified. "Whaddaya mean, Joe? Why would anyone wait fifty years to rat you out? Income is income, right?"

"Well, yeah, it was income, but I didn't know that some of these San

Francisco club owners were from the wrong side of the tracks. I never had anything to do with those types of people. I would be polite, and that was it."

I'd never seen Joe so upset.

"This bastard's going to set me up and leak this story to the *San Francisco Chronicle* or the *Examiner*, or I gotta pay, which is no real protection. It makes me sick. All the years of a good reputation, gone in a few stories in a newspaper!" Joe shook his head. "Fifty years later, I'm bothered by this thug. Imagine getting pulled down for something so innocent fifty years after the fact. You know how crazy I am about my reputation. I don't want people to think I was involved with this guy or any of his type in any way."

"So, these owners were hoods." I summarized what he said in plain English. "You think this guy will score big time either way if he mounts your head on the wall like a trophy?" I knew that any Italian-American smeared by a brush with the Mob never got the stain off.

"Yeah, that's about it, Doc." Then to my surprise Joe asked for my help. "Do you have any advice for me? You have friends everywhere. You know that I'm not a guy to ask anyone for a favor. I've never asked a favor of you, but I'm really worried. Think of my grandkids and great-grandkids. I don't want them to think that their grandfather was in with mobsters. I can just imagine what . . ."

Eager to calm him down, I interrupted him. "Don't ever hesitate to ask me a favor, after all you've done for me. You've never asked me for anything."

I was friendly with some top federal law enforcement officers who had connections in San Francisco and told Joe my plan. "I know someone in San Francisco, an FBI guy who's a crazy fan of yours. Maybe he'll speak to this bigmouth and iron something out."

I saw his entire body relax. "Joe, there's nothing to worry about." I assured him that I would make the problem go away.

The next time I saw him, Joe looked lighter and happier. I asked him what was up.

He grinned and said, "Doc, I gotta hand it to you. Really. I don't know what you did. That FBI guy musta done some job talking to that bigmouth in San Francisco. I don't know what happened out there, but this guy just went away. He made himself scarce."

"That's what friends are for, Joe. I've never seen you frightened of anybody or anything, but it shocked me to see how worried you were about this lowlife. I don't know what happened out there either, but I do know that your old mobster rat got a talking to by the right people. They told him to leave you alone . . . or else."

Joe laughed softly. "I'll never forget the favor, Doc. It could have been a disaster. I would be tried in the newspapers, and you just know what the verdict would be. 'Joe DiMaggio, friend and business partner to the mob in San Francisco.' God bless you, Doc! You are a stand-up guy!'"

I had proven myself to Joe. Any reservations he might have had about trusting me were gone. It was a defining moment in our relationship. It was extremely difficult for Joe to ask for a favor. He knew he could count on me, and this was not the type of situation he could speak about to most people. That does not mean he told me, or anyone for that matter, everything, but he did open up more and told me stories that revealed a lot about him.

Later on, Richard Ben Cramer, a brilliant Pulitzer Prize winner, made a comment during a radio interview to promote his book, *Joe DiMaggio: The Hero's Life*, about the near fiasco in San Francisco. He gave me credit for the save. To this day, I do not know how he found out about the debacle and my intervention on Joe's behalf.

I LEARNED THAT Joe was even a stand-up guy for the United States Supreme Court. Justice Ruth Bader Ginsburg told a story at a New York

University commencement dinner the night before she, Joe, and James Earl Jones were to receive honorary degrees. I was fortunate enough to be at the event as Joe's "date," and to make sure that he showed up.

Justice Ginsburg began by saying that not too many people knew the story she was about to tell. Joe DiMaggio had done some undercover work for a Supreme Court case. Justice William Brennan, who had delivered the opinion of the court on this important search-and-seizure case, had told her about the Yankee Clipper's involvement.

I leaned over to Joe and said sotto voce, "I don't believe you, Joe. Talk about friends in high places! I can't wait to hear this one."

Joe looked down, smiling modestly.

Justice Ginsburg, a DiMaggio fan, proceeded to tell the story to a rapt audience. In May 1959, Federal narcotics agents in San Francisco had a man named Hom Way under surveillance for six weeks, arrested him, and found heroin in his possession. After his arrest, Hom Way said he had bought an ounce of heroin the night before from a man known to him as Blackie Toy, a proprietor of a laundry on Leavenworth Street. At about six the next morning, six or seven federal agents went to a laundry at 1733 Leavenworth Street. The sign above the door of the establishment read "Oye's Laundry." James Wah Toy operated the laundry. An agent rang the bell, and told Toy he was calling for laundry and dry cleaning. Toy told him the store didn't open until eight o'clock. As Toy started to shut the door, the agent took his badge from his pocket and identified himself as a federal narcotics agent. At that, Toy slammed the door and ran to his living quarters at the back of the laundry. The federal officers broke open the door and followed Toy to his bedroom.

They searched the premises and found no narcotics. One of the agents told Toy that Hom Way claimed he had scored narcotics from him. Toy responded that he hadn't been selling narcotics, but he did know someone who was. When the agent asked who that was, Toy said he only knew him as Johnny, and he described a house on 11th Avenue where he said Johnny lived.

The agents left for 11th Avenue and located the house. They found Johnny Yee in the bedroom. He turned over several tubes that contained less than one ounce of heroin.

Within the hour Yee and Toy were taken to the Office of the Bureau of Narcotics. There, Johnny Yee stated that Toy and another Chinese man called Sea Dog had brought the heroin to him a few days earlier. Toy identified Sea Dog as Wong Sun. The narcotics agents went to Wong Sun's home. A thorough search of the apartment uncovered no narcotics. Wong Sun was led from the bedroom in handcuffs. All three were arrested and released on their own recognizance. This case went through trial and appeals courts and ended up at the Supreme Court. The threshold question in the case was whether the officers should have gotten a warrant for the arrest of Toy on the information that impelled them to act. Nothing in the record of the original trial and appeals identified James Wah Toy as the same person as "Blackie Toy."

Edward Bennett Williams was to argue the case before the Supreme Court. Williams, a brilliant litigator, realized he had forgotten a fundamental issue as he prepared his case. There were almost as many Toys as Chins in Chinatown. He woke up in the middle of the night and realized his mistake.

Williams was in D.C. at the time—three thousand miles from Leavenworth Street. He needed a big favor. Whom could he call at three in the morning for such a big favor? He had to find someone in San Francisco who would drive up and down Leavenworth Street looking for other Toys who owned a laundry in the area. Williams pressed his friend Joe DiMaggio into service to do reconnaissance. Joe, celebrity gumshoe, trawled up and down Chinatown's narrow alleys looking for another laundry-owning Toy. Joe did his job, came up with the needed answer, and Williams won the case. Joe's participation helped form the basis of the landmark "Won Sung v. United States" case, 371 US 477 in 1963, a pivotal search-and-seizure case still cited frequently.

Sometime after the decision, Williams told Justice Brennan about Joe's involvement. Also a fan, the justice was impressed enough to pass the story along to his colleagues on the highest bench in the land. Justice Ginsburg's retelling of the tale brought down the house. Joe was amused and couldn't completely mask his pride. He was accustomed to praise for his athleticism. A Supreme Court Justice had just recognized that he was a stand-up guy and a top-notch gumshoe.

At the end of the NYU commencement, the Justice, wearing her adorable professional hat, which DiMaggio got a kick out of, asked as a proud and doting mother, and not a Supreme Court Justice, if I could do her a favor. She wondered if I would ask Joe for two autographed baseballs for her family. I couldn't say no to a fellow Brooklynite.

When I asked Joe, he was happy to sign the baseballs. He loved the story Justice Ginsburg had told at the commencement dinner. He wanted to be known for more than being a great baseball player, his hitting streak, and his marriage to Marilyn Monroe. He was proud to have been recognized by a Supreme Court Justice for something beyond baseball. He was beaming.

Joe's participation at the commencement was nothing short of magical and mystical. I will never forget how all the graduates were cheering for him during the procession.

New York University trustee and Joe's friend Lew Rudin turned to me and said, "Rock, can you believe how these kids are responding to him? They love him."

The weather was very threatening that day, then it started to rain. It was a mess. Washington Square Park turned into a rainforest packed to capacity with graduates and their families. Joe had just arrived on the stage, and James Earl Jones was speaking. The rain stopped. Jones seized the moment and timing of Joe's arrival and said in his distinctive, Darth Vader voice, "Mr. DiMaggio, thanks for bringing out the sun." The park went wild!

Two weeks later, the receptionist at the office called back to me to pick up the intercom. When I did, she nervously told me there were two men, wearing U.S. Marshal star badges and flashing IDs, in the waiting room who wanted to speak to me and me only. I wondered what I had done.

When I went up front, I found two very tall, physically fit gentlemen wearing their ID badges.

One said to me, "Dr. Positano, we are here to secure a very important package for a Justice of the Supreme Court." This was another example of how valuable any gift from Joe was and to what lengths people would go to procure them safely.

I'll never forget when Joe let me know that he included me high in the ranks of stand-up guys. I was trying to set up a dinner to meet Sonny Grosso, the archetypal New Yorker, the hard-boiled detective portrayed in *The French Connection*, who broke up the greatest heroin smuggling ring in history. A mutual friend told me Sonny would be starstruck if he could meet his idol Joe Di. I thought it could work, because Joe loved *The French Connection* and other things that Sonny Grosso had done. Though I knew how much Joe hated strangers at his dinner table, I thought I'd ask him about Sonny Grosso.

Joe and I were having a bite at La Maganette, a midtown restaurant. I was eager to set up the meeting with Sonny. I had to strategize to make this work.

"Joe . . . one of the places we've just got to eat at one night is up on 114th Street in Spanish Harlem, a joint called Rao's . . ." I eased into the subject.

Joe just blinked.

"A friend of mine, Sonny Grosso, the producer," I introduced Sonny into the conversation, "you know, the *French Connection* cop, has a table up there on Monday nights. He would love for us to join him there one night."

If the cloud over Joe's head was any indication, he was not pleased. "No thanks, Doc!"

I couldn't figure out what was going on. "Joe, it's not like you to turn down a free dinner." I checked myself. I might have gone a little too far.

Joe scowled. "Doc, the place isn't new to me. I used to go there when the original Rao, Vince Rao, ran the place," he said.

"So what's the problem?" I asked.

"Well, my sources say that about two years ago you called up to ask if you could grab a bite to eat. Now, if my memory serves me right, you were flat-out refused, even though you had helped their families out with medical problems."

His intelligence network impressed me.

"Do you know why?" Joe asked.

"I think so," I replied.

"Because one of Sinatra's pals was up at Rao's seated near you one night. He was badmouthing me to everyone with a good ear. I was told that you stood up to him and defended my honor and my reputation. Doc, you didn't care that you were in Sinatra's territory. You didn't fold into the crowd."

I started to talk, but Joe silenced me.

"Don't downplay what you did. Let me finish, Doc. The loud-mouth's pug nose was even more out of joint after you stood up to him." Joe was proud of his information. "He pulled one of the managers up there to one side and told him to blackball you from Rao's, because you defended my good name, and on top of that he claimed you didn't treat his woman with respect when she was late for an appointment with you."

"But, Joe, that's all in the past." I didn't want a feud on my hands. "It was nothing personal between the guys and me. They were put in a difficult no-win position. Solid people understand these things aren't personal."

Joe didn't wait to hear me defend anyone else for their actions, which he felt were disrespectful and inappropriate.

"Exactly, which is why I would never go to Rao's again until things change. Respect and loyalty go both ways. After you defended me in that kangaroo court, what makes you think that I would return to that place if they don't do the right thing by you?" Joe was adamant.

Well, that settled that.

"That loudmouth is dead, Joe," I tried to calm him down. "The guy who blackballed me is not with us."

"Good, he's probably kissing Sinatra's ass in hell."

"He wasn't really a bad guy," I said about the loudmouth.

"There you go, Doc, always giving people the benefit of the doubt."

That was not a problem for Joe.

But Joe relented. "Well, if this Sonny fella is really a good guy, and he's also been good to you, then tell him I have no problem sitting down to dinner with him, just not at Rao's, Frank Sinatra's cafeteria in East Harlem."

I arranged the meeting at a good Italian restaurant, Manducatis, a place renowned for homemade pasta on Jackson Avenue in Queens. Both Joe and Sonny were harsh critics of Italian food, and I knew the place would pass muster. It was one of Sonny's favorite joints.

I called the owner, Vincent Cerbone, who was thrilled that Joe was going to have dinner at his place. He was so appreciative that he reserved a private room, one of his two dining rooms, for the meeting.

"Hey, let's make it a surprise meeting," I said to Sonny's friend. "Tell Sonny that it's a business meeting with you. Don't mention Joe at all."

Our friend agreed to the plan. Grosso would turn up for a business meeting in a Queens restaurant and instead meet his childhood idol.

During the drive to Manducatis, Joe brought up Rao's again. Though he wouldn't admit it, he secretly liked the place. "So, this Sonny fella has a table reserved permanently for him at Rao's?"

"Yes, he does."

Having a table at Rao's was a privilege that few enjoyed. After his diatribe about Rao's, I was surprised by what Joe said next.

"Doc, how about you getting a table at Rao's?" he suggested, as if that were easily accomplished.

I knew that a permanently reserved table at Rao's was passed down to the deserving few.

"Joe, that just isn't done," I began. "It's not just a question of making a reservation."

"You're going to the table with Joe DiMaggio," he explained.

Before I could object, Joe listed my sterling qualifications, "Doc, you're a Yale man, a doctor at a prestigious hospital, and an Italian-American. You've earned that table."

I knew Joe wouldn't make such a recommendation for anyone. In fact, Joe didn't make many recommendations at all. I would have been happy to have a table at Rao's, but I was hesitant about trying.

Joe didn't relent. "Besides, I knew Vincent Rao," Joe said.

"Yes, you told me," I reminded him.

No doubt, Vincent Rao was a friend of Joe in former years, and probably, like Grosso, idolized Joe. Connecting the dots made me realize that more than a table at a restaurant was involved. It was Joe's way of saying that I had made it.

Joe wanted to speak with Sonny at dinner about putting me in first position regarding the Rao's table. I asked him not to do or say anything. When the time came, Sonny would do the right thing. We have a very strong personal and professional history as I was always and continue to be his medical *consigliere*.

I was moved by Joe's vote of confidence. I stood up for Joe, and he returned the favor.

I expected Joe and Sonny to get along extremely well, and was glad I had set up the meeting. Sonny and Joe shared an important skill.

They knew a phony when they set eyes on one and could detect a lie in a New York millisecond.

Not only was Sonny enthralled by Joe, which was always a good quality in Joe's eyes, he was also a well-known television and movie producer. He practically patented the New York gritty cop drama. I knew that Joe admired the look and feel of Grosso's movies. Joe was not a mean judge of movies. Having been married to two actresses, he had inside knowledge. Joe loved real street stories, not the stuff that passed for crime stories.

That night, Joe met an open-mouthed Sonny Grosso, who glazed over like a starstruck teenager meeting one of the Beatles.

"Nice to meet you," Joe greeted a still shocked Sonny. "You can let go of my hand now." Sonny had gripped Joe's hand and held on.

A heaping plate of homemade pasta was served to the Clipper and his great fan, the supercop, the scourge of real-life criminals. The dinner turned into a three-hour lovefest between them. They chatted about life in New York. Joe was very much the senior partner. Deferential to the older man, Grosso listened more than he spoke. Grosso talked some about moviemaking, and so did Joe. Grosso told Joe a New York childhood story. Though he made a career of chasing lawbreakers, his story showed that he could break the rules, too.

Sonny played hooky one day for a special mission at Penn Station in New York. The Yankees, including their star player, Joe DiMaggio, were returning from a triumphant road trip and their train was scheduled to arrive at the station.

Sonny and his friend George were trackside waiting for the Clipper to walk by. When Joe came alongside them, George was equipped for the stakeout with pencil and paper. Sonny had neglected to bring his kit.

Sonny just watched Joe signing the autograph for his friend. Then Joe looked at Sonny and asked George, "What about your pal?"

Joe was enjoying this story.

"Yeah . . ." George responded. "He wants your autograph."

Joe walked over to Sonny, but the kid had no pad or pencil.

"I'll get you next time," Joe said. As a consolation prize, Joe tousled Sonny's hair and walked off.

When Sonny returned home that night, his dad was reading the evening paper. Sonny tried to breeze by, and thought he had made it when his father asked, "How was school?"

"Okay," Sonny answered.

"Got much homework?" his father asked.

"No, not much. I finished it at school, Dad."

He folded back the paper with deliberation and said, "Okay, okay. C'mere."

His father pointed to the paper and to a photograph of Sonny with the Yankee Clipper and a gang of other kids.

"Do you know this guy?" his father asked.

Sonny confessed.

Fortunately for Sonny, his father was an even more rabid admirer of Joe DiMaggio than his hooky-playing son. All was forgiven.

"Let's keep this from your mother," his father conspired with his delinquent son. "It would really disappoint and hurt her to know that you didn't go to school and went down to see Joe instead."

Joe found the story amusing and was delighted that they met again fifty years later.

Sonny and Joe continued to talk about movie history. Sonny mentioned his part in the original *Godfather*. Sonny had been involved in one of the most famous scenes in the movie. The young Michael Corleone was going to make his bones and replace his father, the ailing don, by assassinating his two dining partners, a corrupt police captain and a drug lord. The handgun he was to use had been hidden behind the pull-chain toilet reservoir tank in the bathroom. The handgun used in the film actually belonged to Sonny.

Sonny showed Joe the gun, which he unloaded under the table. Joe was beside himself with excitement at seeing this iconic movie prop.

Joe enjoyed meeting Sonny. It was one of the few times that I broke up the party, because I had to be up at five in the morning for work. Joe would have kept going for another couple of hours.

Joe had a fabulous time that night and would often remind me about getting together with Sonny again. This did not happen often. Dinner with DiMaggio was most often a one-shot deal with little likelihood of a repeat performance, but Joe had made it clear that Sonny was now on his very rare list of people who would be invited to sit at Joe's table again.

CHAPTER 7

Take Me Out to the Ball Game

Wednesday June 23, 1993

I went to 350 Park ave to pick up my all Star game tickets, that Bobby Brown made sure I got. He was not in, but, I gave her secretary a check for them.

I t's not surprising that "Take Me Out to the Ball Game" was Joe's favorite song, his anthem. If I were ever near a piano, he always asked me to play it, and he would sing along, no matter where we were and who was listening.

The song is so evocative. Whenever I hear strains of that tune, it turns back the clock for me. It brings back my excitement as a kid watching ball games with my brother and father.

Joe told me, at one event, Al Gore Sr. invited him up to the bandstand to join him in singing "Take Me Out to the Ball Game." Joe liked Gore and had met Al Gore Jr., the future vice president, that evening. Joe thought Al's son was a cute, chubby little kid, so Joe obliged to the delight and excitement of Al Gore Jr. The only reason Joe joined Al Gore Sr. in song was to make his son happy. He achieved his objective, and the duet brought the house down.

When we were kids, our only connection with professional baseball was television. We were New York Mets fans with a sweet spot, as Joe would say, for Mickey Mantle. We'd only watch the Yankee games he was playing in. Invariably, the Mick was a disappointment in his later years. After his last out, we'd put on the Mets. In the 1960s, the Mets were struggling to get out of last place in the National League, and the Yankees in Mickey's last years were doing the same in their league. They were poor teams. We saw the Yankees play live only once, because Yankee games were largely out of the reach of working-class budgets, then and now.

I told Joe how we managed to get to Mets games. Every summer, Sealtest and Borden, the local milk companies, ran a great promotion. We had to cut coupons from the back of milk cartons. If we collected enough coupons, we'd earn tickets to a Mets game. Elsie the cow was the neighborhood's favorite farm animal, and the closest us street kids would ever get to a farm, our version of the Fresh Air Fund.

We drank a lot of milk. My mother bought our milk at the Key Food on 65th Street. We'd go through five quarts a week, easily. Since we were big and brawling, we got all the smaller kids, which was practically everyone else, to turn over their coupons to us. We also recruited family members, who had no interest in baseball, to collect and gather the milk-carton coupons.

Joe liked the story. He had been a big kid, too. He knew that physical size and suggestion could make such bargains possible.

Twenty coupons got a free Mets ticket to a nosebleed seat. There was a catch, of course. It was first come, first served. I told Joe that, in the end, not many tickets were redeemed.

When Joe asked why, I explained that the cheap seats were so high up that when a plane was landing at La Guardia airport, you could read the newspapers in first class.

Joe laughed. "Good way to see the game," he said.

"If that wasn't enough, our father was afraid of heights. And you know that the game was cheap for a reason. Seeing the Mets play was not an exciting experience."

"So, what about the Yankees?" Joe asked.

"Here's how it was. We were tired of the free nosebleed seats in Shea Stadium . . . and so was Dad."

Joe appreciated that.

"So, we nagged our dear mother, who nagged our long-suffering father to invest in three Yankee tickets, also in the bleachers."

"The Detroit Tigers were in town, Joe, and we were thrilled. We couldn't afford the Yankee parking lot, so we scrounged around the Bronx neighborhood. Our father saw a bum."

The Bronx was not safe in those days.

"You asked a bum to help you find a parking spot?"

"Yep. He led us to a broken-down train track, which had other cars on it, somewhere just short of the river and far from the stadium. The bum took three dollars from us and led us to a spot where Dad parked.

When we got out of the car, Dad kept looking back to the abandoned railroad tracks, wondering if his 1960 Ford Falcon would be there when we got back."

Joe began laughing again. "Whoa, Doc, that was risky in that neighborhood."

"We went to the game, hauled my father into the bleachers, and waited for Mickey Mantle to wow us. We bought those friggin' tickets, Joe, he owed us."

"I know what happened next, but go ahead." Joe had a smug smile on his face.

"Mickey let us down . . . as usual. He popped out to Al Kaline in right field, struck out, and then walked. We were deflated. We were even sorrier when we found that our Falcon was wedged in the railroad tracks. It took my father an hour to get out of the spot . . ."

"Oh, Doc . . . poor Dad, poor Dad," Joe sympathized. "Guess it was no more Yankee games that season."

"You're right about that—no more Yankee games. When I visit Yankee Stadium today, I still think of my father cursing the Yankees and Mickey Mantle."

BUT BACK TO "Take Me Out to the Ball Game." The song is so upbeat, so innocent in its way. I can imagine the nostalgic feelings it stirred up in Joe. The song captured his enthusiasm and love for the sport, which he never lost. The familiar tune brought him back to the time when he was a star, the player fans came to see, and all the opening days of his storied career.

Joe's baseball stories were the best. I never got enough of them. It was a privilege to see how the game is played through the eyes of one of the greatest baseball players of all time. He played every bit of the game with a fierce passion, regardless of the score.

One story, which has become part of his legend, involves Joe's giving Yogi Berra a hard time. For the record, Joe was a big fan of Yogi's and often remarked how great a player he was. The Yankees were losing badly going into the late innings of a game. Yogi was at bat, and he hit a little squibbler down the first base line. Yogi committed the cardinal DiMaggio sin. He wasn't going to run it out to first.

When Yogi entered the dugout, Joe shot Yogi a look that was simultaneously stern and disappointed. He turned to Yogi and said, "What's the matter, Yogi, did you hurt yourself?"

Yogi never took it easy again.

Joe did not mind recounting mistakes he had made on the field, especially ones he made at the beginning of his professional career. I was surprised at how good-natured he was when speaking about his major screwup. This is one of former Baseball Commissioner Fay Vincent's favorite DiMaggio stories.

"Back in 1936, my rookie year, I lived at the Mayflower with Lefty Gomez. Lefty was a big star, so he had a car. I caught a ride with him each day to Yankee Stadium."

I did the math. He was twenty-two at the time.

"There was a big story in one of the Sunday New York papers about Tris Speaker. The article called him the greatest center fielder who ever lived," he continued. "I read that Tris played very shallow and still could go back on the ball." Joe stopped for a moment to reflect.

"Later that Sunday, I caught that ride with Lefty and asked him if he had read the article about Tris."

"Had he?" I asked.

"Lefty answered, 'Yeah, kid, what of it?'

"I told him that I would be the greatest center fielder who ever played the game." Joe smiled at the memory of his brashness. "I said that I could play real shallow and go back on the ball, too.

"We were playing a doubleheader that day against the Red Sox. I played real shallow in the field, and we won the first game. Lefty pitched the second game, and he was in trouble. A few runners were on base, and a big hitter was up. We were behind late in the game.

"Now, I was playing real shallow in center field. The big hitter was up. Lefty was about to wind up when he stopped and motioned me with his glove. He waved his glove at me and said, 'Hey, kid, back up.'"

Lefty outranked Joe and should have been strictly obeyed.

"But I was the new Tris Speaker, so I didn't move. The next pitch, Lefty was really waving at me to move back, but I still didn't move." Joe shook his head. "Well, the big hitter put a shot over my head, and it rolled around out there all the way to the monuments. The opposing team cleared the bases."

Joe had messed up big time.

"He hit a triple, and we lost that game. To make matters worse, I had to ride all the way back into town with Lefty, and I knew that he was really pissed at me. I got into the car with him, but I didn't say anything, and Lefty said nothing to me.

"He just sat there all the way back to the hotel. I knew he was upset with me, but we just sat there without saying a word. When we got close to the curb in front of the hotel, I had to say something.

"'Lefty,' I said, 'you know what?'

"He looked over at me and said, 'Yeah, kid, what?'

"'I am still going to be the greatest center fielder. I'm going to make them forget Tris Speaker.'"

I couldn't imagine how Lefty responded to that.

Joe grinned. "He said, 'You keep playing like that, kid, and they'll forget Lefty Gomez.'"

NOW AND THEN, I could get Joe to tell a story if I asked the right question. At dinner one night at Vivolo Restaurant with the Bat Pack, I gave it a try. Joe was a big fan of the Vivolo brothers, Angelo and Carmine. At the infamous Columbus Day Parade, Joe suggested that he would like to take a picture with Angelo and his young son. Talk about a rare event.

"You know that I like history, Joe. Do you have any memories of Yankee Stadium that stand out?"

"You're not paying me enough, Doc, to tell stories that no one else knows about." Joe had a knee-jerk reaction, but he relented. "But for you, Doc, I'll go the extra mile." He thought for a moment, and his memories brought a smile to his face.

We couldn't wait to hear what he considered an outstanding moment.

"I remember that we had a special guest in the House that Ruth Built in the 1936 World Series. The president of the United States, FDR, was there. The series and the game were both on the line."

Everyone at the table settled in for what we knew would be a great story.

"A towering rocket soared to Death Valley. I thought the ball would never stop moving and come down. I made a great grab that saved the game." Joe described his play in words that brought us all there. "So the game was over. I ran in from the outfield toward the dugout." Joe paused.

Mario Faustini took the hook this time. "Okay, Joe, what happened?" he asked.

"FDR got into a big limo parked on the infield. Members of the Secret Service were standing on the running board of the car as they started to move. Then FDR shouted to his driver to stop the whole show. The president leaned against the side of the limo and cupped his hands." Joe mimicked the gesture. He was enjoying the response of his rapt audience.

"What did he say?" I asked.

"FDR said, 'Joe, great catch!'"

Joe swelled with pride.

Everyone smiled, but Joe wasn't finished.

"Then with a wave of his hand, the limo got moving. Now that was probably my most thrilling moment as a ballplayer. I'll never forget it. I mean, FDR was my hero, and he was admiring me . . . admiring me." Joe smiled as if he had traveled in a time machine back to 1936. "That man had the world on his shoulders at the time, and he stopped to let me know that he admired me. How can I ever top that?"

FDR, the wealthy scion of a Dutch burgher family from the Hudson Valley, who served as president of the United States through the Depression and a World War, had shown respect for an uneducated fisherman's son from San Francisco. Watching Joe tell the story a half century later, it was clear to me how much he venerated FDR and how proud and humble he was about his accomplishments.

JOE'S PERFECTIONISM DROVE him. He was happy to talk to me about players who slacked off. Just as Joe was unforgiving when Yogi Berra failed to go all out, he was critical of players who took sick days. "I always played ball no matter how sick I was," he told me. "Not like today's players. If they have a hangnail, they sit it out." Joe was outspoken in his criticism of modern ballplayers.

"So, besides the pain in your heel, when did you play sick?" I asked him.

"I remember back in the season of 1940 having a terrible cold. I could barely breathe," Joe began his story. "The team doc checked me out and told Joe McCarthy, our manager at the time, who decided that I could play. I had a 101 degree temperature. To make things worse, we were going through a heat wave. It was over a hundred for a week. We were playing in uniforms made of heavy wool."

"That must have been miserable," I said, shaking my head.

"I felt lousy. Just talking made me lose my breath. I was sweating and that wool uniform soaked up all that sweat. It weighed twenty pounds when it was wringing wet."

Joe made the moment come alive.

"It was late in the game, and I got hold of an outside pitch and drove it to right center over the outfielder's head." Joe looked pained just thinking about it.

"What was wrong with such a great hit?"

"Doc, I wasn't happy about it, because I had to run it out. I could barely breathe. I felt like I was running under water. Somehow I made it to third base on a hook slide. I'll never forget how I was gasping for air. It turns out that I was playing with walking pneumonia.

"The ball went back to the pitcher. He was about to pitch to the next batter. Suddenly, the third base umpire yelled 'Time!' Play was stopped. No one knew why.

"The ump walked over to me and said, 'Joe, I just wanted to give you a few moments to catch your breath.'"

"Nice guy," I said.

"Doc, I lost eighteen pounds that game. I played my best even with walking pneumonia. Williams would not have been able to do that," Joe concluded his story. "I saved the uniform."

"Joe, players and managers were different in those days." I couldn't understand why McCarthy wouldn't give Joe a break.

Joe had another valiant tale of playing sick.

"Doc, it gets even worse than playing with a fever."

"Okay, tell me."

"In '39, with two weeks to go in the season, the Yankees had already locked up the pennant. I was on a hot streak, batting over .400. I was a sure bet to hit over .400 for the season, the first time since Bill Terry did it in 1930." He grimaced. "Do you know how difficult it is to hit over .400?"

"Of course, I do." Who did he think he was talking to? "What happened?"

"As luck would have it, I developed a terrible infection in my left eye. Now," he felt he had to explain the problem to me. "For a right-hand hitter, that's the eye that picks up the pitcher's motion and the spin of the ball. So, my eye was completely shut!"

I was horrified. "That had to be a dangerous situation. Fast balls going a hundred miles an hour are tough enough for a man with two working eyes."

Joe nodded.

"McCarthy had the team doctor give me a numbing shot in my eye that made it even worse. But that son of a bitch McCarthy wouldn't sit me down. He said he didn't want a cheese champion. If I was going to hit .400 that year, I would have to do it no matter what the circumstances. If he had kept me out of the game, as he should have with the season already locked up, I would have easily batted over .400." Joe was still mad about it.

"Instead, he made me play and bat with one eye." He was so vehement it could have happened yesterday. "Most ball players at that time couldn't hit Bobby Feller's 100 miles per hour fastball with two eyes. Imagine trying to do it with one."

"What was the outcome, Joe?" I asked.

"My batting average dropped twenty-five points in two weeks." Joe was smoldering. "I finished in the high .300s, .381 to be exact. I still can't understand why he didn't sit me."

"You really were robbed," I commiserated. It was hard for me to imagine a manager doing that to a player who was famously not a slacker.

I WAS ALWAYS curious about what Joe had to say about his brothers, Vince and Dominic, who also played in the majors. To me, the DNA miracle of three Major League ballplayers from the same generation of the same family was mind-boggling. Their Sicilian fisherman father was no athlete. You have to wonder how he had three sons who became prominent in the all-American game. Somehow I feel Mama DiMaggio's genes had something to do with this.

In all the time I knew Joe, he never mentioned his older brother Vince, who first broke from the family business to play ball with the San Francisco Seals. I knew that Joe and Dominic, who played for the Boston Red Sox, had a turbulent history. I once asked him how his brother Dom was as a player.

Joe thought it over, before saying, "Not bad, Doc, but not a great player."

I had the sense that Joe measured other players against his own performance. In that case, most baseball players would come up short.

"Do you think he would rate inclusion in the Hall of Fame?" I knew I was stepping into dangerous ground, but I was curious about how he would respond.

"He didn't have enough good seasons to be voted into the Hall of Fame," Joe was quick to respond. "Yeah, he was good, but Hall of Fame? No, he didn't earn it."

It hadn't helped that Dom was a teammate and good friend of Joe's archrival Ted Williams, both playing for the Boston Red Sox.

"But he had a very capable record," I persisted.

Joe leaned back in his chair. "Yes, a good player—not a great one. He was a good fielder and batter—yeah—an asset to his team."

I asked Joe if it was hard to play against his own brother.

"Yeah, and we both knew it was hard. Everyone was watching how we reacted to one another. I mean, from when we were little boys, we played ball on the sandlots. I was used to talking to him, rivals or not."

"Why was it so tough when you were in the majors?"

"Well, the baseball commissioner at the time didn't like the idea of what he called fraternization. He didn't want players getting too friendly with each other on the field or off."

"What's wrong with an occasional drink off campus?" I wanted him to spell it out.

"He was worried about collusion—you know, point shaving, throwing games. I believe that the commissioner was really worried about me and Dom colluding together. I'm sure he noticed our ballfield demeanor. But, hell, we were more than friends, we were brothers, and meant to fraternize."

"That was a strange situation," I commented. "How did you two guys handle that?"

"Awkwardly, that's how we handled it. You can't turn being friendly off, but it's even tougher switching off the brother in you."

Joe was speaking from the heart.

"I mean, we came from a close family. I wasn't used to not looking over at my brother, saying hello, or waving, baseball legends or not." I could see that it still rankled him. "I knew it was a personal thing, Doc. Being successful brothers meant that we were under scrutiny by the commissioner himself, the press, and maybe even the teams.

"I didn't like that rule and neither did Dom. But we were playing Major League ball, not on some sandlot behind the piers in San Francisco. It was the nature of the business." Joe was cooling down.

"I guess it didn't help that the Yankees and the Red Sox vied almost every year for the pennant and for World Series titles." I knew my sports history.

"That was a friendly rivalry at least," Joe responded.

Talking about his brother Dom and the Red Sox naturally brought up the subject of Ted Williams. Joe and Ted had a classic love–hate relationship. They respected each other as competitors, but once they left the ballpark they took separate cabs.

Joe had great respect for Ted, considering Ted the best natural hitter in baseball, even better than himself. But here's the hook. Joe believed that being a great ballplayer meant that you had to be excellent in all areas of the game. If you were great in only one aspect of the game, you couldn't help your team win a championship. In Joe's eyes, Ted fell short in fielding and base running.

Ted, to his credit, had no problems worshiping DiMaggio as a player. He once told me that there was no all-around player who could hit, run, and field better than DiMaggio. He concurred that had Joe not lost all of those crucial years in the military—as he had, too—Joe's records would have been even more out of reach. Williams believed that Joe's fifty-six-game hitting streak would probably never be seen again.

There was very limited contact between the two players off the field, especially post-baseball. Though they would occasionally bump into each other, there really wasn't very much to talk about besides exchanging the usual pleasantries and professing mutual admiration.

Joe was threatened by Ted's relationship with Dom. Joe's devotion to family made him a bit jealous that Ted may have been closer to Dom than he was.

"Well, how about the rivalry between you and Ted Williams? You contended for records."

"That had nothing to do with it. I knew that Dom was friendly with Williams. Hell, he had to be. Every spring and summer they lived together on the road or in Fenway Park."

"What did your parents feel about your not fraternizing with Dom?"

"They didn't understand it," Joe explained. "My mother was more vocal about her displeasure, but my father was weighing in as well. To them brothers were brothers, and to hell with the commissioner's rules. They were at the very least disturbed that their two sons couldn't talk on the field or exchange glances. And my parents were right, of course."

"I can see why it bothered you."

There was a pregnant pause, and a foxy smile appeared on Joe's face. "Of course, the commissioner could have been a little right," he said.

"Huh?" I couldn't believe my ears.

"You should see the expression on your face, Doc."

Joe was definitely amused. I was ready for a bombshell.

"One year, the Yankees were out of the running for the pennant. We had a bad year. It just happened that Boston was better positioned.

They were a single ball game away from clinching the pennant. But the Red Sox had to win against us to get the pennant."

"Both Dom and I were slated to play the game in question." Joe set the scene. "It just so happened that my father came to see me before the game. He asked me to do something that he never asked me to do before."

"Oh, no," I said.

"Doc, my father asked me to 'calm it down a little bit.' "

"He asked you what?"

"You heard it right. Without saying it in so many words, he asked me to throw the game. I couldn't believe he would do that." Joe shook his head. "He figured that if I played off my usual game that day, the Red Sox would beat the Yankees and win the pennant. I guess it was fraternization through a father."

"That's pretty shocking."

"My father figured that since the Yankees were out of contention anyway, what harm would it do to allow Boston a clear shot? Let your brother win one. It wasn't like he was asking me to hurt the Yankees."

"What did you say to your father? You must have been angry."

"I was pissed. I said, 'Listen, Pop, I'm a professional and so is Dom. We aren't going to play the game that way. You shouldn't even think of asking me not to play 100 percent.' "

"It must have been unnerving to play that game."

"Doc, I played my heart out. I had a multi-hit game, scored some runs, and we beat the hell out of the Red Sox. I ruined their chances to get the pennant that year." Joe was gleeful as he told me the outcome.

"Did Dom hold that against you?" I knew Joe and Dom had been estranged.

"Of course not. We were professionals," Joe stated matter of factly. "We did have bad blood between us, but not because of that game. It was later."

"What was wrong between you?"

"There was a problem with real-estate investments and with Dom's wife."

I knew I had to tread lightly. He was talking about family, and that was private.

"How's that?" I asked.

"I let him take over a real-estate property I owned. Let's say that I believe I got the raw deal in that one. And when a woman gets between two brothers," Joe explained in an old-school Italian way, "it's not right, and it's not pretty either."

Knowing Joe, I'm sure he bore that grudge until death. Joe could be pigheaded about perceived slights, and four were involved in this situation: Joe was told by his father to throw a game for Dom; Ted Williams had a close relationship with the same brother, whom he was forced to ignore on the field; a real-estate deal went bad; and his sister-in-law had interfered. It was too much for Joe. By the time the real-estate deal imploded, both of their parents were gone. There was no one there to knock their heads together. In the end, Joe was disappointed, not bitter. In all fairness, Joe did share with me that in the 1990s, Dom's wife, Emily, had made a valiant attempt to get the brothers together for a week to reconnect. Joe was receptive.

JOE MADE A contribution to baseball players that most people do not know about. It was none other than my Brooklyn baseball hero Sandy Koufax who told me about it. Every year, Joe attended the B.A.T. Dinner in New York City, which supported retired baseball players who had neither sufficient savings, nor health insurance to tide them over in their later years, which is a very common occurrence. After their contracts ran out, ballplayers often fell into poverty. I attended these dinners with Joe many years to help out the old timers. Ted Williams, Ralph Branca, and Fay Vincent were always in attendance, and so was Sandy Koufax. Joe held Sandy in high esteem.

"He's a great pitcher," the tough critic of talent and work habits admitted. "Koufax had a monster curveball that wouldn't stop breaking. But, Doc, it wasn't his curveball that impressed me most. The most impressive thing he ever did was not to pitch the ball."

"How's that?" I asked, ready for some brilliant pitching insights.

"He did what he believed was right, not what everybody expected him to do. He refused to pitch in one of the biggest games of the year, because it fell on one of the highest holy days for Jews, Yom Kippur. People tried to make a villain out of the guy, when all he was doing was observing his faith. My respect for him was that much greater after he did that."

So, Koufax did the right thing, a major plus in Joe's book.

"And let me tell you something else, Doc. They always talk about black baseball players being discriminated against. Well, the Jewish boys didn't exactly have a picnic either. Guys like Koufax and Hammering Hank Greenberg—boy, could he hit that ball a mile—these fellows had their own problems.

"There weren't too many Jewish players in the league then, and there were a lot of people in professional baseball who didn't like Jews. Greenberg would get heckled and even received death threats because of his religion. Their faith and values always came first, baseball a distant second."

There is no question in my mind that there was another reason Joe admired Sandy. He was a fashion plate, as well groomed as Joe. In addition to that, Sandy had impeccable manners, which Joe valued. He knew how to talk to people. He spoke clearly, intelligently, and civilly. *La bella figura* was important to Joe, and Sandy embodied a Jewish version of this concept.

Most ballplayers I'd met, especially modern ones, lack some, most, or all of the Yankee Clipper's traits. It was rare to find them at all, let alone in one of my icons from Brooklyn, Sandy Koufax.

At one of the B.A.T. Dinners, Joe introduced me to Koufax.

"Sandy, I'd like you to meet my dear friend, Dr. Positano."

I was flattered on two counts. He used my professional title and he called me a dear friend, which he reserved to few men. I had graduated from a trusted friend to a dear friend. I was pleased he acknowledged that we were close

I extended my hand. "Mr. Koufax, it is a pleasure to meet you," I said. I was effusive.

"Hey, Joe, you're teaching this guy well," Koufax commented. "He knows about manners, I see."

Sandy, like Joe, was formal. He liked that I called him "Mr. Koufax," not Sandy.

Joe was beaming, almost fatherly about Sandy's comments. I had never seen Joe proud of our connection in this manner. I was happy that Koufax attributed my manners to hanging out with Joe.

Later in the evening, when Joe was working the crowd, Sandy Koufax took me aside. "You know, Doctor," he began, "all of us ballplayers have to thank Joe for a life after baseball."

I wasn't ready for that.

"If it wasn't for Joe," he continued, "a lot of us wouldn't be able to make a living. Joe started this whole memorabilia business for us. For that, we are forever grateful."

Joe always insisted that ballplayers deserved to make a living in dignity. Sandy made it clear to me that Joe was a hero for more than his ballplaying. His mission for economic dignity for ballplayers was equally important.

As I grew to know him better, I admired Joe for his dedication to those less fortunate than he was, but I would have expected that. I was even more impressed by his business savvy. Joe led the entire sports profession in business acumen. Not bad for a high-school dropout.

Autographs and memorabilia became a major source of income as Joe grew older and further away from the stadium. Joe had to thank Morris Engelberg for helping him accumulate wealth and exponentially increase the size of his estate from his autograph. Morris explained to

Joe that every time Joe signed a picture or baseball, the Yankee Clipper was just giving away money that would have been put in his family's treasure chest for when he was gone. That statement gave Joe the motivation to develop this business, because he was always concerned first and foremost with the welfare of his family and their ability to live a good life after he checked out. Today, *Forbes* estimates that the volume of autographed sports memorabilia has reached $1.5 billion annually. And to think that it all started with Joe, at least according to Sandy Koufax.

Morris Engelberg, the lawyer from Brooklyn's Borough Park, was a crazy Joe DiMaggio fan before and after he met Joe. It all began when an associate from Morris's Florida law firm was impressed by Joe's popularity at a sports memorabilia show. Morris made the pitch to manage Joe's slipshod business practices. Later he successfully and brilliantly helped Joe resolve an IRS problem in California. Joe was impressed by the Brooklyn boy and vice versa.

As his business manager, Morris standardized Joe's practices and made sure that they conformed to tax codes and the like. He was a skilled negotiator.

"I wish I had met Morris when I was younger. He saved my life, Doc, helped me to be financially comfortable, and allowed me to provide for my family," Joe told me. Joe DiMaggio relied heavily on Morris Engelberg, and their profound respect and admiration was mutual.

Morris and Joe played good cop, bad cop. Joe was always the good cop, politely passing requests to his business manager, Morris, "Big Mo" to the initiated. Morris would take responsibility for killing the deal or declining the invitation, keeping Joe and his reputation above the fray, intact, and in demand. Joe never wanted to look bad in front of people. Morris trusted me to do the same in New York for Joe, which ended up making me an indispensable part of his life.

Morris, Dick Burke, and I were essentially Joe's three adopted kids. What were the chances that two people in Joe's iron-clad inner circle, though separated by thousands of miles as adults, were born and raised in the same neighborhood in Brooklyn? Morris and I were both from the Borough Park area, which was predominantly Jewish and Italian.

Mo and I grew up in cultures that were soothing to Joe Di. Not only were we family oriented, but we were loyal and protective to a fault. These qualities helped Joe to feel free of the prison walls of his iconic fame and stature.

Morris was responsible for Joe's fiscal health, which was so important. Joe was always worried about his family, and Morris made sure they would always be provided for and never in need of anything. Some detractors considered Morris just to be Joe's lawyer. They were clueless and dead wrong. Mo kept the Clipper alive financially and was his admiral in Florida.

I was Joe's New York admiral, keeping him entertained, amused, and out of trouble and potentially problematic situations. His whirlwind social life in New York was great for his psychological health and kept his mind sharp. As he aged, Joe's biggest fear was that he would develop Alzheimer's disease, one of the few things that scared him. Keeping the Clipper stimulated and always on the go was a sure way to keep him engaged.

There was a time when Joe kept a diary of many of the things he did and people he met each day. He didn't write everything down. He edited what made it to the DiMaggio Daily Diary, leaving out some of the pieces of the puzzle to protect himself and his intimates just in case the notes ended up in the wrong hands. He was fiercely protective of his inner circle.

I grew to respect and admire Mo as time went on. I was one of the few people who appreciated what an important role he played in Joe's life. Morris protected Joe from all the people trying to live off his fame, and there were many of them. Mo and I didn't always get along or see things the same way. I guess part of it was sibling rivalry. After I arrived on the scene, it took some time for us to understand each other's essential role in Joe's life. Mo was one of the few people who could send me a very tough e-mail, and there were many, and get an xoxo back. In essence, he was my big brother in the DiMaggio family tree.

Morris wrote *DiMaggio: Setting the Record Straight*, with Marv Schneider in 2003, four years after Joe's death. Morris told me that writing the book was a healing process for him. He felt the need to clear his mind of all the things he remembered about Joe. Working on the book was cathartic for him, especially after the difficult last six months of Joe's life. The father-figure factor was an important part of their relationship. Morris didn't have it easy coming up. As I also found out, Joe could be very fatherly. The book was excellent and showed yet another accurate piece of the DiMaggio jigsaw puzzle. Morris had asked me to enlist the support of Dr. Henry Kissinger, which I did without hesitation. Dr. Kissinger wrote the foreword to Mo's book.

Morris realized that I was one of the few people who actually lost money with Joe. The hours I spent with Joe cut into my work time and resulted in lost revenue.

Joe was a demanding man and would not accept anything less than 100 percent from me. For the most part, I wanted to live up to his expectations. He was a role model for me, and a good part of his example was to be fully engaged. His demands could be irrational, and I had to learn to draw a line I wouldn't cross.

Joe took his own role in the business of being Joe DiMaggio seriously. He knew that working the crowd, admittedly a very select crowd, was an important aspect of letting the show go on, and contributing to the value of his brand. Joe DiMaggio could always satisfy people, and he viewed this as part of his business. The business of entertainment occurred off the field as well as on it. Since he no longer had many occasions to appear on a field, he used off-circuit events like autograph shows, charity breakfasts, lunches, and dinners to extend his celebrity. Joe was adept at polishing his image and collecting loyal fans. His appeal was irresistible as was his desire to be as perfect as possible.

CHAPTER 8

A Legend on Legends

Sunday - June 13, 1993

On the 20th Phil Rizzuto will be celebrating their 5th anniversary at Yankee Stadium (cold) I'm leaning towards the invitation, to spend a couple of hours with all the other invitees, in Steinbrenners Box.

Thursday - April 7, 1994

we discussed other things of importance regarding statue in Central Park.

Morris also mentioned about a catholic university Sacred Heart in connecticut wanting to present me with an honorary degree.

*H*anging out with a legend could be complicated, but there were plenty of benefits. When I was a kid, I wondered what it would be like to sit in the dugout or the owner's box at a baseball stadium. Knowing that this was not likely to happen made me sad. I was one of 56,000 fans, all dreaming the same thing. I made up my mind that, one day, I would be sitting with the players in the dugout and hanging out in George Steinbrenner's box.

It all came true in 1991, a year after I met Joe. It was Old-Timers' Day at Yankee Stadium. The Yankees were honoring Joe for the fiftieth anniversary of his fifty-six-game hitting streak. It was an amazing day. All the past Yankee stars attended, dressed in uniform. They were there to honor the most famous Yankee of them all.

Joe invited me to escort him that day. We were in Steinbrenner's box, and the traffic to come up to meet Joe was out of this world. Past players, politicians, celebrities all wanted to say hello and pay homage to the Clipper.

The Yankees owner, George Steinbrenner, prized Joe's presence in the Owner's Box, because Joe was not merely good for business, not just a great box neighbor for George's upscale guests, but, according to Steinbrenner himself, an indispensable lucky charm for the Yankees. Echoing Rizzuto's opinion, George felt that when DiMaggio was in the house, there was no way the Yankees would lose the big game. When things were going bad for the Yankees, Steinbrenner would often say, "Joe, can you go out there on the field and help us." He meant it.

Joe was not always so accommodating. He even evolved a seating strategy. I would take the seat to Joe's right and another favored guest was on Joe's left to box out any interlopers who wanted to sit next to him. It didn't matter who the interloper was—the governor, the mayor, or the president of the United States. He knew how to control his interactions with people.

Joe was a different person at the stadium. This was his place, and he commanded respect. It was his operating room. Once I stepped into the hallowed grounds of Yankee Stadium, I became one of Joe's "teammates." No preferential treatment was extended even to me. I always trod carefully in that place.

Joe once said to an intruder trying to speak with him during a game, "Listen, buddy, I am a regular guy enjoying my peanuts and trying to watch a game with my friends."

The view was great from George's box. My attention shifted to the upper deck in left field, the nose-bleed seats. I remembered being in those seats with my brother back in June 1978. The Yankees were playing the Red Sox on that hazy, hot, and humid night. I needed binoculars to get a good look at the field, the dugout, and George Steinbrenner's box. And, in 1991, I was sitting in George's box with Joe DiMaggio to my immediate left, not viewing the game with binoculars from a remote location. I couldn't believe my luck.

Nat and Natalie King Cole's duet, "Unforgettable," started to play. A screen in center field came to life to show a video of many of Joe's star moments. I turned to look at him and found him mesmerized by what was on the screen. He was caught up in the moment and enjoyed watching his accomplishments. At that point something clicked in me. I viscerally experienced the cultural and iconic significance of the person sitting next to me—an epiphany in the Catholic sense. I felt like a parochial grade-school kid hanging out with Jesus Christ in the hallway.

Joe was remote and wistful.

"Nice day . . . good game," was all that he said.

When the video was over, Joe signaled to me to come with him downstairs to the field. He wanted to say hello to the Old Timers as well as the present-day Yankees. He didn't have to ask me twice. I followed him like a puppy.

He took me into the clubhouse and showed me where his locker was. Then we went through the tunnel between the clubhouse and the stairs leading to the dugout. We passed the famous sign that Derek Jeter always tapped on his way to the field. The sign was a 1941 quote from Joe: "I want to thank the good Lord for making me a Yankee."

We passed Pete Sheehey, the legendary clubhouse manager, who used to shave down the callus that protected Joe's botched-up heel surgery scar every Old Timers' Day.

"How's the heel feeling, Joe," he asked.

Joe responded, "All better now, Pete, because the Doc fixed it good. No need to shave the callus anymore."

I was seeing blue sky from the bottom of the dugout steps. I'd never seen a more beautiful sight. It reminded me of former Yale President and Commissioner of Major League Baseball Bart Giamatti's poetic book, *Take Time for Paradise*, and how he described the game, the baseball diamond, and home plate.

Joe turned to me and said, "What do you think, Doc?"

I was speechless.

We made a right turn, and we were in the dugout. He motioned to me to sit down next to him. That beautiful field looked endless. Green grass, perfectly cut, the infield diamond groomed and manicured. I was living my 1978 dream from the nose-bleed seats. It could not get any better.

I tried to explain to him what it meant to me, and did so with more emotion than I normally show.

"Glad you got a kick out of it, kid," Joe replied.

I got the impression that Joe viewed my account of that day in 1991 as a delayed honor. After all, not long after we met, I had told Joe that Mickey Mantle was my favorite baseball player.

"I was a good tour guide. Yankee Stadium is, well, special to me.

Good years there, good friends. Most gone," Joe concluded. He was wistful and happy at the same time.

The Yankee Clipper held strong opinions on his fellow athletes. You've already learned about some, but there were plenty more. I discovered that he had two sports heroes: Muhammad Ali and Lou Gehrig.

During dinner one night, we had a major disagreement when I criticized Muhammad Ali for being, in my eyes, a draft dodger. I was touchy about the subject, because we had lost our cousin Michael Sessa Jr. during his second tour of duty in Vietnam. They brought what was left of his body back to Brooklyn in a canvas bag. His sacrifice had affected his family deeply. After I stated my opinion, Joe turned pensive. He told me that Ali was a hero, and that he admired him.

When I objected, Joe explained his position.

"Doc, you're not supposed to be judging the guy in that arena. You're supposed to look at him as a fighter, an athlete. It is not right to look at him as a citizen."

I continued to argue.

"Listen, Doc," he countered, "I may not have agreed with what he did, because I am a veteran myself, but Muhammad Ali is an athlete. He's one of the greatest ever. In fact, he was as good as me."

That is something I had never heard the Yankee Clipper say.

Joe continued to compare himself to his hero, Muhammad Ali, "People could have said the same thing about me. I served for three years at the peak of my career during World War Two, but I didn't fight. Think of how that time away from playing affected my numbers. I never had a missile fired over my head or a bullet whizzing past my ear. I went around the world doing exhibition games for the troops." Joe reached for a breadstick, and continued, "And they could have said the same thing about Elvis Presley. He never saw a day of action. All he did was go from camp to camp to entertain the troops."

"Well, Joe, what are you trying to tell me?"

Joe took a minute to respond. "I think that Muhammad Ali was the greatest. He was a fabulous boxer, a fabulous athlete, and that is what we should remember him for. Not for his religious or personal beliefs. When you judge people professionally, base it on their accomplishments in their area, not for what they believe or what they say and do in their personal lives."

Joe was once again teaching me the meaning of being a stand-up guy.

Joe made his affinity for boxing and boxers clear to me. He loved the sport almost as much as baseball. I never saw him show interest in any other sport. I assume he respected the demanding skills and rigorous physical conditioning required by boxing. He used to make visits to Madison Square Garden matches with his buddies, as long as he could avoid Frank Sinatra, another boxing fanatic, taking pictures ringside.

At Bamonte's one night, he told us a very moving story about Joe Louis, for whom he had great respect. Joe Louis was a towering black boxer who had had a run-in with Adolf Hitler and the Nazis during the 1930s. His two bouts with Max Schmeling from Nazi Germany made him the first African-American sports hero in the U.S. in 1936. The Nazis considered him inferior because of his race. Joe disagreed vehemently. The Clipper thought Joe Louis was one of the best-conditioned and gifted boxers to ever step into the ring.

When we talked about Joe Louis, I asked Joe what he thought Louis's biggest weakness was. I was referring to his boxing skills. Joe floored me when he replied that Louis's biggest weaknesses were his generosity and big heart. He told me that for many years, Joe Louis took care of many people who needed money, shelter, food, and other necessities.

According to Joe, "Louis died a very poor man. It was a shame to see him in this condition after his career as a champion. The people he helped were nowhere to be found."

I believe seeing a champion reduced to these circumstances propelled Joe to start the cottage industry of autographs and signed memorabilia described earlier. The shadowy fear stayed with him. His compulsion to hoard money to provide for his family had its roots in the sad story of Joe Louis. Joe was intent on not letting history repeat in his own life.

Joe's other major hero was his predecessor, Lou Gehrig. Lou was as reticent as Ali was garrulous. Lou, a first baseman, is remembered more today for the disease that killed him than his athletic ability. Lou was vibrant in Joe's memory. Joe was impressed that Gehrig had attended Ivy League Columbia University for two years before he dropped out to join the Yankees.

Lou and Joe shared adjacent lockers during Joe's rookie season with the Yankees. Joe remembered him as an intelligent and shy man. He compared Lou's strong, stocky legs to piano legs that were matched by a body builder's upper torso and Popeye the Sailor-Man forearms. But Lou wasn't muscle bound. According to Joe, Lou had agility as well as strength.

Joe told me that when Lou hit a line drive, it was as though the ball was attached to a taut rope. "It would take off like a rocket and ping off the facades and bleachers of the Stadium in right field. You could hear the balls all the way in the Yankee clubhouse ringing like a bell when Gehrig was in batting practice," Joe said with admiration.

Lou's advice to the rookie was straight and powerful. Joe told me that Lou's example had guided him to develop valuable personal attributes, in Joe's words, "being dignified, never speaking out of turn, conducting myself properly under any circumstances, and, most important, not volunteering any information to the wrong people." These lessons were Lou's direct contribution to Joe's nascent legend.

Lou was keeping a brother's eye out for Joe. The rookie was under the impression that his teammate was there for him at all times, but Lou was suffering from the initial, barely noticeable, symptoms of the disease that would overwhelm him. Joe began to realize that something terrible was happening to his big brother and lockermate.

Joe first noticed that Lou had started to shave unsteadily. Then Lou had problems tying his laces. Joe noticed Lou dropping things. By 1937, Lou seemed slow and even more deliberate. Despite what he was observing, Joe said nothing to anyone. Joe chalked it up to Gehrig's having another slow start in spring training, which was a common occurrence. Though Lou's eyes communicated everything in the privacy of their adjacent locker-room stalls, Joe was true to the creed of the stand-up guy.

Eventually, that something was seriously wrong with Lou became apparent. He couldn't hit well and was having trouble fielding and getting around the bases. It got so bad that Lou was dropping the bat in the batter's circle, had problems with his glove, and wasn't up to the tactics of the opposing team.

One day, he and Lou were talking alongside their lockers. Joe told me that he would never forget it.

"Lou said to me, 'Joe, I don't think that I can play baseball anymore. I want to take myself out of the lineup before McCarthy takes me out.'"

The Clipper was shocked by Lou's words. He had told no one else on the team what Lou was going through.

Decades later, thinking about the conversation made Joe tear up.

"Doc, this was the first time I ever showed any emotion inside the locker room. It was just the two of us, alone, and Gehrig started to cry. I cried, too."

I could see the pain in Joe's eyes even fifty years later.

Joe had kept his mouth shut about the growing evidence of Gehrig's infirmities. He was the stand-up guy's stand-up guy. Dignity had to be maintained. The model for Joe's famous dignity was his own hero, Lou Gehrig.

———————

JOE SURPRISED ME with his assessment of Pete Rose. He was more generous about Pete Rose than I would have thought possible, given Joe's straight-arrow values. Rose was accused of betting on the baseball games he played in or managed, a violation of Major League Baseball's Rule 21, which made betting on ball games a "misconduct punishable by permanent ineligibility" from consideration for Baseball's Hall of Fame.

Remembering what Joe had done when he was playing exhibition games in the Army, I would have expected him to come down hard on Rose, who was banned from the Hall of Fame. To make matters worse, Rose served five months in a medium-security Federal prison for income tax evasion. He was a bad boy by any standard.

Though one biographer says that Joe would hide money in plastic sacks, he was never remotely involved in gambling. He had been so upset by the threats of the San Francisco blackmailer casting a shadow over his reputation, I expected him to be vitriolic about Pete Rose. Mr. Clean delivered his judgment in private.

Joe believed that Rose really did earn the Baseball Hall of Fame award. Starting in the big leagues in 1963, he played for the Cincinnati Reds. Rose earned the nickname "Charlie Hustle" for his explosive energy, even in middle age. He broke Ty Cobb's hitting record by slamming 4,256 hits, which was a critical stat for Joe. In addition, Rose played the most games in baseball history, a total of 3,562. The team was called "The Big Red Machine," referring to a talented group of players, including Joe Morgan, Johnny Bench, and Rose.

"Joe, what do you think about Pete Rose being barred from the Baseball Hall of Fame?" I asked, prepared for a torrent of censure.

Joe thought my question over. I actually believe that handing off Rose's case to a judge like Joe—an athlete and a legend—would have been less damaging to baseball than the media trial that harmed the sport.

As he grabbed a wedge of bread and removed the middle only to be left with the crust, Joe announced his judgment.

"Now, Doc, if moral character was a prerequisite of admission to the Hall of Fame a lot worse people have been admitted."

Joe went on to give me an example.

"Ty Cobb beat up his wife."

"I'm surprised by what you're saying, knowing how you feel about gambling and sports."

Joe took a gulp of coffee, then continued, "Rose is a great athlete, and really delivered for the Reds and baseball."

I thought over what Joe had said. Rose had his flaws, like Ali, but legends defend legends. I have little doubt that, if he had a say, Joe would have admitted Rose into the Hall of Fame and criticized him at the same time. For Joe, merit in baseball, which Rose unquestionably showed, trumped his many misdemeanors. The same premise with which he judged Muhammad Ali applied to Pete Rose. Joe was consistent.

In recent years, Barry Bonds and Roger Clemens, neither of whom have had Rose's record and impact on the sport, have fared better on eligibility, despite accusations of steroid abuse. These athletes, who broke records for hitting, RBIs, home runs, improved their play by using performance enhancers. In the end, performance was sacred to Joe, and talent was a virtue.

Just as Joe was quick to praise his heroes and those he admired, he was outspoken in his criticism of other legends. He once made a comment about Don Larsen. Joe was amazed and perplexed that Larsen's performance in one game in the 1956 World Series, a perfect no-hitter, immortalized him in the sporting world for the rest of his career. On the basis of a single game, Larsen received a lot of attention and accolades.

I went with Joe to the Yankees' Old Timers' Game in 1994. Retired Yankees were asked to come to the stadium to make an appearance for their fans. This was a big deal for Joe. He did it for the fans, not for the owner or the Yankees.

Joe DiMaggio enjoying pasta prepared by his mother, Rosalia, in 1934. Joe didn't like his pasta *al dente*.

Before the start of the 1936 World Series in New York, Joe hugs his brothers Vincent (left) and Dominic.

Joe, brother Dominic, and father, Giuseppe, 1937.

Joe loved children. Much of his charitable work was focused on children. He is pictured here giving batting lessons to a young orphan.

In 1939, Lefty Gomez and a dapper Joe DiMaggio consider a purchase while a salesperson looks on.

Joe and Dorothy Arnold arrive at their Joe's Café wedding reception on November 19, 1939, in San Francisco. Twenty thousand fans showed up at the cathedral for the wedding.

Baby Joe DiMaggio III holds a mini bat as his parents look on in their New York City home in December 1941.

Sergeant DiMaggio gets some help from Brigadier General William J. Flood, sponsor of the 7th Army Air Force overall sports program, on June 9, 1944. Joe spent three years at the height of his career playing exhibition ball in the South Pacific.

Frank Sinatra, Toots Shor—the proprietor of the legendary saloon and restaurant—and Joe admire a portrait of Joe. He would eventually be estranged from both of them.

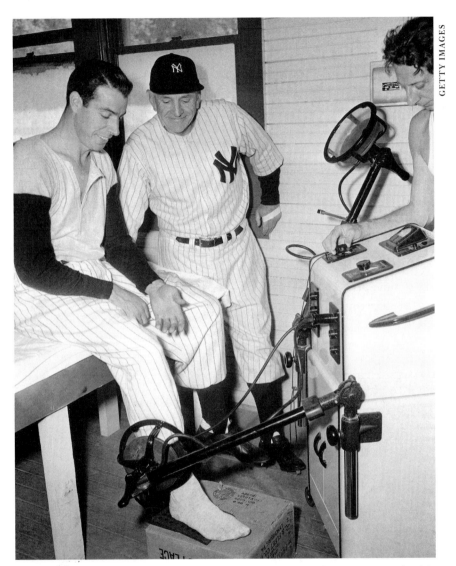

Yankees manager Casey Stengel looks on as Joe receives treatment for his problem heel in 1949. This diathermy treatment once resulted in Joe developing a severe burn on his already injured right heel.

Marilyn Monroe and Joe celebrating at Chasen's after she left her handprints in cement at Grauman's Chinese Theatre, 1953.

Father and son devastated at Marilyn's funeral, 1962.

Joe Jr. in 1975.

Joe with Bill Gallo, the man who introduced us and one of Joe's most trusted sports journalists.

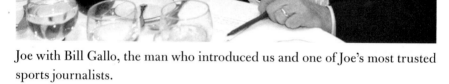

One of the few pictures of Joe and me together. We were both fiercely private and protective of one another.

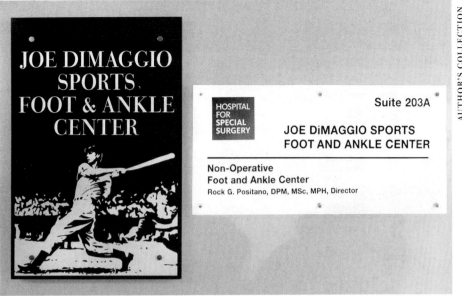

I founded the Joe DiMaggio Sports Foot and Ankle Center at the Hospital for Special Surgery with the blessing of Joe and his estate.

Joe with Anthony Bamonte, the owner of one of our favorite places for dinner, and his daughter Lisa. Joe's table was last and back on the right in front of the dessert refrigerator.

Joe, the Grand Marshal of the Columbus Day Parade, with Mayor David Dinkins. Joe admired the mayor's sense of style and fashion.

Joe and Woody Allen with Soon Yi and the three Bamonte sisters after a terrific meal. (Left to right: Soon Yi, Laura, Woody, Lisa, Joe, and Nicole.)

Joe with former Baseball Commissioner Fay T. Vincent.

My son, Rocky, with
George Steinbrenner.

Joe gave Rocky VIP treatment
at Yankee Stadium. He took
this photograph of Rocky with
Mayor Rudy Giuliani and Jack
Lawn, Vice President, COO, and
troubleshooter for the Yankees.

The mayor returned the
favor with this photo of
Rocky, Joe, and Mel Allen.

Joe served pizza slices at my children's party. My daughter, Riana, is on the far left, and Rocky is on the far right. People from the neighborhood congregated outside to get a glimpse of the Yankee Clipper in their local pizzeria.

Joe arriving at the *Time* Magazine 75th Anniversary party. He chose to sit with Dr. Henry Kissinger rather than President Bill Clinton.

Phil Rizzuto presents Joe with a set of World Series rings on Joe DiMaggio Day at Yankee Stadium in 1998. The Yankees gave Joe the rings to replace his set, which was stolen in the 1960s. He wore his original 1936 World Series ring until the day he died.

By 1994, he no longer wore the Yankee uniform, because his body was showing signs of aging, and he didn't like the way he looked in it. As usual, Joe was perfectly turned out in a well-tailored navy blue suit and tie. He often criticized his former teammates, Rizzuto, Berra, and Mantle, for their poor appearance in uniform. He was less harsh about Phil and Yogi. He expressed his firm opinion that the elder Yankees should show up in suits for Old Timers' Games and other events.

On our way up to the owner's box in an elevator that day in 1994, we stopped between the ground level and the box floor. The doors opened, and there was Mickey Mantle. I didn't recognize the stocky, strong-looking guy in a warm-up suit for a full five seconds, but Joe did immediately. He gave Mickey a stern look.

An eternity passed in those minutes. Both men were avoiding eye contact, looking anywhere but at each other. Joe was waiting for The Mick to blink and acknowledge him first. It was a pecking order thing or the ballplayer's version of chicken. Mickey was the first to break the painful silence between the legends.

"How ya doin' Joe?" Mickey asked with his eyes down.

Joe studied Mickey. "I'm okay, Mick." He paused before asking, "You stayin' out of trouble?"

Neither man spoke after that. When Mickey left the elevator, Joe turned to me and commented, "Doc, some guys just never learn. He will never change."

That was the longest elevator ride I ever took. It seemed endless. The tension was indescribable and something right out of *High Noon*.

The Clipper did not let go of the grudge. As Mickey Mantle was dying of cancer, I thought Joe would relent. It didn't happen. Joe never forgave Mantle for replacing him in center field and not taking his advice about how to conduct himself as a Yankee. Despite getting updates on Mickey's condition, which was bad and worsening, Joe would not soften.

When I ventured to ask him about it, he said, "You know, Doc, I don't really feel sorry for the guy. He did it to himself."

He could be a very tough man.

Joe made himself unavailable to the press seeking his words to honor the dying and departed Mickey Mantle. It fell on me to pass press requests to Joe, who declined all of them. Even at a posthumous Mickey Mantle Day at the Stadium, Joe did nothing more than show up. I found his behavior disturbing.

He told a Steinbrenner special assistant, Brian Smith, that he had no intention of talking about Mickey. "You make sure they know that I am not getting up to that mike to say anything about anybody. I was asked to come here to show up and walk out on the field. That is exactly what I am going to do. Then I am going to turn back and walk off the field."

Joe really liked Smith and was able to relax in the bowels of the stadium. Brian and I made sure Joe made it onto the field.

I was surprised by how rigid and bitter he allowed himself to appear. People remember that sort of behavior. It didn't do much to enhance his reputation. It seemed so petty to me, but what I thought didn't matter. I was disappointed that he dug in. He should have been bigger than that. He expected others to rise above their grudges.

A few minutes later, Joe DiMaggio stepped onto the playing field with the other ballplayers. He got the lion's share of the applause. Then he turned tail, walked off, and headed home.

"Come on, Doc," he commanded, "we're getting the hell out of here." And so we did.

Joe's wrath extended to others as well, including George Steinbrenner, the owner of the Yankees and a sharp businessman. Though very fond of Steinbrenner personally, Joe was never quite comfortable with him, because Steinbrenner was always asking him for some favor, whether to work out a baseball memorabilia deal or to meet people who would help advance the business interests of the New York Yankees. One story has become the stuff of legend.

At dinner one night, Mario Faustini was feeling his oats. He made a comment that I was too cautious to ever try, because I didn't want to risk provoking Joe to clam up about his memories.

"Hey, Joe," Mario jumped right in. "You have the best stories. How come you never wrote them down and shared them with your fans?"

Joe clenched his jaw. He shifted in his chair and looked Faustini in the eye.

"I'll tell ya why: Too many people have made a great living off me, especially at Yankee Stadium. Steinbrenner now wants me to do all these things for the Yankees. He says it's good for baseball."

"Well, isn't it?" one of the Bat Pack asked.

"That's a lot of crap! It's good for Steinbrenner and his cronies," Joe added, "so, listen to this." He leaned forward as if he was about to tell us something confidential.

All of us at the table leaned forward so as not to miss a word. Joe knew how to wrap an audience around his finger.

"He asked me once, 'Joe, what would I have to pay you if you were playing for the Yankees today?'" Joe shifted back in his chair.

The sports news was full of ballplayers fighting with owners for money and perks.

"We can't wait to hear this," I said.

"I didn't skip a beat. I shot back, 'George, I would walk into your office, extend my hand, and say, "Hello, partner!"'"

Joe knew how to get a laugh. That's one of the reasons that having dinner with DiMaggio was never boring. Joe's temperament could be challenging, but when he was on, there was no one like him.

Steinbrenner was obsessed with DiMaggio. He considered Joe a good luck charm. He believed that the Y   couldn't lose if the Yankee Clipper was in "the house that Ruth   t." When the Yankees were in the playoffs in 1996, George made sure that Joe was at the games, sitting in what was nominally George's box, which wasn't the case when Joe was in attendance.

George was intent on commissioning a statue of Joe to be placed in center field at the stadium. He even tried to get another statue of Joe planted in Central Park. There was only one problem. George needed Joe's blessing. It was a respect thing.

Joe was adamantly against being memorialized anywhere in New York while he was still in the upright position.

"As long as I am still walking," he insisted, "there is no way I will have anyone build a statue of me in this city. When I am dead, they can do whatever the hell they want."

It was a closed issue. Joe told George no, and that was it.

In fact, Joe vetoed every statue and monument, as well as East 56th Street, which New York City tried to name after him. On a drive to Yankee Stadium on the Deegan, Joe told me that the city had offered to rename the Major Deegan the Joe DiMaggio Expressway. The expressway in the Bronx passes right by Yankee Stadium and leads to the New York State Thruway. Major William Francis Deegan, a buddy of Mayor Jimmy Walker, served in the Army Corps of Engineers and built many local Army bases.

"I told them no, because I felt it was disrespectful to Major Deegan's memory," he explained. "I won't have them knock his name off to replace it with mine. It wouldn't be right, and I wouldn't feel good about it."

Soon after the confrontation about the statue in center field, we were invited back to Steinbrenner's box. In all fairness to Steinbrenner, he always went out of his way to make Joe feel at home. He made sure that Joe had his Bazzini shelled peanuts and Cracker Jacks in the owner's box. During this visit, George had a new food vendor who made Philadelphia cheesesteaks. He persuaded us to try them out. Joe was resistant to trying anything new. He was a culinary snob. The thought of eating a premade cheesesteak didn't sit well with him, but he enjoyed it.

Not long after finishing, he turned to me with visible discomfort and said, "Doc, we better get out of here soon. My stomach is really bothering me. I have to get back to Burke's place."

We sped back to Manhattan in under fifteen minutes. Joe made it to the bathroom just in time.

From behind the bathroom door, Joe started yelling. "Doc, I don't know what the hell Steinbrenner fed me, but I think he's trying to kill me so he can put up that statue of me in center field."

I think he believed it.

JOE WAS DISPLEASED with the feud between Yogi and Steinbrenner. I am talking about the same Lawrence "Yogi" Berra who flacked for the Yoo-Hoo beverage company. Yoo-Hoo was the official chocolate soft drink of the brothers Positano during the '60s. In my mind, to attack Yogi was to attack Yoo-Hoo. Yogi was on bottle caps, cartons, and print ads of the popular drink. Mickey also promoted Yoo-Hoo when we were kids. Rumor has it that, aside from the photo ops, Mickey told everyone that he wouldn't touch the stuff.

At dinner one night, I got up the nerve to ask Joe about what his take was on the Steinbrenner–Berra feud. He didn't hold back. He felt that Yogi Berra was wrong, and that he was being stubborn.

I did not remind him of how intractable he was about Mickey Mantle, who had only replaced him, not fired him.

Joe did concede that Steinbrenner treated Berra shabbily by firing him as the New York Yankees' manager, but he felt Yogi's response was an overreaction.

I told Joe I had heard that George tried to make amends to Berra unofficially, through the media and through third parties.

"How many times can a guy say he's sorry before he stops saying he's sorry?" Joe knew that Steinbrenner would eventually give up trying.

According to Joe, Yogi suffered from Italian-American disease: He was prone to manufacture slights. With Southern Italian spite, Yogi refused to return to Yankee Stadium after George Steinbrenner fired him. Until his dying day, Joe tried to get the Yankee Philosopher to back down and return to the stadium.

Joe thought Yogi was foolish, because Yogi wasn't just slighting George, who deserved it, he was insulting the Yankees, the fans, and Joe Di by association. Joe took Yogi's behavior as an affront. He thought Yogi's continued boycott of the stadium was a stupid gesture and a direct insult to the fans, who paid everyone's bloated salary and pension.

At Joe's last appearance at Yankee Stadium, Joe DiMaggio Day in September of 1998, he said the same thing to me, again.

"Doc, isn't it a sin that Yogi isn't here? I don't know why he's acting like an asshole, but he should be here. I would have liked him to be here. He was a teammate of mine, and I think it would have been good for baseball, for the fans, and for the Yankee organization."

Regardless of what Joe wanted, Yogi Berra did not show up at the stadium on Joe DiMaggio Day six months before Joe's death. Joe told me how unhappy he was about the slight.

"I was a little pissed at Yogi that day. He was a famous and noteworthy no-show, and I was good to Yogi. He could have done a one-day truce. He would be there for a few minutes and gone," Joe said.

I could see that my friend's pride as well as his team spirit suffered.

"Yankees don't slight Yankees," Joe explained, "and certainly not in front of the fans.

"He could have buried the hatchet with George that day. If he had a problem with George that's one thing, but to take it out on the fans and me was another."

Joe had no trouble communicating what he thought to Yogi. "I've even told him that he was acting like a spoiled kid. What did he think he was proving?"

In fairness to Yogi, Joe agreed that there was some validity to what Yogi felt, but, as Joe always said, Steinbrenner was still the owner, and baseball was a business. Joe certainly had his run-ins with owners of the Yankees while he was a ballplayer, specifically when it came to contract disputes. In the end, Joe always tried to do what was in the best interest of baseball, the fans, and the New York Yankees.

Yogi and Steinbrenner resolved their dispute in 1999. Mike Lupica reported in his *Daily News* column that Joe learned of the reconciliation and commented how glad he was that Yogi and Steinbrenner had patched up their quarrel. Joe died soon after.

We talked about other Yankees as well. Take Derek Jeter, a more recent hero. Joe may have been admired by the Yankees' star Derek Jeter, but Joe's first mention to me of Jeter was hardly complimentary. He was even dismissive.

Joe met Derek Jeter for the first time in March 1996, when Joe was throwing out the first pitch on Joe DiMaggio Day at the Yankee spring-training facility in Florida. Joe flew in from New York. George Steinbrenner and his driver Eddie picked up Joe on the runway.

Steinbrenner was effusive about Jeter. Close to the first words out of his mouth were to tell Joe that they got this new kid named Jeter, who was a sure Hall of Famer.

Not impressed, Joe replied, "How can you say that when he hasn't played in the Majors yet?"

George stopped grinning.

In the first inning, Jeter was hit by a pitch and broke his wrist.

"Some Hall of Famer!" was Joe's remark.

Though he may have reserved judgment on Jeter's Hall of Fame potential, Joe did think that Jeter was a good-looking guy.

After shaking hands with Jeter in the dugout prior to the first pitch, Joe was heard saying to George, "This kid looks like a movie star."

THE FORMER FACE of Mr. Coffee and Bowery Savings Bank, Joe disapproved of another baseball legend working as a spokesperson. One day, we were watching television at the Burkes' apartment. A Tommy Lasorda SlimFast commercial came on the air. Lasorda was the head honcho and field manager of the Los Angeles Dodgers at the time.

"Great manager—one of the best ever—too bad," Joe commented.

"Too bad for what, Joe?"

"Tommy will never get the credit or recognition that he deserves, because he is always so out there," Joe explained. "Everywhere you turn, he's appearing on TV shows, doing commercials for that weight-loss stuff."

"What's wrong with that?" I didn't mention Joe's stint as a spokesperson for Mr. Coffee and the Bowery Savings Bank, whose TV ads were everywhere.

"People don't take you seriously if you try to do other things that are beyond your main job. It would be different if Tommy was already retired, but to do this," Joe said as he pointed with disgust at the TV set, "while actively managing a ball team, well, that is a different story."

"Joe, did you ever tell Tommy about this," I asked. "He really looks up to you. That would be the compliment of his life if you told him how you felt he was one of the best baseball managers ever."

"Doc, I don't give out compliments too often."

"No kidding," I thought to myself. Joe rarely praised anyone.

Joe went on to explain his behavior, which did make him appear stingy to critics. "It goes to people's heads, and the next thing you know they start slacking off.

"This conversation is between you and me, but someday, when I'm not around, you may want to tell him how I feel."

"Joe, you have a strange way of telling people how you feel about them," I had to say.

"Don't go there," he said to end the conversation.

FAY VINCENT WAS arguably the most decisive, talented, honorable, and most unfairly derided commissioner of Major League Baseball. Joe and Vincent had a reciprocal respect. He earned Joe's regard at the cost of being forced to resign by an eighteen-to-nine vote of the owners of the Major League ball teams. The Major League franchises were all about business. A group of owners gunned for Fay Vincent and got him.

Vincent, like Joe, saw baseball sliding down the slippery slope of false economics, corruption, labor bashing, and law breaking. Fay had done a number of things that Joe admired. He sat through the earthquake in 1989 San Francisco during the World Series. He confirmed the ban of Pete Rose from baseball for gambling offenses. He stopped the owners' lockout of the players in 1990. And, finally, with an act that brought great joy to Joe's heart, Vincent excluded George Steinbrenner for consorting with gamblers. Of course, George was reinstated after Fay was forced to resign by George's fellow owners. The owners applauded Pete Rose being banned from the game for life, but wealthy old Steinbrenner—well, boys will be boys!

Before coming to Major League Baseball, Fay Vincent was an athlete, a graduate of Williams College and Yale Law School, CEO of Columbia Pictures, a leading corporate lawyer, and a Coca-Cola executive, among many other achievements. He started a crusade to reform Major League Baseball.

One day, I picked up the phone at home to find Fay, then the former commissioner of Major League Baseball, on the line.

After we exchanged friendly greetings, Fay told me the reason for his call.

"Something's been on my mind, Rocky," he began. "I really miss seeing Joe. I feel so bad that he doesn't want to talk to me anymore," he said in his New England–accented, soft-spoken voice.

I couldn't imagine why Fay was in Siberia, what he had done to provoke the wrath of DiMaggio. Though I didn't think I could do much about it, Fay was a great guy, and I wanted to help a very close friend, who had always been generous to me and treated me with respect.

"Fay, it's a damn shame," I said. "After all, he did introduce you and me some years ago."

Fay was silent on the other end of the phone.

"You know how tough he is when someone is on the outs with him," I explained. "He and Dick Burke call me Lazarus, because I came back from the dead a few times after he was pissed off at me . . . probably a more impressive feat than his fifty-six-game hitting streak in 1941."

Fay laughed on the other end of the line.

"Rocky, if anyone could get me back into good graces with him and clear the deck, it's you," he said, "He has such respect for you, and he trusts your judgment."

I was flattered. The men shared too much to slight each other. During his tumultuous Major League Baseball career, Fay was motivated by the idealistic dream that baseball was a people's game. And Joe saw himself as the people's icon. The stumbling block for Fay was that Major League Baseball was no longer the people's game.

I realized that, since it didn't take much to set Joe off, the rift might be mendable. What complicated the matter was Joe's habit of not telling people what he was mad about in the first place. Although what prompted the exile was undoubtedly clear in Joe's mind, Fay had no idea what his transgressions might have been.

I had committed to try to help, but I was well aware that my intervention could earn me the next ticket to Siberia, the same outcome as when Bill Fugazy tried to do the right thing and patch up a rift between Joe and Steinbrenner. I had to find a way to get these two brilliant men and dear friends of mine together. The first step was to bring the matter up with Joe. If I emerged alive and unblistered, I had to set up a meeting in a neutral territory. It was the ultimate sit-down.

It would be a shame if the two prominent men, who saw Major League Baseball as a sacred trust for the American people, remained estranged, so I set the gears into motion knowing that I, the messenger, might get shot.

I broached the subject at the Gardenia Café on Madison Avenue. As we were surveying the menus, Joe seemed to be in a good humor. I decided to be direct, and said, "Joe, I haven't heard you talk about Fay Vincent in a long while."

Joe gave an annoyed huff. "No need to talk to the commissioner, after that crap they pulled on me at Major League Baseball a while back," he said.

"What crap," I asked, hearing the whistle of the Siberian Express coming off Madison.

"C'mon, Doc . . . you know what I'm talkin' about. One of the commissioner's underlings was feeling his oats one day," Joe began to narrate the story. "I had to talk to this young asshole about a memorabilia-licensing matter." Joe was getting increasingly peeved as he talked. "You wouldn't believe the balls on this guy, Doc. He looked me straight in the eye and said, 'Mr. DiMaggio, you haven't done enough to help baseball.'"

"He said what?" I asked, astonished that the guy would say something like that to a man whose entire life was baseball.

Joe reloaded.

"Yeah, you heard right. The nerve of that son of a bitch saying that to me. I went directly to the commissioner and told him what had happened." Joe shook his head.

"What did the commissioner say?"

Steam practically started coming from Joe's ears when he answered. "He gave the guy a slap on the wrist."

I didn't know what to say. Fay Vincent must have had the impression that the issue had been resolved after their talk. Vincent didn't suspect that Joe had remained angry about what the staffer had said to him and that Joe believed Vincent had not taken the slight seriously enough. Maybe Joe had wanted the guy fired.

Maybe an apology now would satisfy Joe's honor and redeem the commissioner. I took a risky step.

"Joe, you know, to his credit, the commissioner is a fair and honorable man, like yourself," I began.

Joe nodded his head with a sad expression on his face.

I took the leap and continued, "I think that you're carrying this a bit too far. I hope that you don't get mad at me for saying this, Joe, but I feel that you two guys should be talking again."

He had never listened to me before on his many rifts, but it was worth a try with Fay Vincent. Getting Fay out of Joe's doghouse was worth it.

Joe took all of twenty seconds to respond.

"Well, yeah, Doc. You may be right on this one," he conceded. "Maybe I have been a little too hard on the commissioner."

I ran with it. "Plus, Joe, you know that he is a devout Catholic. He goes to church every week. He donates thousands of dollars to the church for kids' programs."

Joe nodded.

"Why don't you sit down with him and talk about it? Besides, Fay has been very good to me and has always been supportive. Would you do it for me, Joe?"

"All right, Doc," Joe caved with a warning, "but I am not going to promise you or him anything. He may not like what I have to say. Make the call!"

I had asked him to do it for me, he had complied. Our relationship had certainly evolved.

I pulled out my cell phone and got Vincent on the first try.

"Fay, it's all set up. Next Tuesday at Bravo Gianni. Gianni reserved the place for you two guys—no other customers—just in case." I added, "Just in case it gets loud, Fay. Gianni is going to lock the front door, so it will only be the three of us."

This was a scene right out of a gangster movie where they locked the people inside so they could not escape.

Fay was too happy and relieved to catch my warning.

"That's terrific, Rock. You're a great friend," he said.

I felt like Henry Kissinger arranging the Vietnam Peace Talks. I got them together, and they exchanged pleasantries. Both men were seated and spoke civilly. Joe asked me to excuse myself from the table. I hovered within ear range, just in case. There were only three of us in the restaurant, so it was pretty easy to get lost.

Joe brought up the slight that caused the rift, and Vincent said he understood.

"What would make this guy think he could tell me such a thing," Joe wondered. "I could only assume that his boss, who was you at the time, felt the same way?"

"Joe, it was an error in judgment. I have the utmost respect for you, for what you've done for Major League Baseball," he said with great fervor.

Joe rolled over on that one. He heard what he wanted to hear, and Vincent got to say what he was dying to say.

Joe was pleasant right back.

"You did some great things for baseball yourself," Joe said. "You and Giamatti handled the Pete Rose gambling scandal with tact and fairness. You protected the integrity of the game whether we agreed with the decision or not."

Vincent grinned. He knew that praise from Joe was a rare commodity.

"And we did have some good times together." Joe went on to recount one such time. "Remember? Me, you, Ted Williams, and President Bush talking about baseball on Air Force One en route to the 1991 All-Star Game in Toronto?"

"Joe, that was a priceless and historic moment for me," Vincent agreed. "The baseball stories you and Williams told about your rivalry and the historic baseball season of 1941."

"Yeah, that was right before Ted took ill with a stroke. But I didn't believe he wouldn't wear a tie, even in the company of the president of the United States. That's Ted."

Some things never change.

Vincent laughed heartily, then reminded Joe, "That story you told about Connie Mack and Bobo Newsom was a classic. It really cracked up the president."

Joe grinned broadly and was game to tell it to me. He called out, "Doc, come back, it's safe now. I have a great story for you."

I sat down with them, eager to hear it.

"Connie Mack, who owned the Philadelphia Athletics, tried to tell Bobo Newsom how to pitch to me," Joe started. "The first time I hit Newsom up pretty bad, with two base clearing shots to the deepest part of the park. Newsom was throwing me fastballs against the wishes of Mack. During an inning break, Mack called Newsom over."

Vincent was already chuckling.

"He said to Newsom, 'Mr. Newsom, let me tell you how to pitch to Mr. DiMaggio. Throw only curve balls to Mr. DiMaggio. That's how you'll get him out. Curveball, curveball, curveball,'" Joe repeated with emphasis, along with the hand motion used to throw a curveball pitch.

"Do you remember what happened next, Mr. Commissioner?" Joe asked, and Fay nodded. "Newsom threw me a curve ball that didn't even break an inch."

Joe was using his hands and fingers to show how the ball was breaking.

"I got every bit of that pitch and sent a rocket into the upper deck for a round tripper!" Joe was triumphant.

"Tell Rock what Newsom said when you were rounding the bases, Joe."

"Bobo came right off the mound and ran toward third base. He cupped his hand and yelled to Mack, 'Oh, Mr. Mack? Mr. Mack? He hit your pitch farther than he hit mine!"

"I'll never forget laughing to myself as I headed home to touch the plate."

Both men had a good laugh—friends again!

"Hey, guys, I'm glad you kissed and made up."

"Rocky, Joe and I were reminiscing about the day at the White House when the President was celebrating the fiftieth anniversary of Joe's fifty-six-game hitting streak, and Williams batting over .400."

I brought up a trivial point.

"Isn't that the day when Bush's staff guy came up to Joe with a box of baseballs and asked him to sign them for the president?"

"Like hell the president asked for them," Joe interrupted. "That guy was full of it. Those balls were for his friends."

"Joe, that day was my fondest memory of baseball ever," Vincent said. "What I found absolutely absurd was when we were about to go on the field at Toronto with you, me, Bush, Williams, and Ted Williams' son, John Henry."

Joe slapped his forehead. "Who could forget what that kid said to the president?"

"What did he say," I asked a smirking Fay Vincent.

"The kid told the president that his father didn't like to wear a jacket and tie on the field. He asked if the president would mind taking off his own jacket to accommodate his father's fashion statement and refusal to wear a jacket and tie, so he wouldn't make Ted look bad!"

"You're kidding."

"No, it happened," Vincent continued. "The president has to wear a special bulletproof jacket, a discreet sort of body armor, when he goes into an open space. The Secret Service would not permit him to take off his protective jacket!"

"Can you imagine the balls on that kid?" Joe said. "Asking the president not to wear his protective jacket out on the open field."

And, just like that, Joe switched gears.

"Commissioner, those guys, the team owners, really screwed up with you, those owners really shot themselves in the foot when they pushed you out of the game. The only owner with balls was President Bush's kid, George, who owned the Texas Rangers. That kid showed me something. He had courage. He could pick out the one asshole in a room of a thousand people. He would make a good president someday if he ever wanted to follow in his father's footsteps."

Joe made this prediction years before George W. Bush's election in 2000.

"He's a solid guy," Vincent agreed. "He didn't bend an inch to the pressure and influence of the other owners. I was most impressed with his character."

"You know, Fay, I hope that history will be kind to both of us," Joe concluded.

"Amen to that," Vincent seconded Joe's wish.

"Joe, thanks for giving me the chance to straighten things out with you," Vincent said before the meeting broke up.

Joe and Vincent shared so much in common: a genuine love of baseball, the utmost integrity, a rigorous discipline, and, for the most part, a reasonable disposition. Fay Vincent was able to return to the dinner table with Joe. It wasn't going to be Fay's version of the "Last Supper." Fay Vincent was welcomed back to the dinner table. A rarity indeed.

Over time, after many meals, what seemed like countless conversations, and never-ending public appearances, I gained a deeper understanding of what drove Joe. He was painfully aware of his place not just as icon, but also as part of history. He had spent much of his life playing to a future generation of journalists, historians, and fans. One of the reasons I wrote this memoir was to define Joe's place in history and in the setting of the town that made him legendary, New York City. He was a complex man, both a demon and a hero, as you've seen in these pages. So many have portrayed him as one or the other, which oversimplifies the man he was. I sometimes thought that Joe's whole existence was designed for future consumption. Comprehending his "I'm one for the ages" point of view explains much of his behavior and illuminates what made him great and what made him impossible.

JOE WAS CONCERNED about Ted Williams's health after his atrial fibrillation made him produce a clot that caused a stroke and other cardiac issues. It bothered Joe that Ted was no longer the big, strong, strapping slugger of the Red Sox. He saw himself when he looked at Ted, because they were both connected in perpetuity for their place in American sports history. He was witnessing the breakdown of one of his contemporaries, who was not aging well. Knowing that I had a relationship with Ted Williams and his son, John Henry, Joe asked me to help out the Williams clan with the important health matters they were facing. He wanted me to look after Williams's health should he ever need assistance.

Ted had numerous strokes in the early '90s, which affected his famous eagle-eye vision. In early 2000, after Joe's death, Ted's heart valve gave out, and he needed emergency open-heart surgery. John Henry, Ted's son, and Ted called me. John Henry remembered what the Clipper had said about my helping out.

I arranged with the Williams clan for Ted to be flown into Teterboro Airport in a specially equipped medical plane. I also arranged for my colleague, world-renowned heart surgeon Dr. Wayne Isom of New York-Presbyterian Hospital/Weill Cornell and prominent cardiologist Dr. Jeffrey Borer to meet us at the hospital Sunday at midnight.

Dr. Borer was no stranger to Ted. He once went to Williams's hotel room with me at JFK airport because Ted wasn't feeling well. When we walked in, Ted had a double bacon cheeseburger and a chocolate shake in his hands. We couldn't believe he was eating these fat-filled junk foods in front of his heart doctor.

Ted's life was in danger and both doctors had to think fast as the clock was ticking. The next morning, Isom performed a nine-hour operation that saved Williams's life.

The news of Ted's health crisis and the surgery spread all over the world. One of the major Boston newspapers ran an article that questioned why Ted Williams had his surgery in New York and not in Boston. After all, he was a Red Sox, not a Yankee. Joe Di had saved the game again, this time for his rival Ted Williams, through our team here at New York-Presbyterian/Weill Cornell. Joe was a stand-up guy for Ted, which reveals the caring generosity I witnessed so often. Even in death, the great DiMaggio exerted his influence.

FEW THINGS COULD infuriate Joe more than the owners' ruthless attempts to make more money. Their business interests took precedence over the game. In 1995, the owners tried to strangle free-agent status for the Major League Baseball players and curtail collective bargaining. Their tactic was lockout.

The players went to Federal Court in the Second Circuit in Foley Square in hopes of winning a temporary injunction forbidding the lockout. The owners hired high-priced lawyers to get the judge to stay the injunction.

The Federal judge on the bench was Sonia Sotomayor, a graduate of Princeton University and Yale Law School, a tough-as-nails Bronx street "girl," as Joe referred to her, who grew up a short walk from the stadium. She blasted the owners and enjoined them from the lockout.

Joe DiMaggio had been following the case in all the New York papers. He was seething over the owner's tricky moves. He was greatly heartened when the Bronx girl ruled against the owners, and when the Appeals panel ruled in the judge's favor as well a few days later.

"Hey, Doc, I gotta say it: This Bronx gal really scorched the balls off George and his buddies with this ruling," said Joe.

"Yeah, Joe," I agreed. "She really let them have it. Imagine what a shame it would have been if an owner's strike crippled baseball for months."

Baseball columnists and sportswriters all said with uncharacteristic universal agreement that Federal Judge Sotomayor from the Bronx saved baseball from a ruined season.

"Hey, Doc, let's send this gal an autographed baseball," he said. "I mean, she saved baseball, and I hear she's a big Yankee fan and a friend of yours."

He really was impressed.

A warning flag went up. Such a baseball would be worth big money, and some pencil-necked lawyer could claim that Joe sent the baseball as a bribe to the judge to preserve the injunction. The owners, including George Steinbrenner, would move to set aside the verdict and stir up trouble with the judge's own bosses. And then, of course, Joe could be involved in the scandal. I had to intercede, to keep Joe out of trouble.

"Errrr . . . Joe, maybe that's not such a good idea."

"And why is that, Doc?"

"Since your sympathies are with the players—as always—and since she ruled in their favor, someone might claim it's a bribe for services rendered to the players' union."

Joe winced, but he got the point. He had begun to listen to me every now and then.

"Maybe someone could make something more out of it than a salute to a sportswoman and Yankee fan?" Joe shook his head. "Too bad. She deserved it."

I mentioned Joe's generous impulse to Justice Sotomayor years later. Without thinking twice, she said she would not have accepted the ball from Joe, though she would have treasured the prize. That would have been a huge hit to his ego. Things have a way of working out.

President Obama appointed Judge Sonia Sotomayor to the highest court in the country more than twenty years later. He cited the baseball case as one of his reasons for selecting her.

BASEBALL PLAYERS WERE not the only athletes in awe of Joe. He had an encounter with another sports superstar in my office that I remember well. Dave Meggett of the New York Giants had an extremely painful heel pain and fat-pad injury, just like Joe. Dave was unable to walk, let alone play, and he was due to face off against the Washington Redskins that Sunday in one of the biggest play-off games of the year. The best third-and-long guy was in trouble. The Giants would have a difficult time beating the Redskins without Meggett.

Dave's physician and New York Giants team doctor, Dr. Russell Warren, and his trainer, Ronnie Barnes, were desperate to schedule an emergency session with me on the Wednesday before the game. Under these circumstances, Dave needed accelerated healing. There was no question in my mind that he could benefit from my specialty, an orthopedic heel strapping I utilized at Yale and the New York College of Podiatric Medicine. Of course, I agreed to see him. Podiatric orthopedics and podiatry to the rescue again.

That same Wednesday Joe decided to drop by my offices at 12 East 68th Street. He enjoyed spending time in the steam room or sauna and liked to use the facilities in the office. He wrapped himself in a big white towel and baked in the sauna that Wednesday.

On his arrival, Dave went to the restroom, which was adjacent to the sauna. He noticed Joe DiMaggio relaxing in the heat. Dave returned to my office and exclaimed, "My God, that's Joe DiMaggio in there. Joe DiMaggio is in the sauna!"

He was beside himself. "I can't believe this. Joe DiMaggio's taking a sauna. I can't believe it."

The DiMaggio Effect strikes again.

"Yeah, I'll introduce you to him."

I knocked on the door and stuck my head in.

"Joe, can I introduce you to someone?"

"Sure, Doc, who is it?" Joe responded as he tightened the towel around his waist.

"Come out here, Joe, I want you to meet Dave Meggett from the New York Giants."

Joe came out and shook Dave's hand.

"Oh, how are you, young fellow?" Joe greeted the football super-star. "I heard that you have the same problem with your heel as I did. Let me tell you something. The doc is the best in the world for taking care of your heel. I should know. My heel nearly crippled me and was a big problem in my career."

I beamed from ear to ear. A professional endorsement from Joe to another athlete was something to write home about.

Dave was still in awe. "I can't believe it's you . . . Mr. DiMaggio . . . it's you."

Joe was used to this sort of response.

"Yeah, Dave, it's me, and, listen—good luck to you in that game on Sunday." Joe gave him his blessing.

Dave left my office believing that the encounter with Joe was a good omen. The Giants, led by a rejuvenated Dave, beat the Redskins that Sunday in a playoff game. Dave told many of his teammates on the Giants that meeting Joe had made all the difference in the world, a good luck omen of things to come that weekend.

The Giants won, and word got around the NFL and the professional sports world that I was the doctor to see for foot problems, which was a great outcome for everyone.

This incident reminds me of another lesson I learned from Joe. He knew how to handle athletes, and gave me advice on dealing with prominent sports figures. His professional advice was spot on and helped to shape my bedside manner with elite athletes.

"Don't tell an athlete that you admire him, Doc," was how Joe began his tutorial. "And don't tell him what a great play he made, because you'll lose the advantage. Good doctors maintain a distance. That's how you keep the advantage. Professional athletes don't want their doctors to be fans. You have to be in control, not them."

No one ever accused Joe of being oblivious to what was happening around him. He was a shrewd man with a gift for reading people. I am still grateful for his perceptive takes on how the world works. His observations, many of which I've internalized, have steered me in the right direction and kept me from making countless mistakes. Life would have been muddier without Joe's clear vision about the need to be a stand-up guy.

I ENJOYED MY spacious offices in a landmark building on the Upper East Side, amid the priciest real estate in the country, but the overhead was crushing, and expenses extreme. Managed care was infiltrating the medical field like a malignant cancer. I needed to change my strategy and develop a new practice plan. I switched gears and moved my practice to the Hospital for Special Surgery, the premier orthopedic and sports medicine hospital in New York at Joe's strong suggestion. My colleague and brilliant sports medicine orthopedic surgeon, Dr. Steve O'Brien, with the blessing of surgeon-in-chief Dr. Andrew Weiland, helped to make this happen, because he was a huge advocate of nonsurgical foot and ankle care. He saw the writing on the wall before anyone else.

My loyal and grateful patients stayed with me. Premium quality health care and access to the best health-care professionals in the world was more important to them than the physical location of my office.

Joe thought the change was the smart and right move. My expenses were dramatically reduced, and the pressures of meeting a payroll vaporized. Joe's practicality and lack of pretension were a great support.

Having interaction with the most eminently qualified orthopedic doctors in the world was a win-win situation.

"Hey, Doc," he asked in a typically sardonic tone, "you liked overhead?"

"No, Joe, but I liked having my own location."

Joe interrupted me before I could finish, "Listen, Doc, you've got a sweet deal. Keep your chin up and do well, okay?"

Joe was right, of course. He helped me to rally and gave his blessings to my decision, which meant a lot to me. All I could think of was Rizzuto's words to me that no matter what the score, just knowing that Joe was out there in center field meant you still had a good chance to win the game. Joe took the position of center field in my life. You couldn't lose with DiMaggio on your team.

CHAPTER 9

Love Lost

Sunday, - June 13, 1993

Emily — Dom's Wife, just Called — wants me to spend a week with Dom and see each other, which is a rarity. Told her that that date is not possible (15th of July). Have obligations. But, will do in time — when convenient to us both. Dinner with Dr. Pastens at Italian restaurant on Madison Street.

Wednesday, - June 16, 1993

Called and talked to my grand-daughter Paula, and Vanessa my great grand-daughter to Congratulate her on her performance on stage for ballet class.

J oe DiMaggio *was not lucky* in love. His first marriage to a star-let, Dorothy Arnold, was probably his first major personal failure in life. Their son, Joe Jr., was a constant source of woe and anguish for Joe. His brief marriage to Marilyn Monroe and her heartbreaking death, the feud with his former friend, Frank Sinatra, and his dislike of the Kennedy clan has been fodder for gossip columnists, journalists, and biographers for decades. Given Joe's unwritten rules about privacy, I knew better than to pry into the drama of his family life. I knew without a doubt that even mentioning Marilyn's name meant, "Good night and pick up the tab for the meal," plus a one-way, express trip to the Siberian tundra.

Over time, Joe trusted my discretion and opened up to me in fits and starts about the loves of his life. I don't think he confided to many people about his disappointing marriages, how Marilyn Monroe's early death affected him, and how devastated he was by his estrangement from his son.

It started over breakfast at the Gardenia Café. We were having a pleasant conversation before our food was served. I noticed that Joe was more talkative than usual. Somehow women and relationships came up. I don't remember what brought us there or what we said, because the conversation that followed overshadowed everything.

"You know, Doc," Joe started, "I was married to two actresses."

"No kidding," I thought.

I kept my head down, looking into a cup of coffee. I knew that Joe would drop the subject if I glanced up. When Joe sensed I was listening too intensely, especially about something personal or private, he would clam up. I don't know how many times he had opened the door and then slammed it shut. I learned to be quiet, listen, and remain expressionless.

"My first wife, Doc, was a gal named Dorothy Arnold. She was a showgirl and the mother of my son, Joe," he continued. "We met on the set of a small movie called *Manhattan Merry-Go-Round*. I played myself in it. I even sang a song called 'Have You Ever Been to Heaven?' When I laid eyes on her, I was hooked."

I looked up briefly and nodded, then went back to staring at my coffee.

"I was always in love with her," Joe confessed. "She was a great girl, but things didn't work out. We had problems getting along."

I uttered a noncommittal, "Uh-huh."

"She was more of a showgirl, and she started to hang out with the wrong type of crowd."

I knew what that meant.

"And—and," Joe hesitated. "I'm pretty sure that she was screwing around on me with some Wall Street banker. Of course, I never said anything about this to anybody."

I couldn't believe he was telling me something so personal.

Thousands of fans had shown up for their San Francisco wedding. Five years later, Joe and his unfaithful wife had a date with divorce court. Joe became involved in a vicious, very public divorce in Hollywood. Joe worried about his son during the ordeal. I had the impression that Joe Jr. was his primary concern.

Dorothy Arnold's so-called Hollywood showcase divorce was her way of manipulating Joe. She was messing around with an investment banker with Joe's son at home. She decided that a public divorce was powerful incentive for Joe to buckle and fade. And she was right. An Italian-American man of the old school would be shamed by his wife's betrayal and his failed marriage. She played on Joe's desire to protect his privacy and to minimize Joe Jr.'s exposure to the media circus.

"Well, the divorce was a bad thing, especially for my little guy Joe," he said with regret.

I shifted my attention slightly, trying not to alarm Joe, who went on to describe the torture chamber his wife, the woman he loved, made of the divorce.

"Dorothy was always trying to get between my little guy and me. Even after the divorce, she tried to drag me back into court saying that I was not giving her enough money to support her and my son."

His voice had a bitter edge. Joe explained that a court hearing had been scheduled for supplemental support and an increase of the original decree after the divorce was finalized.

Joe had been ready with a report from a private detective on his former wife's post-divorce spending sprees.

"She wasn't aware that I knew she was spending a lot of the support money on getting her hair and nails done. It was obvious that she had been using the money I was already giving her for running her household on her own personal stuff."

Joe shifted in his seat and studied my face for a reaction. I didn't dare say a word or blink an eye.

"I will never forget when the judge called us both up to the bench and talked to my wife in front of me."

I lifted my eyebrows slightly.

"That judge turned to Dorothy and said, 'Mrs. DiMaggio, I think that you're spending a lot of money on your hair stylist and on your other personal needs, so I am not granting you any more money. I suggest that you avoid making a public spectacle of my decision, because if you do, I am going to rule in favor of your ex-husband. I will make it a more difficult situation for you."

After all the unwanted exposure generated by the divorce, Joe was still in love with Dorothy. She was the mother of his son and the love of his life. It didn't end with the divorce. He carried a torch for his first wife. Though he publicly cried for Marilyn, he was equally devastated over his first failed marriage.

Joe told me on many occasions that he always tried to be a good father, even if he was a failed husband. He continued to worry about the physical well-being and emotional balance of his only son. He would take a train all the way to New York in between away games with the Yankees just to spend a day or even a few hours with little Joe, then head back to meet the team. In the end, he felt he had failed in raising Joe Jr., who outlived his father by only a few months.

He once told me that he and Frank Sinatra—in better times—shared parenting tips. Both understood that their sons would stagger under the shadows of their iconic fathers. And they were right. To make matters worse, the boys had the same names as their fathers.

"Frank and I discussed our boys often enough," Joe confided one night. "It was real hard for our sons to deal with their fathers' fame."

Their concern for the welfare of their sons was common ground. At the end of the day, Joe DiMaggio and Frank Sinatra were both very caring men. Their love for their kids could never be underestimated. Even though they didn't speak any longer, that was the one bond that would always keep them together. I got the impression that neither Frank nor Joe thought his efforts were effective. Speaking about Junior was always a painful subject for Joe. Failure on his part was not something he digested well.

On another night, we were having dinner at Three Guys Diner. Joe was finishing up his Yankee bean soup. He acknowledged my comments with a nod, then meticulously wiped his mouth with a napkin.

"Let me tell you a funny story," Joe began. "Back in the fifties, my going out with Marilyn wasn't so popular and my marrying her caused even more problems. A lot of people were unhappy about it."

"That's hard to imagine now."

"One day, I got a phone call from Archbishop Fulton Sheen's office telling me that the Archbishop wanted to meet with me. Of course, Doc, my first response was, 'Why the hell would he want to meet with me?'

"Of course, being a good practicing Catholic, even though I had divorced once, and doing what I was supposed to do as a person who grew up Catholic, I thought 'Hey, better pay the guy a courtesy call.'"

The American Archbishop Fulton Sheen was the first televangelical leader. A handsome and iconic figure, he had a popular television show, *Life Is Worth Living*, a precursor to Reverend Robert Schuller's *The Hour of Power*. Archbishop Sheen discussed Catholic doctrine through the infant medium of television. He was an extremely popular figure in the Church, and his influence was extensive.

Joe was not in New York when he received the call. He decided the summons was important enough to fly to town for the meeting.

His Excellency, along with his entire staff, were there to greet Joe, who had expected a private audience. He knew that there was a reason for the group-think session.

Sheen invited Joe to sit down. They exchanged pleasantries for a bit, then the conversation ceased. The Archbishop transformed into a missionary. He proceeded to lecture Joe at length about the value of Joe's image and the power of his influence on young Catholics.

Joe reported their conversation to me.

"Mr. DiMaggio, you know that we are concerned about your relationship with Marilyn Monroe. You should have never married her in the first place."

Joe said he was baffled and wondered, who the hell was *we*? Was *we* the Pope? Was *we* the North American College of Cardinals and Bishops? Was *we* the diocese or archdiocese of New York?

Joe said his face turned red and then purple. His spine stiffened.

Archbishop Sheen wasn't finished. "This isn't the type of woman who gives people moral values."

Joe had listened long enough. "Now, look here, Archbishop Sheen," he said firmly. "No one is going to tell me who to love and who to marry. As far as I am concerned, this meeting is over."

That said, Joe got up and stormed out of the Archbishop's residence.

Archbishop Fulton Sheen was speechless, perhaps for the first time in his life.

"Now that was impressive! What did he expect you to do—annul the marriage?" I asked, amazed at the Archbishop's audacity.

Joe shrugged. We both laughed at the thought of Joe's not taking any guff from Archbishop Sheen and the cleric's stunned response.

I THINK THAT Joe opened up to me about his marriage to Marilyn Monroe, because I never mentioned her and always steered clear of the subject. He gradually told me the Marilyn Monroe–Joe DiMaggio story. He shocked me with his candor as he spoke about his volcanic relationship with her.

"Doc, I was married to this great gal, named Marilyn," Joe said to me, as if I didn't know.

I had to contain myself to keep from revealing how eager I was for him to go on. Joe was about to speak to me about his number-one taboo subject. He wasn't accustomed to speaking bluntly about Marilyn. I know he also spoke with Morris Engelberg, my Brooklyn brother, about Marilyn, but I never knew what he told each of us, and Morris and I never compared notes. That Florida, California, and New York information blockade was at work again.

I have to preface Joe's account of their marriage by saying that Italian men don't talk about what happens under the sheets. The never-kiss-and-tell edict is always in play. In the divorce his first wife Dorothy Arnold brought against him, Joe refused to even mention her affairs as she sued for more and more money. Joe would never make his family or his kid look bad in the public eye, regardless of what personal and professional trauma it brought to his doorstep. Turn the other cheek, get your face bashed in, it didn't matter. Always protect the honor of your family, especially your children.

Realizing that Joe was in a revelatory mood, I had to keep a poker face and let him talk without interrupting him.

"Yeah, Doc, Marilyn was a good kid, but she was a confused kid," Joe began, sounding more like a father than a husband. He dismissed a lot of rumors out of hand. Then he began to talk like her husband. "We got along exceptionally well in every possible way."

I knew where this was going.

"When we got together in the bedroom, it was like the gods were fighting; there were thunderclouds and lightning above us."

Picking up my fork, I thought, "Oh, my God, now Joe is talking to me about his sex life with Marilyn Monroe, the sex goddess."

Joe went on to say that their physical compatibility was the basis of the best relationship he ever had and a big part of what brought them together. Great sexual chemistry was what made Joe love Marilyn, and vice versa. They mutually achieved a physical intimacy neither had before. Still very protective of his physical interaction with Marilyn, he spoke in circumspect ways. He was very respectful in his descriptions.

Joe was still checking me out for a reaction, but I was silent, as if barely noticing the conversation, not an easy thing to do under the circumstances.

"Doc, Marilyn told me that no man ever satisfied her like I did," Joe added.

Unwilling to meet his eyes, I shuffled my fork around in the plate of phyllo pastry.

Joe revealed that the only big issue he had with Marilyn was her personal hygiene. He complained that she wouldn't take a bath for days, probably because of her bouts of depression. DiMaggio was always immaculately clean himself, but he couldn't say the same about Marilyn.

Joe offered his explanation of why the two really split, not what was reported in the press or anywhere else for that matter. From Joe's point of view, they didn't stay married, because Marilyn was not able to have children. It was as simple as that. It was not about the published reports of jealousy and not wanting to take a back seat to her fame. It wasn't about the photograph that captured an upward blast from a subway grate in a Hollywood movie that was everywhere. It wasn't about her hunger for fame that he knew was a prison. It was because he wanted to have kids with Marilyn. Whether or not she was willing, she proved to be unable.

"Marilyn was hurt," Joe said, stumbling on his words, "by the woman thing—her inability to have children."

Joe's eyes looked to me like what combat soldiers call the "2000-yard stare." He was focused on some invisible horizon.

I felt bad for him, and this proud man would never want to be pitied.

With this simple explanation, Joe summed up what the gossipmongers, commentators, and writers had missed: Joe wanted kids, and Marilyn could not have them. Brides of Italians delivered babies. Joe wanted kids with Marilyn, and Marilyn wanted to reward him with a family. In Italian terms, sex meant kids. Great sex meant great kids. Marilyn gave goddess sex, but no kids.

Though Joe saw Marilyn's behavior become erratic, he was unsophisticated about mental illness, which was not uncommon for men of his age and background. I had the impression that Joe did not understand what had happened. He was to regret it for the rest of his life.

Joe surprised me with more revelations about Marilyn on another occasion.

"They," he paused, before delivering a line that took my breath away, "they did in my poor Marilyn."

I knew enough not to ask who.

"Yeah, Doc, they did her in. They did in my poor Marilyn." Joe was losing his composure. "She didn't know what hit her." He seemed to be holding back tears.

"Come on, Doc," he snapped, "let's get out of here. I think that I've talked enough."

Several weeks went by before he brought the subject up again. We were eating at La Maganette, a restaurant in midtown Manhattan known for its good food and for the portraits of well-known people hanging on the walls. Frank Caridi, Jr., one of the co-owners, hero-worshipped Frank Sinatra, as so many Italian-Americans did. A three-foot-by-three-foot portrait of a smiling Frank Sinatra in a tuxedo with his arms crossed beamed down at us.

Joe noticed the portrait and looked away. At that moment, Frank Caridi approached the table to welcome his famous guest and said, "Your friend, Frank Sinatra, comes here often."

Obviously annoyed, Joe barely nodded. The owner excused himself and made a fast retreat.

"Some friend," Joe said when the owner was out of hearing distance. "We were friends, all right, but he failed me in the one thing that mattered, then and now. And that was Marilyn." Joe was fuming.

"Yeah, Marilyn . . . poor kid. She didn't know that she was dealing with sharks. Those high and mighty Kennedys were low-class shanty bastards. That's all they are," Joe continued, using a familiar Italian-American malediction.

Joe looked around to make sure that he wasn't being overheard. "And my good friend, Frank Sinatra, was their pimp." He was emphatic when he said pimp.

"The whole lot of Kennedys were lady-killers," Joe said vehemently, "and they always got away with it. They'll be getting away with it a hundred years from now."

Joe wasn't finished. "I always knew who killed her, but I didn't want to start a revolution in this country. She told me someone would do her in, but I kept quiet."

As I listened to Joe indict the Kennedy family from the mouth of Marilyn Monroe, I was stunned. She had told him that people she was involved with were worried that she would expose them. I wondered why he had never said anything to the press or the district attorney. It might have had to do with the fact that the United States Attorney

General at the time of Marilyn's death was the brother of the president of the United States, a Kennedy. Joe did the only possible thing for a stand-up guy. I believe that Joe would have ended up like Marilyn if he had voiced his suspicions. The press at the time reported that she committed suicide, though rumors have surrounded her death ever since.

Now I understood why Joe harbored a hatred for all the Kennedys of that era.

"When Sinatra pimped for the Kennedys, he thought they'd accept some Jersey grease ball if he threw them some goddess ass," Joe explained. "I tried to protect Marilyn, but she was harder to handle than any Bobby Feller fastball. I could hit in fifty-six straight games. I won nine World Series championships. I could make a catch in center field look easy every time. There wasn't a king or a politician who wouldn't kiss my ass.

"But with Marilyn," he looked, "the ball hit the sweet part of the glove and popped to the ground."

I could see how sorry Joe was that he hadn't had more influence over her.

"I'll go to the grave regretting and blaming myself for what happened to her," Joe concluded

Joe did not wallow in his remorse. He soon changed the subject. "Sinatra told me later that Marilyn loved me anyway, to the end," he said with a small smile.

"You know, she married that asshole playwright, Miller."

I cringed at his assessment of a great American writer. And it got worse.

"Dogface was homelier than homemade sin. She told Sinatra that she always thought of me when she made love with Miller and that she kept a picture of me hidden in one of her closets at their home. That drove Miller crazy and right to divorce court," Joe boasted. "After Dogface divorced her, Marilyn wanted to remarry me. But it was over—my goddamned pride—the same old story for me."

Much has been written about the end of Marilyn Monroe's life. As her confidant and protector, Joe had a unique perspective. I felt privileged that he was sharing such a painful time of his life with me.

"I remember being called to the mortuary," he went on. "She always said that she wanted me to make sure that she was dressed up right when she died."

I realized how difficult it was for him to talk about this.

"Doc, I helped the undertaker pick out her dress, made sure her makeup was right, and that she looked good when her hair was done.

"I banned my good friend Frank Sinatra and all the other bastards from the funeral."

I stayed silent for a time. I knew better than to comment on Marilyn's death, so I asked a question that seemed safer than discussing his marriage.

"So, what happened between you and Sinatra?"

"We used to be really close. Last time I saw him, he was wearing a monstrosity of a hair piece."

Joe was thoughtful for a moment. He went on, "Now, he has been there for me at times, like when I thought Marilyn was balling someone else in some L.A. pad. We broke the door in, with a little help from his friends, only Marilyn wasn't there. We terrorized a dowdy, middle-aged lady. *Hollywood Confidential* wrote a sordid story about it a year later."

My jaw dropped. I had missed that one.

"I was mortified."

"Then there was the time when Frank smuggled me out of a woman's room at four in the morning before Walter Winchell rolled into the hotel." The memory brought a smile to his face. "I mean, in those days, baseball players didn't have dicks. We were cereal-box champions, right?"

I nodded.

"Okay, Sinatra's draft dodging didn't bother me. He claimed all kinds of illnesses and stuff. He faked it all, believe me. He told me so, and laughed about it." Joe seemed to enjoy having something on Frank.

"That war movie he was in—*Von Ryan's Express*—the director told him to hold off two hundred Nazis with a machine gun. I hope they didn't have to tell him too many times about what end to fire."

We laughed at the thought.

"But it did go both ways," Joe continued. "I stood up for Sinatra, too. When those high-living, trash friends of his began circulating the story that the Great Crooner had lost his voice, I helped him get gigs at some of the hotels in Vegas, in exchange for my promise that I would also appear there and just show up."

I wondered if Frank knew about what Joe had been doing.

"And, when Ava Gardner twisted his heart like a pretzel, I refused to make a move on her, though she indicated she wanted me to." Joe looked down. "I refused to even take her phone calls out of respect for him. Real men don't screw around with a friend's woman, especially when there are still feelings. He clearly didn't feel the same way."

He looked up at the portrait of Sinatra, and continued, "That's what friends are for. But Frank Sinatra hid behind his friends. But only one guy stood up for my good friend Frank Sinatra. Me."

Joe hated his old friend Frank Sinatra for using Marilyn to get in with the Kennedys. He believed it cost her her life.

They did have a lot of history between them.

"You know, he wanted to play center field for the Yanks, and I wanted to sing like he did," Joe said, then grudgingly added, "Frank was the greatest singer of them all, my good friend Frank Sinatra."

Joe turned to me and said, "Yeah, we were close, Frank Sinatra and me, but we are close no more."

He took a swill of his light beer, and said, "Let's get out of here. I just lost my appetite."

Learning Joe's body language was essential to knowing how to be his friend and keep him and others out of harm's way. Joe had a "stare."

His eyes would often stare straight ahead without focusing on any particular object. Sometimes he displayed the stare when he was angry, but other times I didn't know what set him off.

After knowing him for a while, I remarked, "Joe, you are always staring into space. What's the problem?"

He looked down and responded in a low voice, "Doc, I get this way when I think of Marilyn. Sometimes thinking of her paralyzes me and stops me from enjoying what I am doing."

I didn't ask any more questions. I was profoundly touched.

The other failed relationship in Joe's life was with his only son. As much as family mattered to Joe, in his eyes he was not a success as a father, and he regretted it. There is so much speculation about why Joe's relationship with his son was so strained. From the point of view of image, Joe was unhappy with the way his son led his life. Joe Jr. became an alcoholic, a pothead, and was living in a garage somewhere in small-town California.

Joe said to me on numerous occasions that the media had exaggerated their problems by spreading lies. Despite their estrangement, Joe told me that he talked with his son regularly, which seemed like a lot for a father and son who were supposed to be on the outs. Joe never stopped loving or wanting to help his son.

While Joe Jr. was out in Las Vegas, he broke his hip when a bus hit the bike he was riding.

"Doc, I can't take this guy anymore," Joe said in frustration. "Here is a kid who is twenty years older than you, and he can't take care of himself."

Joe began by telling me that his son went to the best schools, including Lawrenceville, an exclusive prep school in New Jersey. I knew how much education mattered to Joe, and I'm sure he wanted only the best for his son. Joe thought Joe Jr. had a tremendous amount of ability but didn't take advantage of his innate talent, a cardinal sin for the Clipper. Joe was proud his son had inherited his father's physique and athletic prowess. Since Joe Jr. didn't dare follow in his father's footsteps in baseball, he opted for football and did well.

What Joe, the high-school dropout, was most proud of was that his son was admitted to Yale University on his own merit. Joe did not use his influence or that of his many friends to get his son into Yale. He always made it a point to say, "My boy got into Yale on his own."

Soon after Joe deposited little Joe into one of the ivied dormitories, his son acted as if he had joined the wild fraternity in *Animal House*. He neglected his studies, because he was too busy drinking and gambling. He was hanging out with the wrong crowd. He was clearly not a chip off the old block. Joe tried to intervene. He told me that he had his brother Dominic get involved and call some of his friends in the New Haven area to keep Joe Jr. out of trouble.

Joe told me what soon happened.

"Listen, Doc, I got a call from the dean of the university, who said, 'Mr. DiMaggio, I am sorry to call about this, but your son is seriously in danger of failing out of Yale.' I didn't say a word, so the dean continued. 'Now, we don't want this to happen. We want to do everything possible to keep your son at Yale.'"

Joe explained how he felt when he got this news. "Doc, I wasn't going to have my kid hanging around and getting by on his DiMaggio name alone."

Joe always stuck by his principles. I am sure the dean was shocked when Joe responded, "Dean, do whatever you have to do. If he doesn't cut it, throw the bum out."

Joe described a stunned silence on the other end of the line. "If he pulls it together, he'll stay," Joe concluded, "otherwise, Dean, he's out."

Joe Jr. flunked out of Yale, which was one of Joe DiMaggio's greatest disappointments. Joe Jr. did odd jobs for a time, then enlisted in the Marines. And there was more trouble brewing. In describing the problems between them, Joe disclosed a father–son conflict that was classic, like a Greek tragedy.

"Doc, my son was making a lot of phone calls to my ex-wife," Joe said uncomfortably. "I think that my son was making time with Marilyn, and I wouldn't accept that."

When Joe started to date Marilyn, Joe Jr. was thirteen. He sometimes accompanied the two of them when they went out. They married and divorced when he was fifteen. He was only twenty-one when Marilyn died.

Joe Jr. remained close to Marilyn after she divorced his father. It wouldn't surprise me that an adolescent boy was smitten by one of the all-time sex symbols, even if she was his stepmother. And Marilyn may have been displaying a maternal side for Joe Jr. But I knew better than to offer my opinion. Joe would not be sympathetic to a psychological take on the situation.

Joe reacted harshly to his son's puppy love. According to Joe, he told his son to just back off. He explained to the no doubt baffled teenager, "This is my girl. This is my woman. If you want to call on her once a week to check up on her, that's fine by me, but calling her five or six times a day, that's gotta stop."

I couldn't help thinking, who wouldn't want to talk to Marilyn Monroe? Joe was inflexible. He banished his only son to Siberia, in part because of his attachment to Marilyn.

In later years, Joe Jr. became a recluse in a small town in California. Joe described his only son to me as a "toothless grease monkey," who worked on cars and motorcycles. I never met Joe's son, and the little bit I knew about him was from what Joe told me.

Though he and his son were estranged, Joe was devoted to and took care of Joe Jr.'s two daughters after his son's marriage failed. Since Joe was heartbroken that Joe Jr. was not a good son, father, or grandfather, he became a doting grandfather himself. I thought that Joe's fatherly skills must have skipped a generation. He made up for lost time with his son's family.

In Joe Jr.'s defense, he learned his parenting skills from his father.

It's painful to think that Joe was a role model for every little boy except his own. Joe may not have done well as a father, and tried to make up for it by being a solicitous grandfather. Joe had the cards stacked against him when it came to fatherhood, and people who cared about him know that he tried his best under the difficult and hostile circumstances. Though Joe was disappointed in his son, the rumors that Joe disowned Joe Jr. are not true.

Joe Jr. died at fifty-seven, a few months after his father. They never reconciled. Each was too stubborn. His son did not fly to Florida when Joe was dying, but he did serve as a pallbearer at his father's funeral. Joe and Morris Engelberg made sure that Joe Jr. would be taken care of for life after Joe's death. Morris was very serious about carrying out Joe's wishes regarding his only child. It was a very short-lived undertaking, as Joe Jr. died the same year as Joe Sr.

Joe's estrangement from his only child was one of the great heartbreaks of Joe DiMaggio's life. I witnessed his generosity of spirit in countless acts of kindness toward children. I can't help thinking that he spent his life trying to compensate for his failure as a father.

Piece by piece and over time, Joe shared some of his regrets, disappointments, and what he considered his greatest mistakes to me. In the end, he judged himself more harshly than I ever would.

CHAPTER 10

Fans in High Places

Monday June 6, 1993

Dick Beerke drove up from Atlantic City to pick me up at 11:30 A.M. We had lunch at the La Relais restaurant on Madison ave. Dr. Rock Positano joined us a half-hour later for coffee. We walked back to 69th street garage and took off at 1:30 P.M. for Atlantic City. Dr. Positano went to his office.

Dick and I went to the Claridge hotel for dinner. Katie stayed behind to take care of business. Had some pasta as my main course and not too much more — as I don't want my weight to be a problem. I don't know what Dick was celebrating, but he ordered a Dom Perignon champagne, while I only had a couple of glasses — and Dick had one glass — as he is not a drinker. I tried to talk him out of ordering that wine. Signed many things for a book that were fifteen in total.

J*oe knew everyone, or maybe* I should say everyone wanted to know Joe. Accompanying him to all sorts of events, I saw a stunning array of famous, rich, powerful people who were in awe of him and wanted to get close to him. The intensity of their admiration surprised me. I couldn't imagine being on the receiving end of that sort of adulation.

Joe was accustomed to causing a stir. Over the years, he constructed strong defenses to protect himself, yet he could be remarkably open to people he met. We had a conversation that illustrates his screening process. As Joe told me early on, everyone started in the negative column for him.

On one occasion, I teased Joe, a staunch Republican, about his admiration for FDR. His measured response surprised me.

"Doc, I give people time to prove their worth to me," he said, getting to the heart of the issue. "That means I could accept someone very much unlike myself, and like them a lot. I hope I'm never narrow enough to attach a label to my likes and dislikes. That would make me something I hope that I'm not.

"I don't think any person should be that way. Take FDR . . ."

"You told me how great it was that he complimented you after a game," I said, intentionally implying that Joe honored FDR, because FDR had honored him.

"You think that was the reason I like FDR, Doc?" Joe narrowed his eyes. "FDR was a man's man. Wealthy as he was, he lived up to his potential, and I can't think of a better way to live."

Joe proceeded to discuss politics DiMaggio style.

"FDR had a country on the ropes. Those wealthy old bastards really screwed up the stock market," he said with disgust. "And the farmers lost their farmsteads, land that was in their families for many years, to the banks. And do you know what those banks did, Doc? They let those farms rot away, unfarmed. That land turned to dust. Ever hear of the Dust Bowl, Doc?"

"Yes, Joe, I've heard of the Dust Bowl," I responded with a sarcastic edge.

"FDR came along and made people forget their problems," Joe declared. "He made them believe that things would turn around someday, and they did."

"It took a war to do that," was my cynical response.

"That was just a part of it, Doc, believe me." Joe was wiser on the subject. "I was there. FDR kept the sharks on Wall Street away from the investors when the investors returned to the market. That took guts. After all, he was wealthy himself."

Joe turned his attention to the war.

"Listen, FDR didn't take crap from Hitler, like those European characters did. They fed him whatever they had and whatever he wanted, until he bit them. Served them right, too," Joe concluded.

Joe's brutal working-class common sense cut through to the core of things. I recounted this conversation to demonstrate that Joe was not as rigid as he is often depicted. He was complicated in a way that was hard for people, especially journalists and biographers, to understand, because he was so private. He talked to me and a few others about his beliefs, opinions, and well-contained feelings. I observed him act with generosity and grace in countless situations regardless of a person's credentials.

Joe didn't judge people by their status, wealth, or celebrity. None of those things impressed him. He'd had it all. He was an unpretentious man. What mattered to him was excellence in any field, people who were committed to giving their all, no matter how humble their achievements.

Staying true to his pronouncement that he didn't label people, Joe was kindhearted to the man who saved Frank Sinatra's career. The story begins when I received a call from my friend, Vincent J. Falcone Jr., in the late '90s. He called to tell me he was in New York doing a gig with Tony Bennett. Though Falcone was doing well professionally, he was at a low ebb emotionally. He was in his early fifties and his wife of many years had just died after a cruel and grueling fight with cancer.

Vincent Falcone was a great musician, a classical music pianist at the age of three. The jazz-and-pop bug bit him while he was in college. He became a legendary arranger for top performers and groups. Frank Sinatra hired him to help revive his flagging voice, and Falcone saved the day. He was behind Sinatra's keynote song, "New York, New York," and the *Trilogy* album.

At some point, Sinatra fired Falcone for so-called band friction, but did hire him back for a second term. In any event, Vincent Falcone had no problem finding other artists who wanted to work with him, most notably, Tony Bennett.

I felt bad for my brilliantly talented friend and wanted to do something to cheer him up while he was in town. I debated whether to mention his situation to Joe. Once Joe figured out that Falcone had plucked Sinatra's chestnuts from the fire, he'd consider Falcone a friend of an enemy, which with Joe's logic would translate to Falcone's being an enemy himself. If Sinatra was Joe's enemy, and Falcone was Sinatra's friend, then Falcone was Joe's enemy.

But I was feeling bold, and Joe seemed to be in a good mood one morning.

"Joe, my friend Vinnie Falcone is in town," I introduced the subject.

Joe nodded as he picked up a piece of toast.

"Would you mind if he joined us for dinner?" I asked as I checked Joe for a mood swing.

"Absolutely not, that would be fine."

I never would have predicted Joe's quick agreement. Even more surprising, Joe called Falcone on the phone himself.

"Hey, Vinnie, why don't you join us for dinner?"

Of course, Vinnie jumped at the offer. He could not believe that the great DiMaggio called him and invited him to dinner. Joe never did that, and neither did Sinatra.

On a gloomy night, with a monsoon rain, we took Vinnie to Campagna, a hip restaurant that catered to the celebrity A-List crowd in New York. Joe was at his best. For all his differences with Sinatra, Falcone was still a Sinatra guy to Joe. Nevertheless, Joe went out of his way to be compassionate to Falcone.

"How are ya' doin', Vinnie?" Joe asked with sympathy.

Not knowing what to expect, Falcone almost crumbled with relief.

Joe was being kind, because Vinnie was bereft over the recent loss of his wife, as Joe had been when Marilyn died decades earlier. Despite being depressed, Falcone was receptive and took to Joe, and Joe took to him. It was what Italians call *simpatico*. In this case it meant, "I have been where you are. It was a bitch, but I got through, and so will you."

"Vinnie, I am there if you need me," Joe added.

Joe knew that Vinnie was flying back to Las Vegas after dinner during the monsoon. He arranged for a car to wait outside Campagna to take Falcone to the airport. Falcone was touched by Joe's solicitousness, empathy, and protectiveness, and so was I.

That night, I had seen Joe treat an enemy's friend with profound warmth and even love. Though he guarded the chinks in his armor well, every so often he let down his legendary reserve and relaxed his guard for the right people and at the right time. He even signed a ball to Tony Bennett, so that Vinnie would have something to give his new boss when they met up in Atlantic City for a concert a little later on. Bennett was thrilled with his Joe Di ball, and still has it today.

AS YOU CAN imagine, many people tried to have dinner with DiMaggio, and tried to use me as the contact person. People tried all sorts of methods to persuade me to arrange a dinner. I could have made a fortune, but I refused all offers, because my friendship was not for sale.

On many occasions, Joe would ask my opinion about his having dinner with someone. It didn't matter how powerful or wealthy you were. Joe relied on his inner circle to vet potential dinner partners. Ken Langone, founder of Home Depot, was one such person.

"What do you think, Doc? What do you know about this guy and should I accept?" he asked.

I said Langone was an honorable fellow, who did a lot of philanthropic work. He passed my litmus test, and my thumb was up.

Joe insisted on my coming to the dinner at Coco Pazzo, but I passed. I didn't want to offend Mr. Langone. He didn't need or want someone else at the table holding the candle.

Joe did get some business done with Langone that night. One of Joe's granddaughters was having trouble with a kitchen cabinet she bought from Home Depot. Joe asked him to intervene. By the end of the following day, the kitchen-cabinet caper was resolved.

Joe would do anything for his family. He went straight to the top to get things done.

JOE ENJOYED GOING out to ritzy places as well as the joints we hung out in in Brooklyn. He was just as happy at Le Cirque or The '21' Club on West 52nd Street, as he was sitting around a comfy table in the far corner at Bamonte's in Brooklyn. The Clipper loved the magic and the formality of '21'—the jackets and ties, cocktails served with finesse, and the whole ambience. Yet he liked the very at-home family atmosphere of Bamonte's, which boasted small tables, an old but clean rug, wood panels, and old-fashioned waiter buzzers on the wall.

Dick Burke called me one night with an invitation.

"Rock, we're going to take Joe over to '21' tonight," he said. "Why don't you join us? You know half the place anyway."

Joe wore his beautifully tailored navy blue suit that night. Joe, the Burkes, and I were sitting at the center table in the A section of the restaurant. As usual, the various types of people who were gawking at Joe during the meal fascinated me.

Governor George Pataki was at '21' that night. He sent one of his aides over to ask if Pataki could come over to the table. The governor obviously knew what he was doing and wanted to make sure the coast was clear and that he would be a welcome guest. He probably had heard about Joe's rules on dinner seating.

When he reached the table, Governor Pataki shook Joe's hand. Joe then introduced everyone to the governor. Pataki was very formal and flawlessly polite.

The evening went well. Even Joe's great fan, Rush Limbaugh, came over. He said he would have never imagined meeting his hero face to face. He made mention of this extraordinary meeting on his national radio show the next day.

As we were enjoying our meal, Joe took a trip down memory lane, to the time when New York City Mayor Jimmy Walker frequented '21' during Prohibition.

"You know, I used to hang out downstairs with these guys in a special room, called the Cellar, which had sealed doors. Walker used to drink his illegal booze down there accompanied by his string of escorts. Prohibition existed everywhere in New York, but not in that room.

"I never cared for Walker or Prohibition, but that room had a lot of history. Winchell would have given his right arm to be a fly on the wall. More dirty deals and bribes went on down there, but I steered clear of it all. Trouble never found me. Walker was out of office by the time I broke into the big leagues in '36."

On another occasion at '21,' Joe and I were the guests of legendary talent agent and president of the William Morris Agency, the venerable Norman Brokaw. Joe loved Brokaw and for good reason. He was a local New York boy, a Yankees fan who started in the mailroom at the agency and worked his way up to the top.

According to Joe there wasn't a deal that Norman couldn't close. "He was that good, Doc."

Their relationship went back to the '40s. Later on, Brokaw introduced Joe Di to a beautiful gal named Marilyn Monroe. Norman had joked about how Joe would always sit at the table closest to the kitchen door so that he could go unnoticed or escape quickly. Even into his eighties, Joe would meet with and call Norman for all types of advice, business as well as social. Norman met with Joe for the last time in Florida on the night that Mark McGwire hit his sixty-second home run of the year, breaking Roger Maris's record. They watched together as McGwire rounded the bases. Joe had business and some concerns to discuss with Norman that night. Joe would be gone six months later.

The night after our meal with the Burkes at '21,' Joe and I were at Vivolo. Remembering Joe's mention of Walter Winchell, I decided to steer the conversation to him and gossip columnists in general. Recent biographies had depicted a love–hate relationship between Joe and gossip columnists, but Joe was remarkably detached and professional about the matter. To him, business was business, and part of his business relied on gossip mongering.

"Joe, you were friendly with Walter Winchell, right? Tell me about him."

Joe took a bite from his supper and delayed a few seconds.

"I liked a few of the columnists, they weren't all parasites." Joe was thoughtful. "There was Army Archerd. He was never malicious or vicious. Archerd was kind, fair, and industrious, and very smart. I have no complaints about him.

"And there was Liz Smith, the Texas gal, who was one of my favorites," Joe added.

"Why Liz Smith?" I asked.

"Well, she never said anything bad about my Marilyn." Joe took a sip of ice water. "Yeah, Liz Smith always honored the memory of Marilyn," he continued. "She was always balanced in her judgment and very kind to her. And she was never cruel. That would have been easy to do, because the dead can't defend themselves.

"Liz Smith . . . she's a class act," Joe concluded.

"Walter Winchell never said anything bad about my Marilyn and neither did Archerd," Joe said.

I had the impression that treating Joe and Marilyn honestly, even negatively, was fair game.

Finally, Joe's attention fixed on Walter Winchell. Winchell was the doyen of American gossip columnists for all time. Joe and Winchell used to carouse together.

"He was a good guy," Joe remarked. He proceeded to tell stories of their friendship.

Winchell was on late-night patrol, which was his usual time to pick up scandal and gossip, because a lot of hanky-panky went on in Hollywood hotels late at night and in the wee hours of the morning.

"It was like this," Joe began. "In the old days, the Yankees were very strict about curfew. I mean, very strict. They wanted their players to get a good night's sleep—no women, no booze."

I thought of ballplayers today. They have nothing like a curfew. Maybe that's why so many of them end up in holding tanks, police stations, and Family Courts.

"I stayed in a hotel room overnight, drinking and visiting a lady friend," Joe said. "I was leaving the room early in the morning, very quietly. I didn't want to attract attention."

I didn't think Joe DiMaggio could go anywhere unnoticed.

"I was out of the room, quiet as can be. When I turned a corner, there was Walter Winchell."

"What did you do?" I wondered how he stayed out of Winchell's column.

"I had to say something. It was early in the morning, and the Yankees were playing that day. So, I just said hello to Walter."

"How did Winchell respond?" I chimed in.

"Well, Winchell said this: 'Joe, I'll forget all about this if you promise you'll win the game today for the Yankees and do it.'"

Joe threw back his head and laughed.

"So you won the game, Joe?" I was eager to hear how the story ended.

"Yes, and no mention of this little hotel-room episode ever surfaced in his column," said Joe with a sly grin on his face.

After this introduction to handling gossip columnists, Joe moved on to the most important discussion that night, regarding Yankee Stadium. Rumors abounded in the media that George had plans to demolish the Stadium.

"I hope George never tears down Yankee Stadium," he began what became an uncharacteristically emotional conversation. "It is sacred ground. So many memories of championships there for me. Ruth, Gehrig, Lazzeri, Gomez, and so many other Yankee greats roamed that field. There are too many memories in that ballpark. I am hoping that George doesn't do it, that he leaves the present Yankee Stadium intact and doesn't tear it down."

"Joe, why don't you make this public and let people know that you don't want the stadium to be taken down," I asked him. "It would have an impact on Steinbrenner's leaning toward a new stadium and could well discourage him and the organization."

Joe shook his head.

"Doc, I don't make public statements like that. This is strictly a personal point of view, and I don't think my personal point of view should affect the day-to-day operations of a business like the Yankees."

"Well, Joe," I persisted, "even considering the fact that you're one of the legendary members of the New York Yankees?"

"I'm not going to get involved. I'm not going to tell George what to do, but I'm letting you know. I hope they never knock the Stadium down. I have too many memories. I can still see myself running around in center field, shagging fly balls, and hitting those liners to left center field. Whether I say it or not, it is not going to make a difference. George is just going to do whatever the hell he wants to do."

I couldn't argue with that.

THOUGH JOE HAD problems with many politicians, he did like New York Governor George Pataki. He and Pataki were sharing a car in the Canyon of Champions for the ticker-tape parade after the New York Yankees World Series win in 1996.

I watched the parade on television and could see from Joe's expression that he was complaining. There was no way Joe would have been happy sharing a car for a Yankee celebration with the governor. Later that day, I mentioned to him that he had looked upset.

"Yeah, Doc, I was. Instead of confetti, people were throwing rolls of toilet paper at the car. We were getting pelted left and right by flying rolls of toilet paper. I said to Pataki, 'Hey, Governor, they are aiming at you, but they are hitting me." Joe grinned. "The governor was not amused."

Joe did find pranking politicians entertaining. One opening day at the stadium, Joe decided to play a fast one on Pataki and Rudy Giuliani, who was mayor at the time. The two politicos were counting on running onto the field when introduced. They were banking on Joe's joining them as it would make a great photo and would minimize their chances of being booed by the 56,000 fans packed in the stadium. Fans were not kind to elected officers regardless of how popular and effective they were, especially at a sporting event. It probably had to do more with the increased beer consumption than anything else.

Joe didn't want to share his glory with Giuliani and Pataki.

They were waiting for Joe to climb up the dugout steps. Joe started to move up the stairs as if to go on the field and waited for the politicians to follow. Just as they reached the top dugout step, Joe pulled back, leaving the governor and the mayor to go out on the field to a resounding sound of Bronx cheers and boos. He faked them out! He walked onto the field alone to a thunderous ovation.

THE RANGE OF Joe's fans never ceased to astonish me. He had touched so many people, because he stood for something in a way few have. I suppose that is what icons do. I remember witnessing the meeting of two icons from very different worlds.

Joe dropped by for a visit at my office while I was busy with patients. He made himself at home with the *New York Times* and the *Wall Street Journal*. Joe read these papers for international news, general business, and the stock listings. He read the *New York Daily News* and the *New York Post* for sports. He was extremely well-informed.

Joe had an uncanny talent for doing well with his stock-market investments. Though he had a conservative portfolio, he did attain a decent return on investment. I asked him about his investment strategy.

"I like blue chips and utilities," Joe told me as he was folding his papers to review his investments.

"Why blue chips?" I asked him. I was never a market force myself.

"Simple, Doc, the stock market isn't what it seems," Joe explained. "There's a lot of insider trading, and the market is rigged against the individual investor."

"My father compared the stock market with horse racing," I repeated some Positano wisdom.

Interested, Joe looked up from his paper.

"Well, the odds and the system are rigged against you, my father agreed with you there. He said that in horseracing, at least the Mafia lets you win every so often to encourage you. The stock market doesn't cut anyone slack for any reason unless you are an insider."

Joe winked and agreed, "He got that right, Doc."

"So you invest in nonvolatile stocks?"

"Yes, that's the way to invest. Deal with known names, proven companies, even some rather slow-moving ones. The ride up will be as slow as the ride down. These really hot little numbers can ruin you in an afternoon."

His advice seemed spot on, so I asked him more. "Why utilities?"

"Utilities are basics, even more stable than blue chips. Car companies have bad years, and recessions cut into every basic blue chip stock. But in good times or not, people need electric power, water, and gas to live, regardless of their finances."

"So, that's your theory?" I asked.

"It's no theory, Doc, just good business advice. I got it from a very learned man in this field, not the average guy working at some big trading firm. That guy is clueless. He doesn't get the inside information from the high yield, old boy network. It's better to be random."

I laughed.

"I mean that, Doc, just point a pencil at a page and pick a stock, or do like I do and stick with really stable stocks."

Joe was right. Studies of investment-bank performances have consistently shown that even random stock picks outperform the better investment bankers and brokers.

I can't say who gave Joe this investment advice, but I have to believe that financial giants shared their investment wisdom with their favorite ballplayer. That's how it worked for Joe. He didn't deal with the average person. He spoke to the boss, the decision makers, and the trendsetters.

"For every Wall Street killing I have heard about, there were at least ten cases where some poor jerk followed bad advice, gambled, and lost his shirt." He was ready to wrap up his lesson in sound investing.

"If a deal sounds too good to be true, know that there is a big hook just beneath the bait," he said, "and expect no mercy from those characters. They will pounce on a working stiff faster than on their own kind, though the working stiff's retirement depends on a decent return of investment. They will shed crocodile tears and protest your complaints. Just know that their business is shearing small sheep to cover big sheep with wool."

Though the investment climate has changed, Joe's basic message about the market remains spot on.

When my receptionist buzzed me, Joe went back to reading the business pages. I took a call from Isaac Stern, one of my patients and a friend, who said he was in the neighborhood and wanted to come by.

I asked Joe, "Would you like to meet Isaac Stern?" I was nervous about asking him, because Joe was averse to meeting anyone cold, and celebrity did not impress him. I was ready for a resounding no, but Joe surprised me.

"Sure. That little fat guy from the Bay Area is a hell of a fiddle player," he said.

A comment like that could only come from a fellow legend.

"Well, he's on his way." I informed him that Stern was a Joe Di fan from way back, when Joe played for the Pacific Coast League and the San Francisco Seals. Though Stern focused on violin seven hours a day at the time, he was also very passionate about baseball and his sports idol, Joe DiMaggio.

Stern arrived later carrying two four-inch-high pastrami sandwiches and took a seat in the waiting room. He was the president of the Carnegie Hall Corporation, and the Carnegie Deli was a neighbor. He knew that I love pastrami on rye with an icy Dr. Brown's Cream Soda and a spear of kosher dill pickle, so he often got sandwiches to go when he came to the office. Growing up in Bensonhurst and Borough Park, my brother and I considered pastrami a gourmet delicacy. We were the only Catholic boys from St. Athanasius who would have lunch at Smolinsky's Deli on Bay Parkway and 65th Street in Brooklyn on a Friday afternoon when we were supposed to be eating only fish.

Isaac Stern loved towering pastrami sandwiches, too.

When I brought Isaac back to my office, I opened the door a crack to reveal Joe DiMaggio in the flesh, reading the paper.

Stern grinned from ear to ear.

As Stern entered my office, Joe jumped to his feet, and said, "It is truly an honor to meet you, Mr. Stern."

It was great to see how thrilled they both were.

The Maestro insisted that Joe call him "Isaac." Not too many people called him Isaac.

The two became fast friends before my eyes. They talked about the old days, growing up in the Bay Area, and their youth. Joe turned down the pastrami and went for the sour pickles

"Joe, I'll teach you how to play the violin," Isaac offered and pantomimed playing his instrument. He stopped for a moment and looked at Joe with an impish smile. "Of course, you have to show me how to grasp the baseball bat, and I will show you how to hold the violin bow."

Two legends were comparing notes in my office. It was rare for Joe to take to someone as he did that day, and the same is true for Isaac Stern. The two shared fond memories from a much earlier time. I was glad I got them together.

Some time later, Joe was honored at the prestigious Lotos Club. As he stood at the podium, he spotted Isaac Stern, seated with Mayor David Dinkins and his former teammate, Dr. Bobby Brown, in the audience. Joe couldn't resist calling attention to Stern as a fellow guest.

"I would like to recognize someone who has quite a few hits himself," Joe said with his usual grace and impact on the crowd.

Stern was surprised and delighted. The applause was thunderous. Stern stood up to acknowledge the warm response and bowed in Joe's direction. Not many men have shared the spotlight with Joe DiMaggio or Isaac Stern for that matter. One of the greatest athletes and one of the greatest instrumentalists of the twentieth century, icons in the worlds of sports and music, shared common ground and respected each other for their accomplishments. Their affection for each other was very moving to see.

The next time we got together, Stern and I were having lunch at the Three Guys Diner around the corner from my office, when a beautiful French intern, Laurence Marchese, who was working with our office, approached our table.

"May I have your autograph, Mr. DiMaggio?" she asked a surprised Stern.

Knowing of our friendship, she assumed the gentleman with me was Joe DiMaggio. Stern got a kick out of that. Isaac had just grown a foot taller and shed fifty pounds.

WE ENJOYED ANOTHER terrific dinner at Campagna one night. Before we pushed back from the table, Joe said, "Doc, I'm not in the least bit tired. I'm in the mood for a little music."

Joe was a man with a plan.

"My granddaughter Paula tells me that the Irish kid you've been helping out has a great voice. Where is he singing tonight?"

"You must mean Pat McGuire. He's at a place called Rocky Sullivan's on Lexington Avenue." I decided to discourage Joe. "You don't want to go there, Joe, it's a kids' joint. The music is too loud for your taste."

Joe waved off my warning.

"Doc, I love being around young kids. It always makes me feel better. It would be a good change. Maybe this Irish fellow will give me more CDs and tee-shirts to take back to the grandkids in San Francisco. They love it when I bring them back gifts from New York."

"All right, Joe," I said with resignation, "but you better not tell me later that this was a bad idea."

When we arrived at Rocky Sullivan's, a double line of college students were waiting to enter the music pub and hear McGuire and his band perform.

"Hey, Doc, that's quite a long line," Joe remarked. "Either they're giving away beer, or this fellow McGuire must be really good."

"Joe, he's a sweetheart. He has great songs, too. He just needs to get a break to get a record deal."

When we got out of the car, a stir in the crowd announced that Joe had been recognized. I commented that even the kids knew him.

"Yeah, Doc, it feels good. They're still so innocent. It gives me a connection from generation to generation." This was the fuel that energized Joe anytime he came to New York City. It was a life transfusion for him. He loved the action.

We made our way to the front of the line, where a human mountain, the bouncer, noticed Joe fast.

"Mr. DiMaggio, what are you doing here? You sure you're in the right place?"

"Tell me something, young fella, is this young buck McGuire singin' here tonight?" Joe turned on the charm. "If he is, I am here to hear him sing."

"Is he expecting you?"

"No, but I'm sure he won't mind an old crooner like me in the room."

The mountain stepped aside, and the crowd of kids parted as we entered the joint.

Pat was offstage and wondered what was going on outside as he heard a big commotion. When he recognized Joe, he said, wide-eyed, "Mr. DiMaggio, I can't believe it's really you."

"Young fella, my granddaughters in San Francisco are very fond of your music. Those CDs you gave the Doc for them were a big hit. I wanted to come here and see for myself what all the fuss was about. Is there a place we can sit and talk for a while?"

Joe started the conversation by asking the rocker, "So, tell me, young fellow, how do you write your songs?"

"I have to feel the situation, Mr. DiMaggio. I can be anywhere: on the subway, in the park, on the street, it makes no difference. It just grabs me."

"Just go out there and sing. We'll be in the front row giving you a good listen," encouraged Joe.

As we listened to the set, Joe noticed some very pretty college students and had to ask them questions.

"Is it my imagination, or does everyone here know the words to all of his songs?" Joe asked a young woman sitting near us.

"Mr. DiMaggio, we've been following Pat for years," she responded. "His songs mean a lot to us."

Joe enjoyed the music a lot. After the second encore, we went backstage again.

"Mr. DiMaggio," Pat asked, "did you like what you heard?"

"Not only did I like the music," Joe responded with a grin, "but I liked all the kids singing along with you while you strummed your guitar. It's hard to believe that you aren't on the radio yet, Pat."

Joe excused himself to go to the restroom. By the time he returned, Joe had decided he wanted to leave to see a John Ford Western at a local retro theater. His ears were ringing from the loud music.

"I don't know where he gets his energy from," I commented to Pat.

When we left through the pub, the place erupted with applause.

JOE'S INFLUENCE WAS far reaching. He unofficially helped to cement the deal when Mort Zuckerman was thinking of buying the *New York Daily News*. During a visit to the office, Mort told me about the purchase he was considering.

"I know you read the *News*, Rock. What do you think," he asked me.

I was all for it, but I wasn't speaking as a businessman. The *News* had cash flow problems and union contracts it had to honor. That didn't matter to me. I loved the *News*. My father would visit the 17th

Avenue Bagel Store in Brooklyn every Saturday night for fresh hot bagels and the night owl edition of the *New York Daily News*. We loved the way the *News* reported anything, though I admit I read the *New York Post* cover to cover these days. There is no New York without the *New York Daily News* or *New York Post*.

Mort was noncommittal. Business was business, after all.

That night, I brought up the topic with Joe.

Joe thought about it for a second.

"That would be a great buy. I always liked how the *Daily News* covered my career. Plus Gallo is over there at the *News*."

Joe gave the issue of buying the paper some thought and came up with an interesting offer.

"As a matter of fact, Doc, you tell Mort Zuckerman that if he buys the *News*, I promise I will come to visit the newsrooms at least once a year. I won't go to any other paper," Joe said, grinning. "Yeah, Doc, you tell him that if he buys the *News*, I will come up and even take pictures with the people on the staff of the paper."

Joe, of course, lived up to his promise. His only requirement was for Bill Gallo to be the tour guide. Joe visited the bullpens, columnists, editors, and workingmen and women of the newspaper where they worked. He did so without fail, every year after Mort Zuckerman bought the paper. I won't say that Joe was responsible for saving the venerable *New York Daily News*, but he certainly helped Mort Zuckerman make up his mind.

Joe's favorite fourth-estate personage was Bill Gallo, the man who introduced us. His relationship with Joe went back for many years. Joe loved Gallo's ability to take a situation and distill it into a cartoon, whether the subject was happy or sad. He was impressed by Gallo's ability to draw caricatures, particularly of Joe DiMaggio, as well as people like Steinbrenner and Muhammad Ali. And, most important, he trusted Bill.

In the early '90s, I got a phone call during office hours from John

Campi, one of the executives at the *Daily News*. Campi told me that the *News* was giving Bill Gallo an anniversary party at the Madison Square Garden Club to honor him for his fifty years at the *New York Daily News*. He wanted to know if I could get Joe to come.

Having handled hundreds of invitations for Joe to attend functions, I still couldn't predict how he would respond to this request. I told Campi I would ask.

I was inclined to recruit Joe to go to Gallo's party because of my friendship with the vice president of the *News* at that time, Les Goodstein, who always treated me with kindness and respect.

The next day, Bill Gallo called himself. I had interviewed him when John and I were both writing for an Italian-American newspaper, *L'Agenda*. I discovered during our conversation that Bill was not Italian. He was Spanish. There was a running joke in certain circles that Bill Gallo went around impersonating an Italian to receive awards from Italian-American organizations.

"Rock, any way of you asking Joe to come to my fiftieth anniversary party?" Bill inquired

I could never say no to Bill.

"I'll do everything I can to get Joe to come," I replied. I knew it was far from a done deal, but if there was anyone I would go the full distance for it would be Bill Gallo. That's how much I loved, respected, and admired him.

Joe was in New York that week, and we were planning to have breakfast at the Gardenia Café the next morning.

I told him that the *News* was giving Bill Gallo a party and that Bill had called himself to see if Joe would come.

Joe accepted immediately, but he did have some conditions. "I'll go with certain rules. Number one: There has to be no press, no interviews with television or writers—nothing."

I was incredulous. This party was a press party to honor one of its own.

"Joe, how can I guarantee that?" I decided to take a reasonable approach. "Gallo is a press person, the *Daily News* is a newspaper. Why would you think it possible for no press to be in the house to cover such a huge milestone for Gallo?"

Joe frowned.

"Let's be realistic," I continued, "if the press is there and they see you, they will undoubtedly want to ask you a question or two."

"Listen, Doc, I want you to do everything in your power to make sure that the press does not bother me," Joe demanded.

The day of the party came, and a white stretch limousine came to pick Joe up.

Joe, already in a poor mood, winced.

"Doc, can you imagine picking me up in a white limousine? Do they think that I'm a dago off the boat? Why didn't they give me a black car?"

This was not a good start.

"Joe, why don't we just get into the car? They're only taking us down to Madison Square Garden. Let's go."

Joe remained silent during the whole trip and started to scowl. We arrived, left the white dago mobile behind, and found the Garden Club. We were just ten feet into the room when a television camera crew came over with CBS newscaster Sal Marchiano. They started to tape Joe in the bright lights.

"Doc, nice job," he snapped at me as the cameras were rolling. "What did I tell you about having the press here?"

Even though we had discussed the certainty of the press being at a press party beforehand, Joe gave it to me in front of the gathering throng. Joe was on a low boil for the rest of the party and didn't say a word to me.

I bumped into Dr. Jay Oliva, who was the president of New York University, my alma mater. Jay had written me letters of recommendation to get into the best graduate schools in the country. Oliva wanted to meet Joe, who was definitely not in a "meeting a friend of Rock's" mood. Not intimidated, I brought Oliva to Joe.

"Joe, I would like you to meet someone. This is Dr. Jay Oliva, the president of NYU."

The introduction prompted Joe to unload on me in front of the press corps.

"There you go again, Doc, always trying to impress me with people's titles. I don't care what he does. Just tell me his name," Joe fired at me.

Dr. Oliva was very uncomfortable hearing DiMaggio berate me in front of everyone. Oliva just shook Joe's hand and walked away.

George Steinbrenner, my oasis and savior, who was at the party, came over to Joe.

With remarkable graciousness, Joe asked Steinbrenner, "What are you doing here?"

Steinbrenner returned fire, unlike me. "What are you doing here, Joe? I never thought I'd ever see you at a party like this."

Joe seemed to lighten up. He was comfortable at that moment with Steinbrenner, so I took the opportunity to punt the Clipper onto General von Steingrabber's—a Bill Gallo caricature—watch. Joe still wasn't talking to me.

At one point, he turned to me and gestured with an imperious wave of the hand, which I translated to mean, "Even though I'm not talking to you, I want to get going."

On the way to the door, we were delayed when Mike Lupica, a renowned syndicated columnist at the *News*, pulled me over.

Joe was press conscious and always read the columns, especially items about himself. At the time, he was not particularly happy with the way Mike Lupica was writing about all of the publicity on the fiftieth anniversary of Joe's fifty-six-game hitting streak. In fact, in one of his columns, Lupica threw a friendly barb at Bill Gallo, telling him to stop making such a big deal of Joe DiMaggio's hitting streak. Joe was not pleased that Lupica had taken what could be interpreted as a swipe at the legendary hitting streak of the Great DiMaggio. Joe kept that column in his mind and on his memory card of slights. I had called Bill on a couple of occasions and told him that neither of us was happy about what had happened. Gallo even took Lupica to task on his comments regarding the streak.

"Excuse me, Dr. Positano, I wanted to know if you would do me a favor. I would like an introduction to Mr. DiMaggio for my wife, my mother-in-law, and myself. Would you be kind enough to do it?"

My first impulse was "Why not?" even though Joe was bothered by Lupica's cynical column about people making such a big deal over his fifty-six-game hitting streak.

"Sure, Mike," I said, "but I cannot promise you anything. You know that Joe reads the papers every day from cover to cover and is especially interested in what people write about him," I cautioned the columnist.

We started to walk toward the door where Joe was waiting, not even looking at me.

"Excuse me, Joe, I would like you to meet Mike Lupica. He is a sportswriter who works with Gallo at the *News*."

Joe fixed his eyes on Lupica and said, "Yeah, I know who you are. You've been doing a lot of writing lately. Have you written anything about me recently?"

I was impressed by his caginess. He was letting Lupica know that he was aware that the journalist had written something benignly unflattering about him, but wasn't giving Lupica the satisfaction of saying he had read and reacted to the piece.

Then, in true DiMaggio form, Joe became a gentleman. He turned on the charm and was gracious to Lupica, his wife, and his mother-in-law, as if nothing had ever transpired.

He explained his behavior to me by saying, "That Lupica fellow has been writing things about me lately in the papers, but I wasn't going to embarrass him in front of his family no matter what he said about me."

I wished I received such tender treatment. When we emerged onto the street, Joe lit into me again.

"I don't know why I showed up, why did you make me do this? And you promised me there was going to be no press."

I couldn't take it anymore. I bundled Joe into the white stretch limousine, said goodnight, and slammed the door of the DiMaggio pimp-mobile. I walked home. I had had enough of Joe DiMaggio for one evening.

Joe was stunned. He was used to my accepting everything he dished out regardless of how unreasonable and rude he was being. It had been a matter of respect. I wasn't willing to sit still for his thoughtless behavior anymore. I was always there for him. He relied on me to protect him, to show him a good time, to keep him in his comfort zone. It was time for him to treat me with the same respect I showed him. His days of taking me for granted had just ended.

In true DiMaggio form, Joe called me the next morning as if nothing had happened. So much for Bill Gallo's fiftieth anniversary at the *New York Daily News*. I did make a call to Bill to ask him to please not invite me to his seventy-fifth anniversary party at the *News*.

Speaking of the *Daily News*, I ran into Mort Zuckerman, the media magnate and owner of the newspaper, at a party. As we were chatting, Mort brought up a strange topic.

"You know, Rock, Fidel Castro is a big DiMaggio fan."

"Hmm," I said. I'd been around Joe long enough to know what Mort wanted.

"Castro really wants a Joe DiMaggio baseball, signed by Joe DiMaggio." He went on to explain, "A group of U.S. newspaper owners and journalists met with Castro in Cuba. He was asked what was the one thing he wanted from America. Without hesitation, Castro said through an interpreter, 'A Joe DiMaggio signed baseball.'"

Mort must have thought I needed to be persuaded, because he went on to explain the Cuban leader's admiration for the Yankee Clipper. Castro was a crazy baseball fan and a Yankee fan. Cubans loved the Yankees, because Yankee games aired on radio in Cuba live from the Bronx during the '40s. Even the most primitive Cuban fishermen's village got live Yankee action. Remember *The Old Man and the Sea*? Hemingway knew all about it. Cubans were as familiar with Joe DiMaggio as the average American.

It got even more interesting. Not only was Fidel Castro a fan of baseball, the Yankees, and Joe DiMaggio, but he was once a decent baseball prospect himself. Castro played baseball for the University of Havana and was spotted by Pirates scouts and others. The agent reports stated that Castro had a wicked curve ball. Fidel was almost seduced into playing ball professionally in the United States, but the offer wasn't high enough for him to make the move.

I was concerned about asking Joe to sign a ball for Castro. After all, Joe lived in Florida, which had a large Cuban émigré population, who were vehemently anti-Castro. Many Cubans suffered under Castro, and some had been forced to flee, leaving their families behind. Being associated with Castro in any way might not be good for Joe in Florida.

I had mixed feelings about it myself. I grew up with the old "Communism is on your doorstep" television ads. The world almost ended in 1962 because of Fidel's missiles. I was raised to think that Commies were the enemy. American kids during that period were sick of spending time under their desks during air-raid drills.

I decided it was worth a shot. Joe was unpredictable in these matters. At worst, Joe would make a go-away gesture with his hands, shake his head, and say, "No way!"

Days passed. I made my move as we were driving over the bridge to Bamonte's in Brooklyn. "Joe, can I ask you a question," I began.

"Sure, Doc," he replied.

I took a deep breath and forged ahead. "If I asked you to sign a baseball for Fidel Castro, what would you say?"

Joe gazed out at the traffic and responded quickly, "Doc, I'd do it."

I was surprised and a little annoyed. "You're kidding me, Joe!" I sputtered. "You'd give that Commie bastard a baseball, a signed Joe DiMaggio baseball?"

"Doc, it has nothing to do with his political beliefs. It has to do with the fact that the guy is a huge baseball fan and, from what I understand, he was an excellent fielder and pitcher."

It took a week for Joe to sign the ball, because he wanted to choose his words carefully. He didn't want the message to be construed as an endorsement of Castro's political beliefs. Joe finally signed the ball, and I delivered it to Mort Zuckerman.

Soon after, Joe called from Florida. He got to the point quickly. "That baseball I signed for Castro—a lot of people are talking about it."

I suspected there would be trouble, but had refrained from saying so. We had already disagreed about the gift to Castro.

"You're kidding me, Joe," I said.

"Yeah, I just got off the phone with Morris Engelberg. He is furious that I signed that baseball, Doc. I asked Morris what the problem was, and he said, 'Listen, you are never going to be able to walk around in South Florida again. You're going to have every refugee there wanting to kill you, Joe!'"

Of course, that had occurred to me as well.

"I repeated what you had said to me—that signing a baseball for Castro could improve relations between the U.S. and Cuba."

So, he was using my offhand comment as his excuse.

Joe continued, "I told Morris that I don't want anyone to tell me who I can or cannot sign a baseball for. Whether or not I endorse Mr. Castro's political views does not prevent me from respecting him as a great baseball fan."

Joe had signed the baseball to reflect his intention: "To Fidel, your friend in sports . . . Joe Di Maggio." With those words, Joe distanced himself from Castro's communist beliefs.

Fidel got the baseball. I was told it occupied a special place on Castro's desk. No one killed Joe, or Morris for that matter, and relations with the doorstep communist state improved a little.

(It turned out that Castro died on the same day that Joe Di was born, November 25.)

At one of our dinners at Bravo Gianni's, Joe told us a story about a reciprocal signing. He got a huge kick out of it.

Secretary of the Treasury Nicholas Brady, who served under President George H. W. Bush, was a big fan of baseball, and of Joe DiMaggio. Joe was at a Baltimore Orioles board meeting and planned to meet the secretary for lunch after the meeting broke up. Having enjoyed their meal, Brady took out a five-dollar bill and wrote a nice note to Joe on the bill above his imprinted signature in the lower right hand corner. Joe was thrilled to have both of Brady's signatures and put the bill in his rubber band wallet.

Not long after, Joe Di was speaking with his seatmate, John Robson, during a flight. As they talked, Robson identified himself as a member of the Treasury Department. He turned out to be Brady's deputy secretary. Joe pulled out his signed Nick Brady five-dollar bill. As a goodwill gesture, he took out a Sharpie and wrote his own note and autograph to Nick Brady on the same five-dollar bill. He asked Robson to give the bill back to Brady. Joe joked that he expected some change.

JOE WAS ALWAYS intrigued by high-level diplomacy. At a Bat Pack dinner, someone referred to Henry Kissinger as a politician.

Joe's response was immediate and intense.

"You are making a mistake," he insisted. "Dr. Kissinger is a diplomat and a statesman, not a politician. There is a big difference."

The man who opened China to the West and who ended the Vietnam War loved soccer and baseball and was especially enthusiastic about the Yankee Clipper.

Henry was a patient of mine on account of an old injury to his right foot from playing soccer in his youth. Given his globe-trotting schedule, Henry sometimes asked me for an appointment between one and six in the morning or nine and twelve at night. I always accommodated his schedule.

Traveling with an aching foot while helping to solve the world's problems added to the challenge. Henry appreciated my treatment and advice. Having foot pain has a negative impact on one's ability to concentrate on the tasks at hand, as Henry had found out. Your concentration is on your throbbing foot, not the peace treaty or negotiation.

Joe once asked me why it was so important for Henry to get a quick fix on his foot-and-ankle issues. I explained that it was important for a person of Henry's diplomatic status never to walk into a room limping or looking in pain when he moved. Any sign of weakness was the quickest way for your adversary to size you up and take advantage. It was all about perception. Joe was amused. He had always operated on the same principle.

THINKING ABOUT JOE'S expressed respect for Dr. Kissinger, I offered to get them together.

"Joe, how'd you like to spend some quality time with Henry Kissinger?" I asked him. They'd had a very brief chance meeting at a Paris hotel some years before when Kissinger was getting into a car and Joe was exiting another, but there was no real conversation, just a handshake and some pleasantries.

"I would love that, Doc." He was enthusiastic. "I've always admired the man, but I've never had the chance to sit down with him and talk one on one."

Henry was immersed in advising the Bush administration on handling Gulf War diplomacy at the time. In due course, Henry appeared for a nine-thirty in the evening appointment. Escorted by bodyguards, he walked briskly into the office, obviously in pain.

As I worked on his ankle, which was in bad shape, Henry reclined and read the *New York Times*.

I had arranged for Joe to show up at the office at nine forty-five.

"Henry, would you mind if I stepped out for a minute? I have a surprise for you."

Henry looked puzzled.

I went out to fetch Joe.

"Doc, does he know I'm here?" Joe asked. He seemed excited.

"No, Joe, it's a surprise," I informed him.

We hurried past the bodyguards, who had been delighted to meet the unexpected guest in my waiting room.

"Henry, here's your surprise," I said as I entered the examination room.

Henry lifted his eyes from his newspaper, looking very world-weary, and saw Joe standing in the doorway.

In his deep Germanic voice, he exclaimed, "Oh my God—I can't believe it! It's Joe DiMaggio!"

"How ya doin', Dr. Kissinger?" Joe asked with boyish charm. "Now just stay right up there on the examining table."

Henry wasn't going anywhere soon. They talked briefly, and then I asked Joe to leave so that I could finish the treatment. I invited Joe back in at the end of the session.

"Why don't you two guys catch up on old times?" I suggested to the beaming men.

While Henry put on his sock and his shoe in record time, he started talking.

"I can remember the time I was in the cheap seats in center field. The seats were a dollar fifteen or a dollar sixty-five each. I used to call out to you from the cheap seats, Joe," Henry recalled. "I used to watch you make those center field catches. You made it look so easy—so fine and so great!!"

Dr. Kissinger was starstruck like anyone else.

Joe took it all in with a smile.

"Dr. Kissinger, you are a true diplomat," Joe delivered his praise in turn. "You've been great for our country. You are a great American."

Henry looked bashful as Joe concluded, "We are very, very fortunate to have had you as our secretary of state!"

They talked for a half hour, during which Henry briefed Joltin' Joe on the Paris Talks, the meeting with Mao, and the crisis of the time, the Gulf War. Of course, I can't repeat Henry's blunt appraisal of the world situation.

The friendship launched in my offices developed into an unlikely buddy movie. During the 1997 World Series, Joe and Henry were inseparable in the Owner's Box. Henry had persuaded Joe to make many more trips to Yankee Stadium than he usually did.

During the game, Henry talked to Joe about baseball defenses, what types of pitches were being thrown by the pitchers of both teams, and many baseball questions that showed a high degree of sophistication about the game. I was impressed that Henry held his own, as he scrutinized the players with Joe's tutelage much as a coach would.

Several innings into the game, Joe went to the men's room and Henry held the fort. Joe returned. They had changed pitchers in the interim.

"Ha, they changed pitchers," Joe said as he took his seat.

"How can you tell, Joe?" Henry asked.

"By the way the ball is being delivered," explained Joe. "Look at the way the ball is moving."

Henry was amazed that an eighty-plus-year-old man could discern the difference in pitching motion and how the ball broke afterwards.

He didn't have to see the electronic scorecard or hear the PA to know this. To his dying day, Joe DiMaggio was the perfect baseball machine.

At a banquet one time, Kissinger said how much he enjoyed coming to our offices, because he never knew who he would bump into. He brought the house down at one of our DiMaggio dinners when he said, "It is very difficult to say no to Dr. Positano when he has electrodes hooked up to your feet." He was alluding to the fact that getting him to any function in New York was a major undertaking.

JOE WAS USED to being the draw when it came to friends. People competed for his affection and approval and wanted to be in his company. Everyone hung on his every word to gain favor. It was rare for him to reach out to meet people. In one case, I think he was both curious about, and jealous of, one of my friends.

Joe often heard me mention Jerry Della Femina in flattering terms in conversations with other people. Jerry this and Jerry that. In the old neighborhoods of Bensonhurst and Borough Park, we didn't find too many role models. Sandy Koufax; Fred Wilpon, the owner of the Mets; and Jerry Della Femina all grew up near the schoolyards I roamed at night. All became extremely successful and role models to us kids.

When I was trying to make it in the Manhattan medical community, one name kept surfacing in the media pages: Jerry Della Femina, an ad executive and owner of a popular Hamptons restaurant, Della Femina, where it was almost impossible to get a reservation.

Jerry was the kid from the neighborhood who made it to the big leagues. He was the talk of the town.

Jerry was the DiMaggio of the neighborhood. He and his wife, TV personality Judy Licht, were the king and the queen of the A-list crowd. Their Fourth of July party was the must party in the Hamptons. I used to imagine what it would be like to be invited. I would have parked and washed cars for Jerry's guests just to see the glitterati party. We had met several times at social events, but that was it.

I knew that Jerry, like most of the kids from the neighborhood a generation older than I, loved DiMaggio. At a charity auction in Tribeca, I saw an oil painting of DiMaggio's beautiful swing. I purchased the painting with the intention of giving this to my neighborhood idol, Joltin' Jerry! I thought it would be a memorable introduction.

I had the painting sent to him and included a little note. Within two hours Jerry was on the phone. He was effusive about the painting and insisted on meeting me.

I told Joe about my gift to Jerry, and his wild enthusiasm for the painting and its subject. "Joe, you are hanging in his living room over the fireplace."

"Who is this Jerry fellow you're always talking about? How come I never meet him?"

I realized the Clipper was jealous because of the attention I paid to Jerry. He must have been curious about the guy I admired so much.

One night we were eating at the Vivolo restaurant on the Upper East Side, and Jerry's name came up again. DiMaggio asked me straight out, "Hey, Doc, why don't we invite this Jerry fellow out to have dinner with us and the boys?"

Floored by the request, I said, "Sure."

Ecstatic was too mild a word to describe Jerry's reaction when I extended Joe's dinner invitation. The stage was set for Joltin' Jerry to meet us for dinner at Campagna. He is still so pumped up about the evening, I thought I'd let him tell the story—his first dinner with DiMaggio from Jerry's point of view.

"I grew up in Brooklyn but was always a Yankee fan. Joe DiMaggio was God.

"In the totally Italian Avenue U neighborhood, you would always hear someone say, 'How did he do today?'

" 'He went three for five, made a great catch.'

"No need for a name. Everyone knew they were talking about 'DiMag.' "

"I couldn't believe that my good friend Rock Positano set me up to have dinner with Joe DiMaggio. I was going to eat with Joltin' Joe.

"Before that night, the closest I ever was to DiMaggio was about a hundred feet from his back. He played center field, and my dad and I sat in the center field bleachers at Yankee Stadium, where the admission was two dollars.

"I watched Joe Di drift back with a ballet dancer's grace and catch a long fly ball to center many times. He made every catch look easy. He didn't run—he glided.

"Once he drifted back for a long fly ball hit by the Detroit Tigers' star, Dick Wakefield. The ball hit the side of his glove and bounced out. The crowd couldn't believe it. Joe threw the ball in and took his stance for the next hitter with his hands on his knees. I saw the back of his neck slowly turn a dark beet red.

" 'He's embarrassed,' my dad whispered to me.

"Why not? Joe was a perfectionist.

"Today, some seventy years later, I can still see DiMaggio's neck turning bright red, because he dropped a ball.

"Now, thanks to Rock Positano, I was going to eat dinner with Joe DiMaggio.

"We went to a restaurant on East 21st Street, Campagna. The whole night was a blur. Was I really standing next to Joe DiMaggio? Was he really talking to me?

"At the restaurant's door, something amazing happened. The restaurant was packed and as loud as can be. The bar was four deep. As DiMaggio stepped through the door, people stopped midsentence and stared. Suddenly, the entire restaurant was silent. God had walked through the door. Nobody talked. Everybody stared. I have never seen anything like this before or since. Silence.

"When we were seated, people came up to the table with the excuse that they wanted to talk to me.

" 'Jerry . . . Jerry,' a complete stranger said to me, not taking his eyes off DiMaggio. 'Do you remember me? We were part of the group that toured Nightingale High School for our daughters?'

"Another man came up insisting we had worked together in an advertising agency I had never heard of.

"They talked to me. They gaped at Joe.

"Though I was a bit tongue-tied at first, DiMaggio was easy to talk to. We discussed his duels with Yankee General Manager George Weiss and owner Ed Barrow. He talked of his holdout for more money in 1938. He wanted forty thousand. They gave him twenty-five.

"At one point he blurted out, 'What were those two guys singing about, "Where Have You Gone, Joe DiMaggio?" I didn't go anywhere. I'm here.'

"For a second, he was angry.

"When the time came to order and we all ordered pasta, DiMaggio called the waitress. 'Miss,' he said, 'make sure that my pasta is well cooked. I don't want any of that *al dente* stuff.' Then he turned to me, and said, 'What is this *al dente* nonsense? Pasta has to be cooked a long time.'

"From that day on I have never asked for my pasta *al dente*. I eat my pasta like the great Joe DiMaggio.

"Then it was over. There were the good-byes. Rock handed me a Joe DiMaggio autographed baseball, which is still one of my greatest possessions, and one of the best nights of my life was over."

I REMEMBER A time when Joe failed to be recognized by someone he wanted to impress. It all began when Joe invited me to relax at his place after dinner one night. He changed into his at-home ensemble: a robe, black socks, and shoes. He was watching a network evening news show, broadcast by the local affiliate. I wasn't paying much attention. The newscaster, Elizabeth Vargas, was reporting on a train wreck in the Midwest. She was an articulate and attractive brunette. I noticed that Joe had a strange smile on his face.

"Joe, glad to see you get so much pleasure from a train wreck," I couldn't help commenting.

Joe smirked and pointed a finger to the screen. "That's one fine lookin' gal."

"Oh, that's Elizabeth," I responded. "She's top notch. A nice woman."

"Doc, do you know her?"

"Sure, Joe, I know her. Want to meet her?"

Joe brightened.

"You bet, Doc!"

I had my reservations about introducing them. Elizabeth could have been his granddaughter as there was a forty-year difference in their ages. Most important of all she didn't know very much about Joe as a baseball player. I decided to give it a try anyway.

"I'll set up something tomorrow at a nice restaurant," I offered.

I decided to hedge my bets. "We'll both meet her, Joe. Just try to contain your schoolboy crush."

Against my better judgment, I reserved the private VIP room at Lattanzi's restaurant for the blind date.

Elizabeth was late. Joe was every bit the nervous suitor.

"Doc, are you sure you told her the right time?" The Clipper was worried. "I don't know about this. What have you gotten me into, Doc?"

He started to get agitated. "A blind date at my age? Doc, you know I hate surprises." The tension was building. "I've never been stood up by a gal in fifty years, and I don't know if I can take it now."

"Elizabeth is notoriously late," I offered as an excuse. "She's looking forward to meeting you."

At that point, Eddie Kostner, the maître d, appeared in the doorway. Joe and I looked up expectantly, but he was alone. Eddie knew what was going on and attempted some small talk to occupy Joe.

"Mr. Di, Paul Simon just sat down inside with his wife, Edie Brickell. Let me know if you want to see him."

"Not now, Mr. Ed, maybe later." Joe was distracted. He turned to me and asked, "Doc, you sure she knows how old I am? I mean, she looks pretty good on television. What do you think she's goin' to do with an old geezer like me?"

"Joe, keep quiet," Eddie said as he scanned the restaurant to the entrance. "Here comes your date." Eddie chuckled. "She's walking through the door and turning every guy's head in this place."

Elizabeth entered the VIP area, nodded to Eddie, and made eye contact with me. She ignored Joe as she approached.

"Hi, Rock, you look great," Elizabeth said, "I'm sorry I'm late."

Joe stood to greet her, but she was too busy with her explanation to pay attention to him. Instead, she focused on me.

"Rock, I've had a hectic week with the sweeps," Elizabeth said. "Thanks for seeing my friend last week on such short notice. She really did a number on that ankle, but she feels much better now."

Joe was still standing and waiting to be acknowledged.

"I'm Joe," he introduced himself.

Elizabeth looked up and said without a glimmer of recognition, "Hello, Joe, nice to meet you."

For one horrifying moment, I thought she might give Joe her drink order.

Joe sat down at the table.

Innocently ignoring Joe, Elizabeth directed another question to me. "Rock, what did you think of my piece last week?"

I stayed quiet and let Joe make his move.

"I think the piece was well-organized. Your interview style is viewer friendly, and your facts and conclusions were logical and coherent,"

Joe commented. He had decades of media exposure and countless interviews to his credit, so he knew what he was talking about. He summed up his appraisal by saying, "Your comebacks were focused and to the point."

Elizabeth was impressed.

"Joe, that was very observant of you." She was now paying attention to the old man at the table. "You can identify with my pattern of interviewing."

"Well, you know, I've had a lot of experience dealing with the press and doing interviews," Joe said, waiting for a sign of recognition from Elizabeth.

"Tell me, Joe, did you ever work in television as a commentator?"

Elizabeth winked at me when she was asking these pointed questions. She was giving him a hard time and pulling his leg. She knew she had the Clipper on the ropes.

While Elizabeth was occupied with Eddie and the menu, Joe leaned toward me and asked, "What have you done to me, Doc? She doesn't even know who I am. I have never been so humiliated."

Figuring that humor might help, I quipped, "At least she didn't take you for a security guard with that blazer you are wearing." I tried to calm him down. "Look, Joe, you are always complaining about how you have no life, because everyone recognizes you, how you are never getting any privacy. For the first time in a long while, you're meeting a lovely woman, who might actually get to know you—and like you—not the DiMaggio legend."

Joe was flustered but game.

Elizabeth turned to Joe and asked, "So what do you do for a living these days, Joe?"

"Actually, Elizabeth, I was a professional ballplayer for fifteen years," Joe began his resume. "I played center field for the New York Yankees when baseball was America's game and number-one pastime. I knew and played against the best who ever lived."

"I don't know much about baseball," Elizabeth explained. "I was an army brat and grew up all over the world. I happen to be a big basketball fan. Tell me more about baseball."

As Joe talked, Elizabeth went into interview mode. "Tell me more. What did it mean to you, Joe?" she asked.

"Lizzie, do you mind if I call you Lizzie? It meant the world to me. Baseball meant wearing nice clothes and going to interesting places." Joe stopped to find the right words. "I breathed baseball. I ate baseball. I thought baseball. I dreamed baseball." Joe's passion for the game shone through. "There wasn't a minute when I wasn't thinking about how to get better at baseball. It wasn't only me—everybody loved the game."

Elizabeth was enthralled by Joe's resume. She asked a leading question. "How about modern ballplayers?"

Joe registered vague disgust.

"In my era, they were all sportsmen, all-round athletes. Nowadays, they are corporate raiders. They might as well be CPAs or sports lawyers. They only play for the bottom line."

Before Elizabeth could protest, Joe continued, "I can only blame the owners for that. The players have no fan loyalties—none of them. And it seems that half of them are in rehab or prison at any one time. Some beat their wives or their girlfriends. They really aren't ballplayers as I knew them."

"Oh, you didn't play for money, Joe?" Elizabeth's tone was challenging.

"The money was good, but I also played for the fun of it," Joe responded. "We all did. No one starved in the Major Leagues. But we all strove to be models for the kids watching us. We kept our dirty laundry inside the clubhouse. No one today will deny that we kept our flaws to ourselves."

"Joe, you had to have flaws. You were ordinary men," Elizabeth retorted.

"We were ballplayers first. Baseball meant the world to us. It meant the world to millions of people in the Depression. We were like the movies. We kept people's minds off hard realities. Our ability made them cheer."

Joe saw baseball as the pulse to American national morale

"That's so fascinating, Joe. I have to excuse myself for a moment. No more stories until I get back," she said and headed past the doorway. She was now intrigued and captivated by the Clipper. He got to first base with her.

"Joe, you are doing pretty well for a guy she didn't recognize," I said to encourage my friend. "You better stop dropping water on your trousers or she is going to think you have a weak bladder and can't hold it in."

"Do you think she'll ever want to have dinner with me again?" he asked.

When Elizabeth appeared, she was ready to pick up the conversation as we ate our dinner.

"Joe, tell me more," she said with a radiant smile. "I'm enjoying your stories."

The Yankee Clipper didn't need to be asked twice. The Clipper, a true competitor, was getting ahead of the count and gaining some leverage with Lizzie.

Joe reached farther back.

"You ever hear of a place called Alcatraz in San Francisco, Lizzie?"

Elizabeth nodded. "Yes, the famous prison."

"Alcatraz had an amusing way of entertaining its inmates. They had a baseball field at the prison, which sat on an island in the middle of San Francisco Bay. There wasn't much space to hit or play, but that field was there, and it was used. The inmates played for special privileges. The games were well guarded, of course. Some of those prison fellas could hit a ball a country mile."

"Into the bay?" Elizabeth asked.

"Yes, into the bay, Lizzie. But there was a major rule change in

Alcatraz—a big difference between baseball played at the island prison and everywhere else. At Alcatraz, if you hit a ball over the fence and into the water, it wasn't a home run like it would be anywhere else. Nope, it was an out!"

"Why was the rule changed?" Elizabeth inquired.

"Well, Lizzie, hitting the ball off the island was an out, because the warden wanted the inmates to know that any attempt at escape would end up the same way—down and out!"

All three of us laughed.

"The same rule did not apply when I was playing in Yankee Stadium. The fences in left center field were over four hundred feet away. I used to hit many long balls to left center field, which was the deepest part of the stadium for a hitter.

"I would tag a pitcher and send a ball screaming toward left field. In any other park in the league, then and now, the hit would have been an easy homer into the parking lot. I can still see one of my line drives heading into this Death Valley for hitters. The left fielder could just wait there for the ball to come down into his glove," Joe explained. "Another four-hundred-plus-foot easy out.

"Some people have estimated that I must have lost over 150 home runs just by playing in Yankee Stadium," Joe ended his tale.

"How did you handle it?" Elizabeth asked.

"I learned to hit with power to other parts of the Stadium. What a place that old Yankee Stadium was. It was like . . . well . . . it was like a cathedral in Rome."

Before Elizabeth could react, Joe went on with his image. "And there's music in a stadium. It's the roar of the fans. It sounds like a strange type of uneven music. It has its own melody." Joe seemed transported.

"You can't hear that music in the stands. It has to wave in when you're fielding out there. You can't hear it anywhere else."

"Music? How can it be music?" I asked.

"It can't be described," he answered. "Thousands of people calling your name . . . Joe . . . Joe . . . Joe . . . Joe.

"No one was jealous. Not even the other team. I can hear it now. It's like the sound of the sea you hear in the seashell you found at the beach."

Elizabeth and I were quiet and mesmerized after Joe's elegantly poetic description. This was a side of him I had never seen. It took an extremely bright and fetching woman to bring this out.

"That's something." Elizabeth broke the silence. "Joe, it's getting late. I have to get up early tomorrow to do the news."

Joe turned to me and scolded, "Doc, how could you make Lizzie come out here so late to be with us, if you knew that she had to be at work early tomorrow? She has to get her rest."

Then he turned to Elizabeth and said, "Before you leave, Lizzie, I want to introduce you to someone."

Joe waved to Eddie, who had been watching attentively.

"What can I do for you, Mr. Di?" asked the loyal Eddie.

Joe half motioned to the next room and said, "Eddie, why don't you get Paul Simon over here? I would like to say hello to him."

"Sure, Mr. Di, whatever you say."

Eddie raised his eyebrows when he looked at me. Joe never did anything like this.

"That fellow over there, Paul Simon. Do you know him, Lizzie?" Joe asked.

"Of course, I know him. He wrote . . ."

Joe cut her off.

"You know he wrote a song about me. Someone said that I am angry at him for doing this, but that's not true at all."

She was visibly impressed and excited at the prospect of having an introduction to Paul Simon.

That night, Paul couldn't ask, "Where have you gone, Joe DiMaggio?" All he had to do was look across the room.

I was able to see Simon when Eddie asked him to come over at Joe's urging. Simon was incredulous. His facial expression and body language were priceless. He turned to his wife and gave her a panicked look, and then he shrugged and pushed away from the table. He clearly had no idea what to expect.

Eddie appeared at the door of the VIP room with Simon in tow. Joe got up, shook his hand warmly, and introduced him to us. "This is the guy who wrote that great song about me, right, Paul?"

"Yes, Mr. DiMaggio, yes, I did." Paul Simon was shy in Joe's presence. "Glad you liked it."

"I'll let you get back to your wife now. I just wanted to say hello."

In other circumstances, Joe might have put Paul Simon on the spot, but he had a lady to impress that night, and impress he did. Elizabeth became a regular dinner partner of Joe, who acted like a grade-school boy with a crush. He even signed a ball for her without her even having to ask.

THE BURKES WERE good to Joe. They were part of his East Coast family. Their place was his home away from home. He wanted to return the favor. He thought he might be able to help Cathy Burke with her acting career. He volunteered to assist in any way possible. I suggested that Woody Allen might be a good person for Joe to meet, and arranged for the elegant and beautiful Jean Doumanian, who produced many of Woody's films, to introduce us. Doumanian was also known for her stint as the executive producer of *Saturday Night Live* during the Joe Piscopo and Eddie Murphy era.

We planned to meet at the Café Carlyle, where Woody Allen has played clarinet with the Woody Allen & the Eddie Davis New Orleans Jazz Band once a week for more than thirty-five years. When Joe and I arrived, the lobby was filled with a boisterous crowd, not to hear

Woody, but because another event was being held elsewhere in the hotel that night.

Eyeing the crowd, Joe had just started muttering to me, "I don't know about this. This isn't The Carlyle that I know. Nobody in that crowd is wearing a jacket and tie. What are you getting me into, Doc?"

He was visibly pissed off, but Jean was watching the action from the sideline. Jean sensed that Joe was giving me a hard time. Her instinct was dead on! She came over to us.

The sight of such an attractive woman changed Joe's mind.

"Hey, Dr. Rock," Jean said when she reached us, "we are waiting for you guys inside. Woody is so thrilled that you are coming to hear him play, Mr. DiMaggio, and you are sitting right next to me."

Joe's entire demeanor changed. He was clearly thrilled by the seating arrangements.

Music was playing in the nightclub, which buzzed with the sound of people enjoying themselves. As the three of us entered, the room turned silent. It was the DiMaggio Effect again. The attention of every person in the nightclub was focused on Joe. Time stopped momentarily. Woody, who was playing up front, skipped a beat and became visibly unnerved when he noticed that Joe had arrived. The audience didn't hear a note of music from the band when Joe walked in the room.

We settled in at our table. Joe said quietly to me, "Don't forget why we are here. We have to give these headshots of Cathy to Jean and Woody. Maybe Woody will use her in his next picture."

"Joe, don't be so obvious. You may actually enjoy yourself tonight. You once told me that you admire Woody Allen's talents as a writer and filmmaker. You know films and movie-making almost as well as you know baseball. This should be a treat."

"After listening for a few minutes to Woody's music," Joe whispered, "I can tell you that I'm certainly not an admirer of his clarinet playing. Glad he stuck to making great pictures."

I just gave him an exasperated look.

"Okay, Doc, I admit that I am a little excited to talk pictures with Woody," Joe relented a bit, "But I am even more excited to sit next to this Jeannie gal."

By the time Woody was about to finish his set, Joe was smitten by Jean and hadn't heard one note of the music. Jean suggested that the party move to Elaine's. Joe was delighted to comply, which did not happen often. As he stood to escort Jean to Elaine's, I was amused to see that he had left the headshots of Cathy Burke on the table. I went back to pick them up, as I did remember why we were there in the first place.

At Elaine's celebrity-studded restaurant on Second Avenue, the mob parted to allow our party to proceed to the A-list table—the third table on the right. Woody and his wife, Soon-Yi, soon joined us. Woody looked unwell.

I asked Jean if Woody was all right. "He looks like he's going to faint," I whispered.

"He gets that way," Jean confided. "He is petrified of meeting his idols. Joe is on the top of that list. He would hate to find fault with any of his idols and be disappointed, and vice versa."

Joe broke the ice. "Woody, you play that licorice stick pretty well for a picture guy. I love that thirties and forties music. I was singing along with your playing."

Woody seemed tongue-tied.

Jean lent an assist by graciously flirting with Joe. "Joe, you look so handsome tonight. Just look at all these beautiful women staring at you."

Blushing like a schoolboy, Joe responded. "Not bad for an old guy of eighty-two."

Woody interrupted the flirtation. "Joe, do you get to see many movies these days?" he asked.

Joe shook his head. "Not too many, Woody. I have a problem with the crowds. They see me and want autographs. I wait until I can see them on television. My favorite movies are Westerns, but I like your movies. *Annie Hall, Bananas, Sleeper,* I've seen them all. I like your style. Your *Crimes and Misdemeanors* was a little too ironic for me."

Woody seemed flattered as well as perplexed. I thought he might have taken Joe for a rube when it came to the movie business. Woody was amazed by Joe's knowledge of movie producers, directors, actors, and music scores. Few people were aware of how much the movie and entertainment business was part of Joe's sphere. I explained that Joe used to read Marilyn's scripts and offered her advice when negotiating her contracts. He knew all the Hollywood players and their creative work. Everyone at the table was in awe of his entertainment acumen.

"Ironic, you say? Well . . ." Woody was ready to defend the film.

Joe was quick to reassure the filmmaker. "But you are consistent. I've never finished watching one of your films and felt unsatisfied."

Woody looked pleased in his nervous way. Woody and his wife excused themselves for a while. When they returned some time later, the table was mobbed with Elaine's regulars wanting to meet Joe. The filmmaker and his wife beat a fast retreat.

It was a good night for Joe, and I think Woody was even more impressed by his idol than he had imagined he'd be. He also passed Joe's litmus test, which meant there would be another dinner with DiMaggio.

In general, Joe didn't interface well with the modern world of entertainment. Some modern icons did not make the grade for him. Joe took exception to Madonna's imitation of Marilyn Monroe, as she copied Marilyn's hairstyle, her speech, her singing style, and her wardrobe. He actually thought Madonna had a great figure when he was shown her naked modeling portfolio. "She looks like a strong gal, Doc, and could probably beat the crap out of most guys, including you.

"Doc, she's not in the same league beauty-wise. So many people think they can be Marilyn just by dressing up a certain way. Look at that Madonna song. She is dressed and made up the same way as Marilyn. She even mentions me in that song 'Greta Garbo and Monroe, Dietrich and DiMaggio.'

"Next thing you know she is going to want to go out with me," he joked.

Director Ron Howard, Opie of the iconic, '60s *Andy Griffith Show*, could have secured Joe's movie rights. Joe became particularly interested in going to Coco Pazzo for lunch after I told him that Ron Howard ate there regularly. Joe was a big admirer of Howard's film *Apollo 13*. He had seen the movie numerous times.

We showed up at Coco Pazzo one day and had just missed Howard by ten minutes. Joe, the man who never wanted to meet anyone, was very disappointed, because he would have liked to praise Howard for his movies, discuss *Apollo 13*, and talk about moviemaking in general.

Joe even said to me, "That fellow would do a great job on a movie about me." But that was not meant to be.

IN ALL MY years of having dinner with DiMaggio, I only once saw Joe go to someone else's table. We were having dinner at Coco Pazzo, when Joe spotted Tom Hanks at a table with his wife, Rita Wilson, Penny Marshall, Rosie O'Donnell, and a number of other guests. Joe told me how much he had liked Hanks in his role as the field manager Jimmy Dugan in *A League of Their Own*. Penny Marshall had directed the film, and Rosie O'Donnell had a hilarious role. There at one table sat many of the people who made the film he enjoyed so much.

Joe went over to the table on his own. Hanks looked as if he was going to fall off his chair. Stunned, he offered Joe one of his chocolate-chip cookies, which Joe accepted without hesitation.

I heard Tom Hanks say, "I can't believe I am sharing my chocolate-chip cookies with Joe DiMaggio."

A nervous silence fell over the table. Hanks started to tell Joe what a big baseball fan he was. When he used to sell peanuts at the Oakland Athletics ball park, he saw Joe dressed in a yellow-and-green Oakland Athletics uniform. In 1968, the Oakland A's first season in California, Joe became an executive vice president, consultant, and hitting instructor for the team. Hanks said he could never get used to seeing Joe in any other uniform but the Yankee pinstripes.

When the Clipper returned to the table, he threw out one of Hanks's funniest lines from the movie that Joe loved, "There's no crying in baseball!" He let out a big laugh.

The convergence of Hollywood and baseball was wonderful to watch. Joe was a big Hanks fan.

Joe bonded with Michael Bolton, a Columbia Records artist, who was an excellent baseball player, aside from being a fine singer. When Bolton was on tour, he traveled with his own team, the Bolton Bombers, to raise money for charities.

Wanting to help him out any way he could, Joe appeared often for Bolton's charity for battered women. Every October, Bolton hosted a softball game and fundraiser dinner in Old Greenwich, Connecticut.

Joe was lukewarm to the idea at first.

"You know, Doc, I really don't know these people very well. Would you mind accompanying me to the game and dinner that night?" he asked me.

No problem, as far as I was concerned. We drove up to Old Greenwich, which is about forty minutes from town. Joe had agreed to throw out the first ball, which thrilled Bolton and everyone else.

We were sitting in the dugout when Joe's superhuman vision spotted Dick Gephardt, one of the candidates for the Democratic nomination for president, headed toward the dugout from left field.

"Hey, Doc, let's get the hell out of here." Joe panicked. "This guy's going to want to take his picture with me, and he's going to want to talk. I got nothing personal with him, but I don't want to be bothered with these Washington types today. I am here to help Bolton's group and nothing else."

"Joe, he's here for a charity. What difference does it make?" I said in an attempt to avoid a scene.

Joe was adamant.

We escaped the dugout, explaining to Bolton that we needed to go to a hotel room nearby, because Joe needed to rest up. Bolton understood.

The dinner later was to be held at Valbella, an A-list local place. As Joe rubbed shoulders with the elite in the most elite of suburbs during cocktails, his mental telepathy about sports kicked in. Somewhere a baseball game was on, and Joe's brain picked up the signals just as surely as a TV set.

"Doc, let's get out of this room to watch the Yankees game."

We left the swanky affair and retired to the lounge, where the Yankee–Mariner playoff game was on over the bar. We took seats at the bar.

Joe observed the Yankee pitcher and said, "I don't like the way this guy is pitching. I'm watching his motion and the movement of the ball. The Yankees are going to lose."

"Joe, what are you talking about?" I argued. "The Yankees are up six to nothing. It's the sixth inning. There's no way the Yankees are going to lose."

Joe grinned. "Doc, you wait and see."

Then we went back to rejoin the swells. After a mess up with Joe's pre-ordered dinner—shrimp and Miller Lite were too hard to rustle up—I straightened things out. In their efforts to please Joe, the Bolton people and the Valbella staff were trying to bring in all fancy food. I told them that it wasn't necessary. When Joe asked for something, especially in public, just do it. I gave one look at the event organizer, and someone was immediately dispatched to get the Clipper his shrimp.

He was a perfect gentleman at dinner sitting with Michael Bolton,

Jane and Dick Gephardt, and me. He asked Michael about his singing projects. Bolton shared that he was going in the opera direction as a performer.

Joe asked, "What do you know about singing opera? Pavarotti, now, that was an amazing and powerful singer."

The table went silent. I kicked Joe under the table to make him shut up and change the subject.

Back at the room, I turned on the television. As Joe had predicted, the Mariners beat the Yankees.

Joe looked me straight in the eye and said, "You see, Doc, I told you so."

"How the hell did you know?" I shot back.

Joe just pointed heavenward.

"Let's just say that I have a connection with somebody upstairs."

I already knew that.

CHAPTER 11

It's Cold on the Tundra

Tuesday, July 6, 1993

Valerie called from Florida — to find out how many people will be with me for the Jim Thorpe awards for ABC network on the 12th. Told her "just one." Dr. Rock Positano called from New York to tell me he will be out in Los Angeles on the 11th — so he will be the one to join me. Told him to take his black tie suit along.

Sunday — July 11, 1993

Dr. Positano will be with me tomorrow night at the Awards ABC appearance. Heard once from the people who are putting the show on. I did not get a call to appear for a dry run. Dr. Positano and group picked me up at 7:15 PM. We drove to the Palm restaurant to have dinner. Got back

As I have said from the start, it wasn't difficult to offend Joe, like a true Sicilian. Though I tiptoed through the minefield for nine years, it was inevitable that I would step on a mine and set him off. When I did, he exiled me for two and a half months. I had heard him rail against people who had earned a permanent place in the negative column. I knew there was a spot for me on that list if I made a wrong move. When I did, I experienced how uncompromising and irrational Joe could be. It was maddening but well worth it, because it changed the tone and dynamic of our friendship radically.

It all began with Dr. Salvatore Ferrera, who was running Xaverian High School, my alma mater. About ten years older than I, Ferrera had been my basketball coach at St. Athanasius, our elementary school, which was also in Brooklyn. I always wanted to pay back Sal for his inspirational sessions. He discovered and tapped into my lack of basketball ability, which pushed me in the direction of becoming a doctor. I was the best "eleventh man on a ten-man team," according to him. I owed him for that.

I had heard Sal was turning around the fortunes of Xaverian. The school was going through tough times. Its enrollment base was a fraction of its former robust numbers. Xaverian was cut off from the Diocese of Brooklyn, left to sink or swim. Sal made it swim.

I called up Sal and told him about Joe DiMaggio's love of children, especially disadvantaged and learning challenged children. I mentioned that Joe might be willing to sponsor a fund-raising dinner. Needless to say, Sal jumped at the chance.

I, unlike everyone else, never asked for a single favor from Joe. By this point, I usually paid for Joe at meals and parties. It was now a respect thing. I hosted Joe and introduced him to the best places and the right people. Not once did I ask for an autographed ball, bat, or mitt for myself. Joe would have viewed such requests as mooching, which was a quick way to earn an all-expenses-paid trip to the DiMaggio tundra.

On the upper deck of the 59th Street Bridge on the way to Bamonte's, I asked him straight out.

"Joe, I've never asked you for anything in all the years I have known you," I started my pitch. "We've spent a lot of time together. I have a favor to ask of you that doesn't benefit me directly."

Joe was quiet and seemed receptive. I used the right choice of words.

"I went to a Catholic high school that now helps working-class kids, who are part of the learning-disabled program at the school. These are bright kids who learn differently from most kids," I explained.

I had used all the DiMaggio charity catchwords: kids, Catholic, disabled, working class. Joe valued education, because he had little. Joe was a devout Catholic. Joe always had a touch for the disabled, maybe because of his crippling heel spur. And Joe had a soft spot for any and all kids. These were the touchstones for Joe's charity.

DiMaggio and I had the same weakness, which is another reason why we got along well. We couldn't bear even the thought of seeing a child who was physically ill or mentally challenged suffer. Neither of us could ever say no to kids or their families.

He remained quiet and allowed me to finish without interruption.

"The man who runs the school now was my basketball coach at St. A's," I added. "I asked Sal if he'd start a benefit dinner for these special needs kids with you as the first honored guest. We'll call it the Concordia Award." I paused. "Would you be the first honoree?"

Joe was quiet in the car. All I could hear was the drone of other cars and trucks on the bridge. More silence.

"Okay, Doc, I'll do it." He agreed to participate that easily. "Just give me the details and let's work it out."

I was elated.

I called Sal after dinner and told him the wonderful news. He was ecstatic. We started to plan a major gala in the very best venue, because this event could not be held just anywhere.

The Marriott Marquis in Midtown was booked for the gala and invitations and press releases worthy of the great DiMaggio were sent out.

Somehow, one of Joe's friends—I've always suspected it was one of the Bat Pack who wanted to cause trouble—got the word to Joe that the affair was taking place in Xaverian's gymnasium, a glorified Communion breakfast with the smell of sweaty, teenage boys, catered by Irish brothers serving corned beef and cabbage. So, that's what Joe was expecting.

With a month to go, I answered my cell phone to be treated to the most obscene, petty, and mean-spirited phone call I have ever received in my life. It was Joe on the line.

After his rant, he finally got to the point.

"What kind of a person are you, Doc," he demanded, "how could you deceive me like this? What is this I hear that this award is being held at the Marriott Marquis for a thousand people?"

"Huh?" I had no idea what was going on.

"I was told that this award was going to be held in a gymnasium in a Brooklyn high school."

"Joe, what are you talking about," I protested. "How could we hold a fundraiser in a Brooklyn gym?"

"Doc, I got a copy of one of those invitations. It says that this event is going to be held at the Marquis in New York City. That's a pretty big place, Doc, and I would never have agreed to this had I known that is what you had in mind."

"Joe, we never spoke about this," I tried to defend myself. "You made it clear to me that this wasn't an issue. Joe, I don't know who told you that this fundraiser was being held in a gymnasium in Brooklyn, but it was totally wrong."

Joe hung up, furious.

This was big trouble. Almost a thousand seats had been sold. The hotel was booked, the lawyers and media alerted. The dais guests were on board, and New York's elite was drafted to serve. Joe DiMaggio, the draw and keynote speaker, might not show up. I shuddered at the thought.

Adding to my agony, Joe switched to radio silence. For two weeks, my calls went unanswered. Even a fax I sent to Joe came back with a scrawled refusal to communicate. And the gala date was approaching.

I called Dick Burke, Joe's longtime friend. Dick told me not to worry.

"Joe would never break his commitment," he said. "He may not ever talk to you again, but he will be at that dinner. When he gives his word, it is his word. You can count on him," Burke reassured me, and I could breathe a little bit easier.

A thousand guests were looking forward to seeing Joe DiMaggio, but the honoree still hadn't called or confirmed by the day of the gala.

At about one, an anonymous caller asked the school switchboard about the time a car and driver would pick up Mr. DiMaggio at his apartment in the city. Altering his voice, Joe had made the call. That was his sole communication. It was ridiculous.

The car was sent at the agreed-upon time. The driver, Angelo, later told us what happened. At five-thirty, Angelo found Joe nattily dressed in his blue blazer, gray pants, white shirt, and red tie.

Angelo told us that when Joe got into the car he said, "So, I understand that the Yankees–Mets game is happening tonight?"

Angelo was so surprised that he turned in his seat to see his passenger.

"Tell me something, Angelo, if I told you I didn't want to go to this fundraiser and wanted to see the Yankee–Mets game instead, what would you do?" Joe asked the horrified driver.

This was a big game as it was the first official, not exhibition, game between the Mets and the Yankees that counted in the win–loss standings.

Angelo, from Brooklyn, thought fast. He reported that he said, "Mr. DiMaggio, I would do whatever you asked me to do."

Joe was satisfied, and so was honor.

"Okay, Angelo, let's go to the Marriott." Joe had finished messing with Angelo's head.

At the Marquis, Sal greeted Joe warmly. "I'm Sal Ferrera, president of the school," he said.

"Well, Sal," Joe responded with ice in his voice, "I don't know if I am going to stay for this thing yet."

They entered the banquet hall together.

This was a big gala, in an elegant setting, a far cry from a gymnasium.

Looking around the ballroom, Joe was obviously counting tables.

"Hey, you've got a lot of tables here," he said to Sal. "A lot of people are coming. You must be making a lot of money here."

"Mr. DiMaggio, all of this money goes toward scholarship money for learning-disabled kids," Sal said in all sincerity, "because we have a special program called REACH. Kids who can't afford the program will get scholarship money to attend."

Joe was softening up.

Lewis Rudin, a prominent real-estate investor, developer, philanthropist, and president of Rudin Management, observed from where he was standing that Joe was being difficult with me. DiMaggio loved Lew Rudin, as did I, because he was the last of the stand-up guys in this town from his era.

Joe had great admiration for the entire Rudin real estate family in New York, especially Lew, the real Mr. New York. Lew had a heart of gold. So many people called Lew for favors, including me. On the very rare occasion he asked for an accommodation in return, the answer had better be yes.

One day his assistant called. When Lew got on the line, he said,

"Rock I know this is a real tough one to deliver, and I'll understand if you can't, but would it be possible to have my brother Jack bring his grandson up to the Stadium and be introduced to Joe?"

Lew was right. Asking Joe to meet someone was a tall order, but since the request was from Lew, it was worth a try.

When I approached Joe to ask him, I explained, "Joe, Lew never asks for favors. But this is his brother and his brother's grandson."

Joe understood. He wasn't going to disrespect Lew by making his brother look bad, especially in front of his grandson. DiMaggio appreciated the bond between grandparents and grandkids. "The hell with the parents" was his attitude.

He responded, "No problem, Doc. Have them come up to Steinbrenner's box this Sunday, and I will lay out the red carpet."

That's exactly what he did. Joe met Jack with a warm handshake and talked baseball with the kid in front of one of the Yankees World Series trophies. The boy was thrilled, his grandfather was even more thrilled, and I was relieved—mission accomplished.

Now Lew Rudin repaid the favor. He sailed right over to save my ass.

"Hey, Joe, how are you doing?" he greeted Joe.

"Lew, what are you doing here?" Joe was delighted.

"Are you kidding, Joe?" Lew Rudin knew what had to be done. "I would never miss this. It's for such a great cause."

Joe nodded in agreement.

"This is such a good thing that you are doing," Rudin added. "I'll be sitting next to you on the dais."

"Great," Joe responded.

Sal and I planned that seating arrangement. Joe had a long friendship with Lew Rudin. I was confident that he would never dishonor Lew by running for the exit. And more insurance was on the way.

Elizabeth Vargas, the news anchor Joe charmed at dinner, was now on site. She walked up to Joe wearing a knockout dress.

"Joe, it's always a pleasure to see you," she said to a beaming Joe, and then kissed him on the cheek. Joe's face turned bright red from this greeting.

"It's such a pleasure to see you, Lizzie," Joe responded with real enthusiasm.

"Thanks so much for doing this, Joe," she continued.

"What do you know about this award, Lizzie?"

"One thing I know is that I'm sitting next to you tonight."

Joe couldn't have been happier. Flanked by Lew Rudin and Elizabeth Vargas, Joe wasn't going anywhere. This wasn't an accident by any means. It was my form of a strategic naval blockade of the S.S. DiMaggio. Sitting between his crush and his prominent and highly respected friend and contemporary, Joe would not think of leaving the dais and heading to the Yankees–Mets game.

He let it be known that he did not want Governor Mario Cuomo to speak, a hardship for Governor Cuomo, who really loved to talk. Joe knew I was a big fan of the governor and his family. He had even called Governor Cuomo a silver-tongued orator and considered him a great speaker. But the governor would not have the opportunity to deliver a speech that night. Joe's demands were accomplished with the precision of a military maneuver. Governor Cuomo was seated in the corner near the banner for the school. It was a night I have tried to forget.

Joe entertained the crowd with baseball stories, remained gracious, and left at an appropriate time. He didn't say a word to me all evening, and left without even looking at me. He stared straight ahead just as he had with Mayor Dinkins and Governor Cuomo at the Columbus Day Mass fiasco at St. Patrick's Cathedral.

I called Joe the next morning to thank him for being there for the charity and to tell him what a hit he had been. Joe refused to pick up the phone. I tried several times, but he gave me the cold shoulder. And I mean liquid nitrogen cold. I had a one-way ticket on the Siberian

Express. I left a message that if he wanted to exile me, fine. I was left out on the frigid tundra for almost three months.

I sent word to Joe through his friends who were still in favor that I had done nothing wrong and would not call again. I had learned on the rough streets of Brooklyn that if you've done nothing wrong, you must stand your ground. It worked.

Some of Joe's friends told me that Joe wanted to speak to me but would not out of pigheaded pride. They said Joe was driving them crazy with his rigidity.

Mario Faustini and Nat Recine, the Westchester contingent of the Bat Pack, called me one day to get me to make contact with Joe.

"Rock, please call him. He is driving us fucking nuts and is not happy you haven't called him. Do it for us, please."

In the back of my mind, I knew one of these fellows caused the problem in the first place by telling the Clipper that the fundraiser was going to be a gymnasium function. I was going to let them deal with the consequences.

"Guys, call him for what?" I responded. "So I can get berated again for something I didn't do? Sorry, but he has to call me now."

I was digging in!

There was silence on the end of the phone.

Two weeks went by. I was working on a chapter of a medical book when the phone rang at twelve-thirty in the morning. I knew it could only be one person.

Without missing a beat, I answered, "Hey, Joe, how's it going?"

"Doc," he said, "I am flying into LaGuardia tomorrow. Will you pick me up?"

"Sure, Joe, see you tomorrow," was my response.

That was Joe's way of saying uncle, and I made it easy on him. When I picked him up at the airport, it was if nothing had happened. He didn't say anything about the exile and neither did I. I knew that, at this point, our relationship had moved to a different level. The bottom line was that we missed each other but wouldn't admit it. I think my time in exile made Joe aware of how much he depended on me and what good times we had together.

Two and a half months of Siberian exile, which I had tried to avoid since we met, made me stronger, because Joe had tacitly admitted that his treatment of me was wrong. There was a shift in our friendship. No longer worried about potential exile, I became much more outspoken. At the same time, I felt more protective of him. Lazarus had risen from the dead.

My very close friend and mentor Commissioner Fay Vincent always reminded me, "Rocky, you have a lot to offer Joe. Don't forget that and make sure he doesn't forget it as well."

I took the commissioner's advice and, as usual, it was right on the mark.

There is a happy ending to this story. Joe's sponsorship of the gala raised more than two million dollars in the next decade for Brooklyn's Xaverian High School. After his death, the Concordia Award was renamed the Joe DiMaggio Award and Gala with the blessing of his family. The gala became the keystone of the New York sports season for many years to come. At least my exile ended up producing a worthwhile charity that still honors the name of Joe DiMaggio. Future DiMaggio Award recipients included Luciano Pavarotti, Henry Kissinger, Regis Philbin, Rudy Giuliani, and Tommy Lasorda. That was worth my exile to Siberia.

SPEAKING OF HONORS, Joe DiMaggio was awarded the Jim Thorpe Lifetime Achievement Award in Los Angeles in 1993. He invited me as his guest.

When Joe was checked in and headed for his room, he stopped to have a few words with me.

"I hope you didn't forget your tux, Doc," he said "The Jim Thorpe Award is a big to-do. ABC is televising it live tomorrow night," he began.

Before I could assure him that I knew how to dress, Joe continued, "That guy who never ages—Dick Clark—is putting it together." Then he turned his laser on me. 'I hope your tuxedo fits. You've put on a couple of pounds since I last saw you in New York."

I was used to his digs.

"Don't worry, I won't embarrass you," I dismissed his nagging.

At that moment, we bumped into ABC sports broadcaster Al Michaels in the elevator. That broke some of the tension, as Joe was a fan of his as well as Bob Costas.

"Are you hungry?" I asked Joe.

"I could eat something, Doc. I haven't gone to Matteo's—we used to call it Matty's place—in over thirty years."

"What did you like about the place?"

"I used to love his escarole and beans," Joe said. He never forgot a good meal.

"Besides, Matty and his brother would sneak me in through the back door, so I could avoid all those Hollywood people. That way, I could enjoy my meal in peace. I sat at the table right outside the kitchen door."

I knew about that. I had spent a lot of time getting out-of-the-way private tables for him.

"I ate more meals by the kitchen door than you can imagine," he said.

"And so have I," I muttered to myself before I swung into action.

"My friends out here in Los Angeles know Matty Jordan, the owner, well. Why don't I give them a call and see if we can go there for dinner tonight?"

"Sounds great, Doc. Let's do it. Give your friends a call."

I followed the age-old Hollywood protocol. I called my friends, who called Matty for a table and told him to keep it quiet.

My friends picked us up to drive to the restaurant. A cell phone rang, and my friend passed his phone to me. Their son had gone to the restaurant to do recon and was reporting back. He had done us a huge favor and averted a major disaster.

Apparently, Matty had called his loyal customers to let them know Joe would be at the restaurant that night. He was extremely excited that the Clipper was coming home for dinner. He called the Sunday night regulars—Jack Lemmon, Walther Matthau, Gregory Peck, Steve Lawrence and Eydie Gormé, Don Rickles—to let them know that the Clipper was coming back to Matteo's.

Word spreads like a brush fire in Hollywood. Matty's little secret filled up the place. But it got worse.

"Listen, Rock, I thought that you should know this," Lloyd said, "I'm here at Matty's at the bar. The phone is ringing off the hook with people trying to get in tonight. I overheard Matty talking to Frank Sinatra on the phone. Sinatra wants to come over tonight, because he heard from Tino Barzie that Joe will be here for dinner. I heard Matty say that the entire Sunday night crowd is coming to see what happens when Joe finds out that Sinatra will be seated directly in back of him. They're expecting a showdown. It's the hottest ticket in town."

"Oh, shit. What am I going to do? If Joe bumps into Sinatra tonight, he's going to blame me and accuse me of setting the whole thing up. He knows that one of my dreams is to get them to reconcile before one of them dies."

Joe, sitting in the front seat, was oblivious to the panic behind him and clueless about what was going on.

Joe turned around to say, "I can't wait to have those escarole and beans. Matty can make them better than anyone."

We drove right past Matty's and pulled up in front of the Palm Restaurant.

"This doesn't look like Matty's place," Joe exclaimed.

"Joe, there's been a slight change of plans," I jumped right in, "Let's all go inside for a few drinks first. I'll give you the lowdown later."

"All right, Doc, I always trust your instinct with these things."

I got off easy. The fact that he did not object to the last-minute change of plans was remarkable. I was relieved that he didn't make a scene and that his trust in me was on display.

We entered the Palm where Joe worked the crowd and got to reminisce with Gigi, the famed manager of the restaurant. Even Mr. Baseball, Bob Uecker, came over respectfully to say hello to Joe.

"Let me tell you about my great-granddaughters. They are doing well on the school soccer team," Joe said, "I'm really proud of them, especially Vanassa. How about that second beer? Where did our waiter go?" Joe asked me.

I looked around for the waiter.

"They're even in the school plays. Vanassa is something else. I don't think much of the other actors, but . . ."

Joe stopped midsentence and asked me, "Okay, Doc, are you goin' to tell me what really happened tonight?"

I took a deep breath and gave it to him straight.

"Joe, my friends' son was nice enough to call me from Matty's to let us know that Sinatra was going to be sitting behind you. Sinatra heard you were coming to Matty's, as did half of Hollywood, because Matty couldn't keep his big fucking mouth shut. . . ."

Joe looked stricken.

"I didn't want you to be in the same room as Sinatra, let alone back to back with him. I know how you hate surprises."

Joe grabbed my arm. He had a look of relief on his face.

"Doc, you did the right thing!" Joe blurted.

I was ready for the outburst that was soon to follow.

"It figures! That Sinatra is a coward!" Joe began his rant. "He can't go anywhere without a fucking crowd. Sinatra needs all his Hollywood pals and pug noses around him just to face me," he continued, "and maybe just to look me in the eye. Lucky for him, Doc, because I would have kicked the shit out of him from table to table in front of all of his friends."

Everyone in the restaurant froze. I had never seen Joe lose control in that way in public. His animosity for Frank Sinatra was so fierce that he made a spectacle of himself. The full blast of his fury at the mere thought of being ambushed by his enemy for the entertainment of the Hollywood crowd was volcanic.

I thought maybe he was disappointed, because he couldn't get the escarole and beans he hadn't eaten in almost thirty years.

Joe regained his composure in a few seconds, which seemed like an eternity to me.

In the end, he was glad we headed the confrontation off at the pass. In gratitude, he stopped hounding me about my tux. He didn't get his escarole and beans that weekend.

JOE WAS NOT a fan of President William Jefferson Clinton. Clinton was the sitting president for much of the time that I knew Joe. I liked the president. He was a working-class guy, like Reagan, who never lost the common touch. He was charismatic, which is a two-edged sword. He was charming, and he could sell just about anything. Joe had his own reservations about "Slick Willy," as he referred to him.

Joe disliked President Clinton's lying about his affair with a young intern, but Joe disliked Hillary Clinton more. He couldn't fathom why Hillary didn't just dump the president. Joe figured that Hillary was willing to sacrifice her personal honor in the hope that staying with her philandering husband would help her career in the end. Joe believed that if Clinton had anything on his wife, he would blow her away. In either case, the breakup would be horrible. Having gone through one of the most sensational divorces of all time, Joe knew all about high-profile split-ups. Though he wouldn't wish the pain and invasion of privacy on anyone, he thought that Hillary should have put honor before ambition.

Since I had openly admired both Clinton and his wife in Joe's presence, Joe held back on his judgment of the Clintons with me. Joe was rarely moderate in his appraisals of anyone.

I found out about Joe's hostility over dinner at the Casa Rosa Restaurant on Court Street in Brooklyn. Joe loved the restaurant's homemade ravioli and roasted chicken made fresh by Lou Catuogno, the owner. The meal took him back to the days of his big family dinners with his mother's "famous" roasted chicken and homemade ravioli. An Italian man feasting on such a meal was a contented man. Lou would open the kitchen for Joe no matter how late at night. I would call Lou and put him on the phone with Joe, who would say "Lou, the Doc and I are coming to Brooklyn for your chicken and ravioli." Lou never said no to Joe.

In the lull after the delicious food, Joe decided to tell me a story about one of his encounters with President Clinton.

Cal Ripken was about to break Lou Gehrig's record for consecutive games played. Joe had been asked to represent Lou Gehrig at the Baltimore Orioles game. Who could better represent Gehrig than his friend, teammate, and locker mate, Joe DiMaggio? Joe was honored to be asked to stand in for the Iron Horse.

The paths of Joe DiMaggio and Bill Clinton would cross at the commemorative event.

The Orioles invited Joe to the game and sat him in a special box near the Clinton entourage. The seats in the area were filled with the elite of Washington society, because they are sports nuts, too.

An official from the Orioles came to Joe's box and introduced himself. The unsuspecting representative made a gracious offer.

"Mr. DiMaggio, President Clinton would like to come over to meet you and say hello," he said.

For almost anyone, it would be a rare honor to be introduced to the president at his request. Showing even more respect, the president offered to leave his well-protected box to meet and greet Joe.

In his inimitable way, Joe was annoyed to be bothered by the president of the United States during a baseball game.

Joe told me he said to the astonished Oriole official, "Listen, I met the guy once, and once was enough. Tell him I'm busy."

I was not entirely sure that blowing off and insulting the president of the United States was a wise thing to do, but there was no stopping Joe in situations like these. He was inflexible.

Joe didn't tell me how the president reacted. I'd guess that Clinton was more shocked than angered. The idea that Joe was busier than the president of the United States was ridiculous, though if you think about it, both men were just holding their hot dogs at an Orioles game. Clinton's hot dog and bun surely got roasted that day.

Joe did say with a sly smile that Clinton and his group did not get within a hundred feet of Joe's box seats.

Hearing the story years later was amusing, but I was not entertained when Joe chose to slight President Clinton again in my presence in 1998. Hell, the president is the president.

I WAS WRAPPING up a long day, dictating a diagnosis, when the intercom buzzer sounded. I tried to ignore it, but someone on my staff was not giving up.

I switched on the speaker.

"Okay, okay, what is it?" I almost barked into the intercom.

"Doctor Rock, It's a Walter Isaacson from *Time* magazine," my receptionist informed me. "He said that he has to speak to you immediately."

I picked up the phone and said, "Hey, Walter, how's . . ."

Before I could finish, Walter interrupted.

"Rock, I have fantastic news! You and Mr. DiMaggio will be sitting with President Clinton tonight at our Seventy-fifth Anniversary Gala!"

I didn't respond.

Walter maybe thought that I was overcome by shock and awe to be invited to sit with the president of the United States at a party attended by the most prominent people alive.

"Rock, you still there? Isn't that exciting?"

"Yeah, I'm still here, Walter. That's exciting all right," I said without much enthusiasm. "Let me give Joe the news and get right back to you."

Stomach churning, I dialed Joe's number.

He answered on the first ring and was cheery.

"Hello, Doc, how's it going?" Joe was looking forward to the party. "Do you have your tux and tie ready for tonight?"

There he was with the tux again.

"You know, me and *Time* magazine go back a while," he said. "I was on the cover twice—in 1936 and in 1948."

"Hmm," I said.

"I can't wait to talk about politics with Dr. Kissinger and Gorbachev." Joe was revved up.

"I gave Gorbachev an autographed baseball when President Reagan threw a party for the commies at the White House. In exchange I got a ball signed by Gorbachev and Reagan. Can you imagine, Doc, that I asked two non-ballplayers to sign a ball? I had the ball in my outer pocket and waited for the right time to ask."

All I could think of was how nice it was that Mikhail Gorbachev would be there when Joe roasted Clinton.

"Doc, Gorbachev specifically asked that Reagan invite me to the state dinner just so he could meet me. Can you imagine that?" Joe asked.

I had to break the news to him.

"Joe, uh, Joe . . . there might be a little change in plans for tonight."

Joe was silent.

"We might be sitting with the president."

Joe exploded.

"You know how I hate surprises," Joe bellowed into the phone.

"That's why I'm telling you now," I said, as I tried to stay calm.

"There's no way I am goin' to be seated with Slick Willy and that wife of his. His people will want me to smile and take pictures with him like we're the best of friends."

He paused for a breath, then started up again, "Doc, it's all for propaganda and publicity. I want no part of it!"

Not many would take sitting with the president and his wife as a death sentence.

"You tell that Isaacson fellow that we made a deal, and I accepted his invitation based on my sitting with you and the Kissingers. And that's where I will be sitting! Otherwise, I won't be going."

Then he smashed his phone in the receiver.

In rapid order, the following highly disorganized thoughts raced through my mind.

"Jesus Christ!"

"Do I need this shit?"

"I was minding my own business, and now I'm in the middle of an awkward and insulting conflict between an American icon and the president of the United States."

I picked up the phone and speed dialed Walter's number. Walter's assistant, Elliot, picked up.

"Elliot, this is Doctor Rock. Lemme speak to Walter."

Walter was on the line in record time.

"Rock, give me the great news. DiMaggio was thrilled. He was happy to sit alongside . . ."

I didn't let him continue. "Walter, here's the bad news." No need to ease into this. "Joe was furious. He is threatening to boycott the dinner if he's forced to sit with the Clintons."

After a stunned silence, Walter stammered, "Oh, my God, Rock, this is horrible. Horrible for the dinner, for the magazine. He can't offend the president of the United States like that."

"You don't know him, Walter. He doesn't care. If you press or try to trick him into it, he would insult Clinton in front of the national press corps, the Secret Service, the Marine Color Guard, and the Boy Scouts of America. Count on it."

"But . . ." Walter was ready to protest.

"Let me set you straight about something. He is the only person in the country who can blow off the president of the United States, get away with it, and still be invited a week later to the White House to attend a State Dinner." I knew what I was talking about.

Isaacson was still trying to reconcile what I had said with Washington protocol.

"But, Rock," Walter tried again. "You can't snub the president."

"Yes, you can, if you are Joe DiMaggio." That said it plainly. "The truth is that Joe couldn't care less about protocol, or who you are or think you are. He's going to call the shots here. It's his decision."

I went on to explain the particulars of the situation. Joe had accepted the invitation to attend the *Time* Gala with one major stipulation. He had to be seated with Henry Kissinger. It was a deal breaker. You could just imagine what this gesture did for Henry's ego. He was beyond flattered.

The musical-chairs shift wasn't going to fly with Joe. Joe asked Henry Kissinger to sit with him first, and politics be damned. Joe would have nothing to do with trading up or upgrading our table arrangement.

"Joe gave his word to the Kissingers to sit with them, and Joe's word is everything. He'll never buck a commitment to sit at a better table."

I had found this out firsthand when I was frantic about his not showing for the Xaverian High School scholarship dinner at the Marriott Marquis. His word was a sure bet.

There was still silence on the other end of the line.

"So, Walter, he sits with Uncle Henry or he doesn't show. That's the way he is. He watches who he sits with and won't break bread with someone he doesn't like. Dinner is sacred to him and has a whole other meaning."

Walter accepted he couldn't win this one.

"Okay, okay, but this is going to be tough to explain," he said.

I knew that it wouldn't be tough to explain, it would be impossible to explain.

The media took the final seating arrangements as a snub, when the real reason was very much in keeping with Joe's adage, "Loyalty goes up as well as down."

When he was asked, Joe told his friends, "I'm not snubbing the president. I have great respect for the office of the president of the United States, but I made a commitment to sit with Dr. Kissinger."

At the table, Joe asked, "Why did they seat Anne Bancroft at this table?"

"Don't you get it, Joe?" I laughed. "You're sitting with Mrs. Robinson from *The Graduate*." Joe got it and grinned.

"Yes, I get it," he said, "where have you gone, Joe DiMaggio?"

The *Time* magazine 75th Anniversary Gala was held at the only venue spectacular enough for the event: Radio City Music Hall, a magnificent art deco landmark. Among the 1,200 or so invited guests were the Clintons, the Gorbachevs, Muhammad Ali, Dr. Jack Kevorkian, Bill Gates, Lee Iacocca, and at one table, Mel Brooks, Anne Bancroft, Nancy and Henry Kissinger, Joe DiMaggio, and me. It would be easier to relate who wasn't at the gala than who was. This was the last great pre–September 11, 2001, gathering of A-list Americans.

After the showdown about seating arrangements, the evening started well enough. When the car carrying Joe and me arrived at Radio City Music Hall, we emerged to a tidal wave of photographers, cameramen, and reporters. Everyone, inside the hall and out, wanted a glimpse and photo op of the last American icon. Joe knew the drill. He stopped for a few photo ops without any reservation.

He turned to me and said, "It's amazing how all these people are here. They must be here to see you, Doc."

"I wish!"

Forty years after Joe retired from baseball, he still caused a flurry of excitement. People wanted to see him, photograph him, and shake his hand.

As we stood in the receiving line, most of the 1,200 attendees seemed to be queuing up to meet Joe. His line was at least one hundred feet long. Joe was beaming as A-Listers waited to shake his hand and get a photo with him.

Joe ate up the respect and the attention. He loved every minute. I stood off at his elbow.

"Doc, they would never wait in line for Mantle, Williams, or Mays," he said to me. "Isn't this great? I'm glad I came." He patted me on the shoulder. "Thank you, Doc, for twisting my arm to come to this party."

Twisting his arm? How about moving a fucking mountain?

Just that moment, Joe's publicity radar picked up a cameraman from *People*. He grabbed my arm.

"When that picture guy comes over here, take my bottle of beer from me and hold it," Joe demanded. "Can't have some kid see me swigging a beer in tomorrow's papers, huh?"

I was already holding my own bottle of beer just for show, because I actually hate beer.

"No problem, Joe, I'm sure that my patients won't mind seeing their favorite doctor with a bottle of beer in each hand," I declared.

Joe ignored my sarcasm and handed his beer to me as the cameraman shot the pictures. I wondered whether the *Yale Alumni Magazine* would run a picture of what looked like a double-fisted night of drinking on my part.

As soon as the photographer walked away, Joe stuck out his hand and said, "Okay, Doc, give me back my beer."

As we strolled around the party, Joe caught sight of Sophia Loren. He made a beeline for her and kissed her on the cheek.

Ever gallant, Joe complimented the legendary Italian beauty, "Sophia, you look like a million bucks!"

"Is that a compliment?" she asked in a sultry voice. "A million dollars doesn't buy a lot nowadays."

Joe blushed. All he managed to say in response was, "Uh . . . uh."

Sophia Loren sashayed away.

"Joe, you should have told her that she looked like a billion dollars," I couldn't resist sticking it to him. "It doesn't pay to be cheap with compliments. Who knows what could have happened tonight if you had played it right?"

Joe did everything to avoid being within photo range of the Clintons. It was the ultimate musical chairs. The president and his entourage moved in one direction in their attempts to get Joe and the president together in the same photo. Joe would immediately move to the opposite location. He pointed out to me that he thought it odd that a waiter was talking into his fork until I explained that it was one of the many undercover Secret Service agents protecting the president.

Another avoidance move was with the doctor of death, Dr. Jack Kevorkian. He wanted to meet Joe and take a picture with him. No way! The Clipper moved with quicker grace from him than he did from the president.

Being a germophobe and shaking the hands of hundreds of friends and strangers sent me downstairs to the restroom to sanitize my hands. A few minutes later, John F. Kennedy Jr. came into the restroom to wash as well. We had been introduced on a previous occasion.

"How are you doing, Rock?" JFK Jr. greeted me as we dried our hands.

"Fine, John. Your aunt Pat was just telling me upstairs that your magazine is going great. Congratulations."

I liked the young Kennedy a lot. He was easygoing and pleasant. Like his mother and his sister, he was a class act. I started to wonder how DiMaggio would react to meeting JFK Jr.

"Do you think that Mr. DiMaggio would mind if I introduced myself to him?" John inquired. John was aware of the history. "Just to say hello," he went on.

I had to give it to him. That was diplomacy in action. I thought that maybe Joe would be rational and genial. Fat chance.

"John, Joe is a gentleman. He doesn't hold grudges against the kids of people he has issues with," I explained. "If you treat him with respect and don't call him by his first name, he will be polite and charming."

I hesitated for a split second then agreed to check with Joe. When I went back upstairs to the *Time* lovefest, I figured what else could go wrong? We had already insulted a sitting president of the United States, so what could be the downside of introducing Joe to the son of the most popular U.S. president?

Sensing a possible frenzied photo op for the media, Joe dismissed the idea of meeting JFK Jr. with a perfunctory shake of his head. JFK Jr. and Joe DiMaggio together for the first time!

"If Junior doesn't chase skirts and takes good care of his wife, he won't have any problems," Joe predicted. "He's a nice kid, especially for that family. Sometimes the apple does fall far from the tree."

That was as gracious a comment as I could imagine from Joe considering his history with the previous generation of the Kennedy clan. But he would not agree to meet him. At least he acknowledged that his beef with JFK had nothing to do with JFK Jr. And Joe felt that JFK Jr.'s work for kids redeemed the young man. Little known to most people, Joe had tremendous respect and admiration for Jackie Kennedy as the mother of JFK's children.

When I thought it over, I had to assume Joe hated RFK more, because he believed that Marilyn was either more intensely involved with RFK or maybe that the attorney general had something to do with her death, as he had alluded to in the past.

At dinner that night, Joe told me that on Mickey Mantle Day in 1965 at the stadium RFK walked toward him and put out his hand to shake. Joe ignored him and walked right by RFK with a glacial stare. RFK was left with his hand extended in front of the SRO Stadium crowd.

WITH ONLY A few exceptions, Joe distrusted journalists. We were mingling in the press lounge at Yankee Stadium one day, when we had an awkward encounter.

The press lounge has a venerable tradition. Joe's usual vantage point was from George Steinbrenner's Owner's Box, from which the media was excluded. At the Press Lounge, reporters could "press" the athletes or other celebrities for interviews. In other words, it was open season if you made yourself available.

Joe DiMaggio took the job of Greatest Living Yankee seriously. He made himself available for public relations on behalf of the Yankees management, at least to a point. His current mission was to shut down Richard Ben Cramer, a Pulitzer-Prize–winning writer, who was working on an unauthorized biography of the Yankee Clipper.

Cramer, who reportedly got a million-dollar advance to sink his literary jaws into Joe's reputation, was stalking Joe and wanted to interview me. Though Joe was streetwise and appreciated tough journalism, he did not want to cooperate with Cramer. Joe made it clear to me and other friends that talking to Cramer meant Siberia. Cramer knew about the hush order.

Charlie Rose had given Cramer my name and told him I was one of Joe's legitimate confidants. I had managed to dodge Cramer until we met face to face in the Press Lounge.

Joe was concluding an interview in the lounge when his expression froze. He saw Cramer approaching the table at which we were sitting. Joe put up his right hand in a stop motion.

"I've got nothing to say to you, Richard Ben Cramer. Leave me and my friend alone," Joe demanded.

Cramer did stop and didn't say a word.

"Why can't you leave me alone?" Joe implored.

"Mr. DiMaggio, I'm just trying to do my job," Cramer protested.

"Well, go do your job somewhere else," Joe snorted. "Plus, you are interrupting my private time with my very dear friend, Dr. Positano."

"Oh, you're the guy," Cramer said, meeting me for the first time with an introduction from Joe himself. "You're the guy who won't return my phone calls." Cramer smiled and walked away.

Joe's radar antenna went up when he realized that Cramer had tried unsuccessfully on numerous occasions to reach me. He wasn't aware because I had made no mention of this to him. Why make him more paranoid?

"Doc, you did the right thing. Thanks for not returning his phone calls." Joe was pleased, then he asked me, "But what did you tell him?"

"I didn't tell him anything," I responded with annoyance. "I never returned his phone calls, Joe, remember?"

"You didn't say anything to Cramer or anyone else that I asked you not to talk to him, right?" Joe continued his Spanish Inquisition–like interrogation.

I rolled my eyes, and gave my last answer, "No, Joe, I didn't tell anyone that you forbade me to talk about you."

"Doc, you did the right thing." Joe praised me again. "I don't want anyone to think that I told you not to speak to anyone."

Of course, that was exactly what Joe had told me. Cramer's book was published a little more than a year after Joe died. Cramer did write a monumental book without Joe's help. I thought that he was only doing his job. In the end, I told him some good stories that put Joe in a very positive light.

Cramer encouraged me to write this memoir. He felt that sharing some of my stories of Joe at the dinner table would reveal a side of him that no one knew existed. As he told me, "Rock, yours is the real story to tell."

I told Cramer years later that under ordinary circumstances, which did not include his writing an unauthorized biography, Joe would have liked him and probably would have enjoyed his company at dinner. I had a solid sense of whom Joe would like, but more important, whom he would dislike and not want to be around.

THE ITALIAN GOVERNOR of New York fared poorly around Joe, but he was at his vitriolic worst with the Italian mayor, Rudy Giuliani, even though he was a big fan of Rudy for many reasons. He knew the mayor was honest and not full of it, came from very humble beginnings, but that isn't enough to exclude anyone, myself included, from a DiMaggio atomic-bomb detonation. There was no such thing as discrimination when dealing with a Mount DiMaggio eruption.

Joe asked me to join him for breakfast at the Gardenia Café on the Opening Day of the season at Yankee Stadium. Nick, our regular waiter, saw us coming in. He knew the drill. "Good morning, Mr. Di, Dr. Positano. The usual? A half a cup of decaf coffee with a half cup of hot water on the side, Mr. Di?"

"That'll be fine. How about a piece of pound cake toasted on one side on the grill, a bowl of Special K cereal with skim milk, and a banana?" Joe ordered his standard country-club breakfast.

I ordered what I've liked since I was a boy in Bensonhurst.

"I'll have a regular cup of coffee and an English muffin with grape jelly."

"So, Doc, another Opening Day at Yankee Stadium." Nothing made Joe more gleeful. "I can't wait to get out there and throw out the first ball.

"This is the only thing in baseball I look forward to, every year," Joe elaborated. "You know, I don't do this for Steinbrenner or the Yankees. I do it for the fans—the kids and all those families who come out to the ballpark."

"I know you love it, Joe," I said as I stirred my coffee. "I forgot to tell you something yesterday."

"What?" Joe asked lightly.

"I spoke with Rudy Giuliani. You know he'll be coming to the stadium today."

My nervousness was a dead giveaway. Joe looked up from his breakfast warily.

"What about the mayor?"

"He'll be bringing a proclamation with him that declares," I stopped for a second. "The proclamation will declare Joe DiMaggio Day in New York City," I eased into it. "Oh, he'll also present you with the Key to the City of New York."

"A key to what? The city! After all I have done here," Joe had shifted to high indignation. "I've spent my whole career here, and this guy is going to treat me like a first time visitor by giving me a key to the city!!"

I guess I should have known better than to think that Joe might be honored by the gesture. He could turn an intended honor into a humiliating insult.

"He should save his key for the mayor of Kalamazoo. That's who the key is for, a stranger. I'm no stranger here. I'm not a visitor." Joe was irate.

This was not one of Joe's better moments.

"Well, Doc, I am not accepting it. I'll give that key right back to him and tell him to shove it up his ass in front of 55,000 people."

Joe had lost it, though I have to admit that the idea was funny.

"Joe, I didn't know that you felt this way." I was contrite.

Still livid, he explained his outburst to me. "Doc, I have gotten so many goddamned keys to the city and lifetime achievement awards that I'm sick of them."

Then his focus shifted to me.

"No way, Joe, I had nothing to do with it." I denied any involvement. "But, I really have to get back to the office. I'll call you later."

When I got back to the office, I frantically buzzed the intercom.

"Please get me Beth in Mayor Giuliani's office immediately."

Beth, the Mayor's executive assistant, was bright and cheery when she got on the line.

"Hi, Doctor Rock, you and Mr. DiMaggio all ready for the big day at the stadium?" Beth asked, oblivious to what I was about to serve up on her plate.

"Yeah, Beth, I'm ready to jump off the upper deck."

"What's the matter?" Beth asked, a bit shaken.

"I need to speak to Rudy urgently!"

She picked up the panic in my voice.

"Well, he's in with his deputy mayors, but I'll interrupt him," she answered.

When Giuliani finally got on the phone, he said, "Hey, Rock, the foot feels great."

I jumped in without the small talk.

"Forget the foot, Rudy. I told Joe about your giving him the Key to the City at the stadium today, and he went ballistic."

"He what?" was the mayor's confused response.

"Listen, Rudy, you have to cancel the Joe DiMaggio Day or you might wind up with that big Key to the City up your ass!" I warned the mayor, "He'll think nothing of embarrassing you in full view of thousands of people. Believe me, you don't want to be the target of his anger."

"Christ, that would be a public-relations disaster for me," the mayor said. "He really is such an odd son of a bitch at times."

That observation was not news to me.

"Okay, Rock, Joe DiMaggio Day is officially canceled. Thanks for the tip."

"Sorry, Rudy. See you up in Steinbrenner's box."

Joe DiMaggio never got a Key to New York City, the city he adopted and which made him its leading citizen. Rudy Giuliani was trying to correct an oversight, but Joe thought himself slighted. Since the Key was first awarded in 1805, many outstanding out-of-towners such as the astronauts, the Beatles, war heroes in no fewer than eight wars, presidents, foreign dignitaries, and other people deserving respect have accepted the Key with pride. Joe chose to regard what is considered an honor around the world as an insult, because he felt that his very close connection to New York City was overlooked, making him no better than a visitor or tourist.

As I saw repeatedly, Joe's volatility and hotheaded reactions sometimes hurt him more than the recipients of his irrational anger. As my mother would say, he cut off his nose to spite his face.

CHAPTER 12

The Patron Saint of Kids

Tuesday, June 15, 1993

Took a ride with Doc Rael Positano to Long Island to see my six year old boy products at her catholic school. Said hello to him and other 5 and 6 year olders, girls and boys. "Doc" and I drove back. We stopped off and had a turkey sandwich. He is watching his weight and he is doing a good job of it — he wants to drop 12 more pounds of the 60 that he already has. I had been watching myself and I'm pretty much back before this last couple of weeks of stuffing myself. No candy — watching T.V. and no picking. I'll be buying dinner for "Doc" tonight at 8:00 P.M. after his office hours are done.

Positano came by at 8:15 P.M. Had dinner at Coco Pazzo restaurant.

Food 25.00
Tips — tea at 15.00
Coco-Pazzo 40.00

J oe had a soft spot for kids, any kids. His face beamed when he was with children. His charities centered on children. His hospital in Florida was a great example of such largesse. I witnessed his kindness innumerable times in public and private interactions. Joe lived this kindness every day.

Though he was estranged from his only son, he was devoted to his granddaughters and great-grandkids, and spent time in California seeing them. Not long after we met, his great-granddaughters, Vanassa and Valerie, were obsessed with the latest fad: Beanie Babies. There was a Beanie Baby shortage, and the girls enlisted Big Joe to find the Beanie Babies they just had to have. Joe would never let them down. And to whom did he turn to save the day? Yes, despite my crazy schedule, I became the leader of the Beanie Baby mission. The quest began when I visited more than twenty-five crowded New York toy stores in the midst of the great Beanie Baby drought. Joe even offered a signed bat for the lucky Beanie Baby seller.

I found a source for those little dolls, a guy who went around Manhattan and bought out the entire Beanie Babies supply to turn over for a scalper price. When I offered him a rare, signed DiMaggio bat, the Beanie Baby hoarder couldn't resist. Beanie Babies for a signed DiMaggio baseball bat might not be as sophisticated a deal as arms for hostages, but we did manage to get results. I had become the Dr. Henry Kissinger of Beanie Babies. The Clipper left New York with a healthy stash of Beanie Babies and was a hero to his great-granddaughters. I couldn't believe the amount of time I spent on this mission in Toyland, but it meant a lot to Joe, so I was happy to oblige. He would never disappoint his great-grandkids. This scored major points with him, establishing me as the ultimate go-to guy who delivers. Something so simple meant so much to him in his quest to make his great-grandkids happy. This was just as important to him as doing an autograph show that could net him hundreds of thousands of dollars. This is another illustration of what I loved so much about Joe. He had simple needs and required simple things to make him happy.

When the girls were older, we went on what I now think of as the CD Caper. We visited a Manhattan record store to find an album his great-granddaughters wanted.

A young African-American man recognized Joe as we stepped into the shop. "Hey, m'man," he announced, "it's Joe Di!"

Other young shoppers mobbed Joe. No one was old enough to have seen Joe play ball at the Stadium. The same was probably true of their parents. But he was still recognizable even to the kids.

A sales associate came over to us.

"Mr. DiMaggio, follow me, sir, the mellow stuff's over here. We have the best selection of the big bands north of 14th Street. It's right over there, past the escalator."

Joe shook his head. "I'm not interested." He was a little short with the kid. "I wanna see the rapper Coolio's latest. My great-granddaughters love him. The song's called 'Gangsta Paradise.'"

"That's the shit, Mr. D." was how one fellow responded to Joe's choice of music.

Joe turned to me and asked, "What's this fella saying?"

I translated. "That means, that's great stuff."

The kids congregating around Joe nodded their heads. They approved of his choice.

Joe loved the attention more from these kids than if all of the Fortune 500 CEOs were milling around him.

"They're for my great-granddaughters," Joe explained.

He bought the CD and tipped the sales kid twenty bucks. As a treat, Joe blasted the black rappin' anthem around town while I drove. My car was vibrating.

———

I WITNESSED EVEN younger fans react to Joe. We had hopped into a cab to visit the manager of the Manhattan Center Studio on West Thirty-fourth Street and Ninth Avenue. My friend was manager of the high-tech studio.

Joe secretly wanted to be a singer. During the '30s, he sang "Have You Ever Been to Heaven?" in *Manhattan Merry-Go-Round*, a film that was a musical revue.

We were met by a solid phalanx of teenyboppers, mostly between twelve and fifteen, as we got out of the cab.

"Hey, Doc, did you tell anybody that I was coming?" Joe asked me, assuming that the crowd was for him.

"Of course not," I responded. "Besides, this crowd isn't your fan base."

We walked parallel to the line of kids, solidly packed for two hundred feet along West Thirty-fourth Street. At fifteen feet, Joe was recognized.

"Joe Di, Joe Di, Joe Di," the teens began to chant. Joe gave them all a big wave and big hello. The crowd roared its approval and applauded. I guess I was wrong.

"Okay, Doc, I think you're on the A-List now, too." Joe had to get a dig in.

Inside, my friend, who was the manager of the center, took us up to Studios Four and Seven. These studios had the latest high-tech gadgets, such as the Neve board. Joe made himself at home at the equipment. Moving hundreds of buttons up and down, he was like a teenager.

"You know, Doc, my great-granddaughter Vanassa would love this."

"Mr. DiMaggio, you can bring her by anytime you want," my friend volunteered.

When we were at the Manhattan Center, Joe asked if the old ballroom was there. The Hammerstein Ballroom was very popular during Joe's heyday. We were taken to the famed ballroom, which now highlighted the music acts of the day. It was beautiful. Joe pointed up to the hand-painted ceiling. He remained mesmerized for a few moments while studying the same ceiling he had admired fifty years earlier. He gave us an art history lesson about that famed ceiling. I was impressed.

Just then a building administrator called to tell us that the Backstreet Boys were in the building, which was why all the kids were gathered below. The boy band learned that Joe was there, too. They wanted a session with Joe Di.

The Backstreet Boys were the idols of many millions of American girls, and here they were ready to fawn over a towering, silver-haired icon. I wondered how they recognized Joe when even their own parents had not experienced Joe's greatness as a ballplayer.

"Doc, why don't we take a pass on meeting these Backstreet kids. We can do it at another time." Joe seemed disappointed, but he wasn't feeling well.

We left the building to a repeat performance of teens for Joe.

"Hey, it's Joe DiMaggio," said one of the teenyboppers.

Again, youth prevailed, and Joe beamed at his happiest. I had seen Joe be glum around the wealthy and powerful men who celebrated him. I'd never seen his dark side when he was with young people.

SOMETIMES ADULTS TOOK advantage of Joe's love of children. Though Joe was aware of what was going on, he was never angry with kids who were fronting for adults. Kids could do no wrong in the Clipper's eyes.

Once at dinner, an adorable little girl approached us. Being interrupted while he ate usually got a rise out of Joe.

"Excuse me, which one of you is Joe?" the girl asked with Shirley Temple charm.

Joe melted. He shifted in his seat and bowed his silver head. "I am, little lady," he replied.

The girl brightened and asked, "Then can I have your autograph on this napkin?"

Joe took the napkin and signed it. Before he gave it to her, he asked, "Young lady, do you know who I am?"

The little girl smiled. "Yes, you're Mr. Coffee!"

Joe's face reddened. "Why would you want an autograph from Mr. Coffee?" he asked.

The child looked down at her feet. "I really don't know who you are," she confessed.

"Then, who put you up to this?" he asked as he glanced around the restaurant.

She came clean and rolled over on her grandfather. She pointed to the door of the kitchen. "My grandfather—he's over there, hiding behind the door," said the little girl. "He made me do it."

I heard a voice from the shadow mutter, "Shit!"

"Here is your napkin. Next time, tell your grandpa not to let you do his dirty work." He smiled at the girl. "Now go and enjoy your dinner with your family."

She thanked Joe. Joe gave her a big smile as she left, and she gave one right back. Joe could never stay angry with a child.

"I love the honesty of little kids," Joe commented. "Look over at the table now. She just got Grandpa in trouble with Grandma—that's the spirit! There's no way I could ever refuse a kid." He thought a bit more about the innocence of children. "Doc, ya know, kids will never hurt you or betray you. Only grownups will do that."

The hospital Joe founded in Florida came to mind. The Joe DiMaggio Children's Hospital in Hollywood, Florida is an enduring testament to his largesse and sincere concern for young people. I asked him about his involvement.

"I am really proud that my name is on that hospital," he said.

"Regardless of how expensive a medical procedure is, no kid is ever turned away from that hospital for lack of money. We wouldn't have it any other way."

I was impressed by his commitment.

"When you are driving down I-95 in Florida," he continued, "there's a big billboard of me cradling a baby in my arms. It says, 'Joe and the Babe.' Get it?"

I got it all right. I nodded with a smile on my face.

"That's how I give back, Doc," Joe said. "That's how I give back for my blessings. I wish everybody did the same—give back what they can. But most don't."

WHEN MY SON was seven or eight, I decided to bring little Rocky to the stadium to meet Joe. I wanted him to see the press box and other places in the stadium most people don't see. I know how thrilled I would have been to have an inside look at Yankee Stadium when I was his age. He had his picture taken with sports legend Mel Allen, Joe, and me. But the best was to come. Joe took Rocky into the offices of Jack Lawn, vice president, COO, and troubleshooter for the team, for a lecture on Yankee Stadium from its king, the Yankee Clipper.

Joe acted like a grandfather to Rocky. He insisted that Lawn take a photo of the two of them. When that was done, he took Rocky to the window of Steinbrenner's Press Box and put his arm around my son.

Joe pointed out to the field and beyond.

"You see out there?" Joe was pointing to left center field.

Little Rocky nodded.

"You see that fence out there? Well, that fence wasn't there when I played here. Instead, the fence was all the way in the back. You know how many home runs I lost because of that fence, Rocky?"

Joe didn't expect an answer and didn't get one.

"How many home runs did you lose?" Rocky asked.

"At least 150 to 200 home runs I lost out there," he estimated. "See, little guy, the players today have it easier than I did, but that was when I played."

Joe pointed to center field.

"Do you see center field?" Joe asked my son.

Rocky followed Joe's finger.

"That's where I played ball, way behind the fence you see right now. I used to roam in the back there, and there were monuments."

Joe continued to describe the field and what he did.

"There used to be a longer fence there. I used to patrol that whole area and catch fly balls, when I was younger." Joe finished up the tour.

Joe wanted to make Rocky's Yankee Stadium visit memorable. He was very successful. Rocky loves baseball, and Joe stoked that love. And the day wasn't over yet.

Mayor Giuliani came into the Press Box and was surprised by the attention Joe was giving to Rocky.

Joe yelled to the mayor, "Hey, Rudy, come over here and make yourself useful and take a picture with the kid!"

Joe ordered the mayor of New York City to take a picture with a kid he didn't know.

Rudy looked confused. Watching him, I thought he was trying to figure out why Joe was being so friendly to this kid. When I introduced him as my son, Rudy's disposition changed. He embraced him as a family member.

The photographer, Joe DiMaggio, took a great shot of the mayor and the excited son of his closest friend in New York in the Press Box.

My son Rocky will never forget that day.

Joe was doing his best to make me pay attention to my son. He knew how crazy and difficult my schedule was, and he wanted Rocky to get a sense that his dad was doing things in his best interest, and had an extremely stressful and demanding job. Joe understood the importance of quality versus quantity of time. He made sure that Rocky knew he was number one that day.

I'VE SEEN JOE treat obnoxious kids with kindness. One particular incident comes to mind. We were having dinner at Bamonte's on a Sunday night, which was rare, when a twelve-year-old boy approached. There was something off about him. The kid didn't have the guileless look kids usually have around Joe. The twelve-year-old held a piece of paper in his hand.

Joe noticed the brown-haired boy and smiled benignly at the kid. The boy had a smirk on his face. He didn't look like an innocent kid to me.

"I guess he's looking for an autograph," I said. "I'll politely send him packing." My sixth sense was rarely wrong.

"No, Doc. I know I usually don't sign them at dinner, but this kid kind of reminds me of my boy at that age, though that was a long time ago."

I got the impression that the boy was a creep, but Joe was convinced that the boy was sincere.

I tried again.

"Joe, I think that . . ."

But Joe wouldn't listen.

"I never refuse a kid an autograph. It's their pain-in-the-ass parents and grandparents that annoy me," he said.

"C'mon, son, want my autograph?" Joe asked.

"Not really, sir. I consider you one of the great athletes of all time, but . . ."

Joe realized that something was going wrong here and that he may have just stepped on a booby trap. His face had a pained look. He tried to save the situation.

"I guess you saw me play at Yankee Stadium," Joe said, as if trying to rally his own ego. He knew that the boy was far too young.

"No, but my grandpa did. He's a big fan of yours." He placed the emphasis on "he's."

Joe arched his eyebrows and asked, "Grandpa?"

"Yeah, I'm a bigger fan of Ted Williams. He was a far better hitter than you."

"Uh, well," was all Joe could manage to say.

The kid didn't know when to stop. Arrogant little brat.

"He outhit you really, really badly," the boy continued.

"Really? I didn't know that." Joe went on to explain. "Williams was a better hitter sometimes, but when the game was on the line, I was the guy you wanted in center field to lead the team in hitting, fielding, and base running . . . really."

Irritation was starting to surface, and the kid saw it.

"But I hear you made better commercials," the kid added.

I was powerless to stop Joe. Anything even half-complimentary said about Williams infuriated Joe even if the opinion was accurate.

Joe went on the attack.

"I was the better all-around player," Joe defended himself against this twelve-year-old. "I could do everything, young man—hit, run, throw, field. And how many World Series teams did Williams play on? None!"

Joe pointed to his ring finger on his left hand where he wore his first World Series ring from 1936. The ring, which had a little diamond in the middle, was so worn you couldn't read the writing. Joe waved his hand at this brat for emphasis.

The boy looked unimpressed.

"I've won nine different World Series rings. Williams has none!"

Joe was floundering in the face of the boy's indifference. Other diners were listening to Joe's defense of his record.

The boy shrugged his puny shoulders and said, "If you say so. Just sign here," then he went on, "Leave room for Williams. Just do the bottom."

Leaving room for his archrival didn't sit well with Joe, but he signed anyway.

The little boy said "Thanks, Mr. DiMaggio," and walked off to his waiting family.

Joe rallied and tried to salvage something from the insulting episode. He laughed loudly and said, "I sure straightened that little smartass out, huh, Doc?"

I thought that the little smartass had actually straightened Joe out.

"Doc, he was expecting a polite nod from me. Instead, I gave him something to think about for the rest of his life."

I wasn't convinced.

"The balls on that kid, Doc!" Joe exclaimed.

He shook his head and was checking for reactions from the other people at the restaurant.

I thought back thirty years to my own indifference to Joe DiMaggio. I didn't even like the Bowery Savings Bank and Mr. Coffee commercials. Young people are not impressed by former glories, a trait that is hard-wired into the species.

We had another memorable encounter with a pushy, opportunistic kid during a bad snowstorm. I have to say that Joe was kinder than I would have been.

Joe and I had planned to go out to dinner. I was at his place to pick him up.

"Doc, I love Lattanzi," Joe announced at his apartment that miserable winter day. "They make a great minestrone soup."

I looked out the window at the falling snow. It was slushy out there, the sort of dirty New York slush that clings to your shoes and pants. Since I was driving, I agreed that our usual jaunt to Bamonte's would be hazardous, a trip I didn't want to take with Joe in the car.

"I could use a bowl of his minestrone soup. It really sticks to the ribs." Joe was already planning his menu. "Besides, Eddie—the guy up front—always takes great care of us. Why don't we go there, instead of Bamonte's?"

"No problem, Joe."

I couldn't have been more relieved. Getting to West 46th Street would be a piece of cake compared to driving to Brooklyn in snow, slush, and ice.

As we left Joe's apartment, three or four school-age kids, waiting outside the building, followed us. They wanted autographs. One of the boys, who tailed Joe closely, was very aggressive.

"You kids should go home and get warm. Since you've been waiting in this mess, I'll sign autographs for you."

Joe took the time to stop in the winter storm to sign the damp papers they held out to him. Joe called Florida home. He wasn't used to the harsh winter weather and hated the cold. Joe always made fun of my lack of sartorial savvy, but he was so cold that he asked me to bring him one of my overcoats. I was flattered. Of course, he made a point of telling me that the overcoat was swimming on him, because I wore a much bigger size.

"Now, get out of the cold or you'll get sick," he said as a good-bye.

We got into the car and slipped and slid our way to Lattanzi's. Joe assumed his usual role as the designated backseat driver, as he barked warnings and commands to me during the trip.

Happy to enter the cozy restaurant, we handed our damp coats, scarves, and hats to the coat check.

Eddie, the manager, came over to Joe. Joe liked Eddie and greeted him warmly.

"Hi, Eddie."

"Mr. Di, I have a favor to ask of you," Eddie said as he was helping Joe off with my coat.

Still defrosting and anticipating the steaming bowl of soup he was about to have, Joe was caught off guard.

"Sure, Eddie, what is it? What can I do?"

"Well, Mr. Di, there's a little boy waiting outside," Eddie began his request. "He's been shivering in the cold just dying to have the opportunity to shake your hand and get your autograph."

"You're kidding me, Eddie." The thought of a kid waiting outside in the storm made Joe big-hearted. "Well, don't leave the kid outside. Let him wait in the front of the restaurant until Doc and I are finished with dinner, then have him come over, and we'll say hello to him."

Eddie went to see the boy outside in the cold.

We enjoyed our bowls of steaming minestrone. When we were done, Eddie brought over Joe's decaf and half a cup of hot water and I warmed my hands on my cup of regular coffee as I thought about the storm we would soon face.

Eddie brought over the little boy, who was wearing a rough hat.

"Mr. Di, this is so nice of you, to see this young kid, who was shivering out there."

I looked the kid over and realized that he was Joe's shadow from in front of the apartment building earlier.

Joe was no fool. He beckoned to the boy and said, "Listen, young man, it is not proper manners to wear a hat indoors. Now, take off your hat."

When the kid removed his hat, Joe recognized him.

"Hey, wait a minute," Joe said, "I saw you in front of the apartment building. I already gave you an autograph."

Joe softened a bit. "What are you doing here?" he asked the kid. "Why aren't you home studying?"

The boy did not respond.

Joe narrowed his eyes. "What are you trying to do, pull a fast one on me?"

I could see that the boy was crestfallen, but I had to put in my two cents.

"Listen, enough is enough," I began my lecture. "You've been stalking this poor man for the last week. Why don't you go home and do your homework?"

It was odd. The boy didn't react. He didn't seem to care that he'd been caught.

Joe looked the boy over, probably trying to figure out just what to do with him.

Eddie felt terrible about being bamboozled by the kid. He knew that Joe didn't want autograph hunters or uninvited guests brought to his table.

All around this was the sort of situation that would have irritated Joe. Eddie had bothered him the minute he walked into the restaurant. The kid had been actively shadowing Joe. No doubt, the boy was dropped off at the restaurant after tailing my car in brutal winter weather. That took adult organization. Joe's good-natured love of kids was being tested big time.

I knew that Joe would do the right thing. He had a lot of experience in situations like these.

"What next, Mr. Di?" Eddie inquired.

Joe gave the boy the once over.

"Well, no autograph." Joe was firm about that.

"Well what, Joe?" I asked.

After a moment's thought, Joe came up with a plan. "Eddie, lemme treat him to a piece of cake and a hot cocoa," Joe said.

Eddie escorted the boy to another table, where he was served the booby prize.

"Joe, that was really nice of you," I said of Joe's decision.

It was an interesting solution, but I doubted if treating that kid to cake and a hot cocoa during a snowstorm would discourage the boy in future attempts.

"Well, Doc, you can't blame the kid for trying. It was a good try," Joe said with a touch of admiration.

I thought that the little ruffian didn't deserve cake and hot cocoa.

But Joe was Joe. He was the patron saint of kids. I couldn't help thinking about Joe's lack of compassion for his one and only son. Maybe Joe saw his own son in the boy. Maybe unconditional acceptance of all kids was a form of atonement for one of the biggest tragedies of his life.

ON THE TOPIC of good parenting, Joe always complained that I never spent enough time with my kids, Riana and Rocky, just as he had done with his son. To help remedy the matter, he asked if he could host a pizza party for the kids and their best friends from St. Joseph's elementary school on 30th Avenue in Astoria, Queens. I was beyond touched by his desire to do something for my children. His offer was testimony to the strength of our friendship.

He showed genuine love and concern for my children. On another occasion, Joe had insisted on showing up at one of the kids' graduation from pre-K at good old St. Joe's. His attendance turned into a riot as he felt obliged to take pictures with many of the little graduates and their families.

I was late picking him up the day of the big event and, to make matters worse, there was a lot of traffic from Manhattan to Queens.

"Doc, I can't believe that you were late." Joe was fuming. "When you promise kids something, you'd better deliver. All those kids are waiting there at the pizza parlor wondering where the hell we are. And I have to say your being late is a reflection on me. Next thing you know, it will be all over the neighborhood that I kept kids waiting."

I knew that was coming. "Rock-bashing" wasn't going to end there.

"Plus, you don't spend enough time with your kids, Doc, so I am doing this more for them than for you. Next thing you know, they're off to college, and you never see them again. I don't want that to happen to you." Joe was speaking from experience.

I explained to Joe that I had no choice but to work feverishly due to my large school loans and building a practice from ground zero. I had no mentoring or financial help and actually worked during school at Tavern on the Green and Maxwell's Plum restaurants as the kitchen expeditor for Warner Leroy, which was against the rules. I didn't want my kids graduating with astronomical debt after they finished their education like their father. That major fear and concern drove me to work around the clock.

"Joe, I'm sorry I was late," my apology was required, "but I'm a doctor, and doctors do have emergencies. I had a teenager in the ER with a piece of glass in his foot. I couldn't just leave him there. I did take the Hippocratic oath, or do my commitments to you transcend that oath?"

Joe was dismissive, and cut me off with a hand slash.

"I'll tell you one thing. You are going to apologize to those kids in that pizza parlor," Joe commanded. "I don't want to be like your politician friends. They pay no attention to the outer-borough kids, only to the kids of rich Manhattan parents. Their parents can't write out thousand-dollar checks for election campaigns. This should be important to both of us. We came from poor families.

"These kids are forgotten, but I'm gonna remember them today. If they can't sit in Steinbrenner's box with me, I'm going to bring Steinbrenner's box to them," Joe defined his mission. "By the way, Doc, I don't always like sitting in that box and entertaining those little, spoiled Lord Fauntleroys, because their parents are big shots. I've wanted to give a few of them a swift kick in the keister."

"That's true enough, Joe," I agreed. "When I was a kid, I couldn't get within two miles of you. I could only see you on television, the Bowery Savings Bank, and in Mr. Coffee ads, or in newspapers. If you were to ask me twenty years ago what were my chances of sitting this close to you now, I would say that it would never happen." I couldn't resist a dig, "But they also say to be careful what you wish for, because you may just get it."

Before my barb registered, the ultimate backseat driver barked, "Watch that car over there, Doc."

As I dealt with the idiots driving around us, he went on, "You see, education is a great equalizer. You grew up piss poor in Brooklyn, right? But you persevered. You attended the most prestigious universities and got in on your own merits, not because you donated millions to the school. Now, everybody wants to be your friend."

I nodded.

"I had the same thing growing up," Joe continued, "we were so poor that I had to borrow shoes from my brothers. I never had new clothes before Major Leagues. They were all hand-me-downs. Do you think that any of those guys in Steinbrenner's box would have wanted to talk to me back then? There's no way. Don't think that I don't know that. I keep that idea in the back of my mind when I'm up there in the Owner's Box, and now they are kissing my ass."

While we were stuck in traffic, my daughter Riana was trying to ensure that everything was ready for the Clipper's arrival at Villa Gaudio, a pizzeria on 30th Avenue in Queens. She had a hard time convincing the owner, Sal Gaudio, that it had to be perfect, because Joe DiMaggio was coming to the party. Sal was dubious about a world-class baseball icon stopping by his Queens pizzeria for a quick slice and a Coke.

"Hold on, Riana. You're a good kid and all, but don't try that hard. You got the special room in the back for your party. You don't have to push this DiMaggio stuff." She reported what Sal had said to her. "We'd give you the party room no matter what. You don't have to make up stories. Why would he come to a pizzeria in this neighborhood, anyway? Poor working-class people, nosebleed and bleacher seats, pizza a dollar a slice?"

When Joe and I walked in from the street, Sal could only utter, "Jesus Christ, Mother Mary!"

"No, Joe DiMaggio and Dr. Positano," Joe shot back without skipping a beat.

"Mr. DiMaggio, the kids told me that you were coming, but . . . but," Sal started to apologize.

"But you probably didn't believe them. Remember, young man, kids don't lie. Only adults do," Joe preached on one of his favorite subjects before turning his attention to the kids.

"Okay, here's the party." Joe gathered the kids to him with a hand motion. "Before the fun starts, Dr. Positano has something to tell you kids, right Doc?"

I did what I was told. "Well, kids, it's like this. I'm sorry that I made Joe late. It was my fault. I hope you'll forgive me."

I turned to Joe and suggested we take a seat. Then I asked Sal to bring the pizza. The kids cheered.

Still doubting his eyes, Sal brought over a stack of pies to us. Joe jumped to his feet and gave a pizzeria speech to remember.

"Kids, I'm Joe DiMaggio, and many years ago, before any of you were even born, I used to play center field for the New York Yankees." His words were met with a booming response from the guests. "They were the best team in baseball. I played with the best. You name them. I played on the same field with them. Baseball was a real game then."

Joe gazed around the pizzeria and continued, "But some things never change. You should always pick what you love to do, not just like to do. When you find what you love to do, work at it. I was always passionate about baseball, and I worked hard. I had the god-given skills, but that didn't mean it was easy.

"Believe me. Your best friends are your family. Family is always first. I remember so much that my father taught me, and he is gone many years now. I still remember my mother's smile. It warms me to this day. So appreciate your family when you are with them and when you are away.

"Now . . . let's enjoy the pizza!"

The pandemonium that followed indicated to me that the kids wanted pizza more than the speech. To my amazement, Joe started serving pizza to the fifteen or so kids and pouring their drinks. He took pains to cut each slice right. One of the kids couldn't eat dairy, so he went back to Sal to ask for ziti for her.

Outside, a line had formed to get a look at the party, which was in the process of becoming a neighborhood legend. Joe noticed, and I could tell that he was getting concerned.

"Word got around about the party, Joe," I informed him. "All of Astoria knows."

"Forget about it," he responded.

He turned to grandfather the kids. "Hold it, kids. Don't eat the pizza until it cools down. I always tell my great-granddaughters, Vanassa and Valerie, the same thing back home. The cheese sticks to the top of your mouth. It can give you a nasty burn." Joe, the pizza server, giving the kids advice.

Sal came over to watch the festivities.

"Oops. Looks like someone's been making phone calls that I'm here having pizza with the kids," Joe remarked. "There aren't enough pizzas for those adults out there pressing their noses against the window."

"Mr. DiMaggio, I made a few phone calls," Sal 'fessed up. "It's not every day that the Yankee Clipper serves pizza pies and soda in my place."

"The pizzas are good, so it's okay."

Joe was in a benevolent mood. He turned his attention back to the feasting party.

"Kids, I want to tell you how proud I am of you. Remember this. Do well in school. Help Mom and Dad with the chores. Go to church. Do your homework."

"I really want to tell you how much fun I've had. I hope you'll have me back for pizza again sometime soon."

Joe posed for photographs with the excited kids.

"Listen, Sal," he said. Joe had this down. "Now don't put this picture in the local papers as an ad for your pizzeria. I don't want to see a picture of my head inserted into the middle of a pizza pie. But you have my blessing to put the picture on your wall. That's okay.

"So long, kids." Joe waved to the cheering munchkins.

As we were leaving, he said to me, "Thanks for taking me to meet the kids. It really made this New York trip special. Youth agrees with me more as I get older. I don't really know why—it just does."

He seemed very happy as we walked to thunderous applause through the amazed Queens crowd packed about six deep, outside.

In June 1995, my professional friends at the Neikrug Gallery were throwing me a party, probably in appreciation for the so-called Mapplethorpe transfer. I've never liked to celebrate my birthday, but when there was practice building involved, I was more than happy to blow out the candles on a birthday cake. Joe was in town for the party.

I thought it would be a good opportunity for him to meet my old friend Joe Piscopo, the comedian who was part of the *Saturday Night Live* ensemble during the Eddie Murphy era in the '80s and who now has a popular radio morning show in New York City on AM 970. He acted in many movies as well. He had experienced triumph and sorrows and had a tumultuous domestic life for a short time. Through it all, he kept a loving umbrella over his son Little Joey. Joe Sr. was a big fan of the Yankee Clipper, and Joe was a fan of Piscopo. In fact, Joe had liked a skit Piscopo did on *SNL* about Sinatra.

I wanted to invite the comedian and his son to meet Joe at my thrust-upon-me birthday party. Playing by Joe's rules, I had to clear it with him before extending the invitation.

"Joe, I would really like you to meet Joe Piscopo." I got right to the point.

Joe hesitated for a few seconds before replying, "Wasn't this the same fellow who had a problem with his wife some years ago because of a custody battle?"

His memory amazed me. Joe DiMaggio knew all about domestic courts, divorces, and custody battles. He worried about the effect of the court system on children of divorce, due to what he went through with his own son.

"Yeah, Joe, this is the same guy. He really wants to bring his son along," I said.

Joe seemed happy about the request.

"Doc, I would like to meet the guy and his son."

I asked Piscopo to come, but he didn't believe Joe DiMaggio would be there to meet him and his son. He thought it was a ploy to get him there.

"I promise you, Joe DiMaggio is going to be at my birthday party."

I gave Piscopo the address and hung up.

When Joe and I showed up at the Neikrug, we mingled with the fifteen to twenty business and professional people there. At first, the guests were hesitant to introduce themselves to the iconic Clipper, but they warmed up after I encouraged them.

Tired, Joe found an easy chair in the corner of the gallery and asked me to get him a beer. The gallery's collie-shepherd-mix dog came over and nuzzled Joe. Joe welcomed his visitor, because he didn't have to talk to the dog.

The doorbell rang and Joe Piscopo and Little Joey entered. As he looked around the room, Piscopo's eyes lit up. He pulled me over.

"Rocky, Rocky . . . I can't friggin' believe you. The last thing I expected was to walk into your party and to see Joe DiMaggio sitting in the corner with a beer in one hand and a collie in the other," he exclaimed.

I took father and son to meet Joe.

"Mr. DiMaggio, I have to introduce you to my pride and joy, my little boy Joey," were the first words out of Piscopo's mouth.

Joe instantly liked the young boy—no surprise there. He invited Joey to be his dinner companion and neighbor at the table. I watched Piscopo tearing up as he listened to the conversation.

"So, tell me, Joey, do you like to play baseball?" Joe asked in grandpa mode. "What teams do you like? What do you like to do?"

Joey had no idea he was talking to a legend. But the boy was game, and his answers were sweet and intelligent.

"You know, Joey, you've got a great dad there," the Yankee Clipper said, as he turned to Joe Piscopo, "you better be good to him."

Joe's words were encouraging to Piscopo, who believes even today that the icon's validation of his fatherhood was crucial in his recovery as a father after his divorce. For me, it was another example of Joe's devotion to kids as well as how stand-up guys stick together.

CHAPTER **13**

Winding Down

Wed. Thursday
Dec ~~to~~ 8th & 9th 1993 ?

Things getting away as I'm cramming in
more than I can handle and trying to
remember places and dates — Did not
keep up on the dates every day

J ust as Joe was unlucky in love, his relationship with modern American medicine was unfortunate as well. The surgeon who originally cared for his heel spur botched the surgery. The resulting crippling pain forced one of the greatest athletes of all time to retire before his time. He was open with the Bat Pack about another medical mishap. He maintained that during a 1988 surgery for an abdominal aortic aneurysm, the doctor cut a nerve that affected his sexual performance. It was a necessary and life-saving operation, and the surgeon could not be blamed. He was seventy-three, and his carousing days were over. But he wasn't ready to accept that. Women still found him attractive, and he was more than interested. By the time I met him, he was open to exploring ways to regain his past sexual performance.

The Bat Pack invited us for dinner at Campagna for what I've come to call a Viagra Session. Viagra was just approved in 1998, a year before his death. Joe was eighty-two the evening his friends set up a consultation with Dr. Commatucci and his bag of sex-function aids at the upscale entertainment hangout on Park Avenue South.

Dr. Commatucci, who I knew was reputable, was late. Joe became restive.

"Doc, where the hell is Commatucci? He knows that I am waiting to see his new toys."

Mario Faustini explained that the doctor was coming in from New Jersey and probably had hit traffic.

"You could be right, Mario, but you know how important this is to me. I mean, I have all these offers from pretty gals, and I can never do anything with them."

This was news to me, but the Clipper was sincerely distressed.

"Joe, did you ever think that they just wanted to sit with you and have a nice dinner? A little conversation," I ventured a different approach. "You always tell me that women are different from men. What's wrong with a nice dinner and some companionship?"

"Doc, conversation only goes so far. I don't want only conversation. I want a normal sex life. If I had a dick that worked for just an hour, I would be one happy fella."

When I noticed that a group of pretty young women began giggling at a neighboring table, I warned, "Joe, keep it down before all of New York knows about your sex life. I think those girls are listening."

"Doc, there was a time when I could have handled that entire table of gals," Joe responded wistfully.

Mario rescued him. "We've all heard stories about your carousing days."

"Enough." I wanted to stop the conversation from spiraling into adolescent dick jokes. "If you start talking about the size of Joe's joint, I'm going to crawl under the table."

"Guys," Joe agreed. "Let's change the subject. We have an audience over there."

The young women looked anywhere but at our table.

Not a moment too soon, Dr. Commatucci was escorted to his chair.

"Sorry that I am late, guys. You know the traffic from the tunnel."

"You're never on time," Joe snapped. "I don't know why I include you in my dinner plans. No one is busier than the Doc here, and he's never late."

Joe eyed the bag Dr. Commatucci was carrying and asked, "What do you have for us tonight?"

The doctor reached into his bag and pulled out a bottle of pills.

"This is a new medication—the vitamin of the gods—Viagra. Take one of these and Joe, you can say good-bye to your problems. You will be able to go all night long."

"I don't know." Joe's reaction was sour. "With all the pills I have to take now, it might not be such a good idea."

The Bat Pack protested.

As Joe examined one of the pills, he explained his reservations.

"One of my friends in the Bay Area took one of these jobs. He had a hard-on for four days. Eventually, they had to take him to the hospital. He was embarrassed as hell when the doctors and nurses had to examine his joint. I'd hate to make the news for that. What would my family think?"

"But, Joe, that was an exaggerated response." Dr. Commatucci tried to be reasonable. "That wouldn't happen to you."

He reached into his bag and said, "Here's something even better than Viagra. Look at this. A urologist colleague of mine, who does these procedures, lent these implant models to me to show you."

He fished out a penile implant model from his bag of tricks. The device had already started to grow erect. He handed the expanding device to Joe to the delight of the Bat Pack and me.

The women at the table nearby began to make exaggerated moans.

"Why are you doing this to me in public?" Joe was livid.

"Mario, you hold it." Joe tried to pass the penile prosthesis to Mario.

"Don't give that thing to me, Joe." Mario declined the offer. "I'm not the one who needs it."

He passed the prosthetic penis off to Nat, who looked terribly uncomfortable.

Everyone at the table, including me, passed around the portable, swelling prosthesis. It reminded me of the game we played as kids called "hot potato."

Joe put on his glasses.

"Give me that thing back," Joe demanded.

He made a very close inspection.

"Where are the balls on this thing?"

"Joe, it doesn't come with balls," Dr. Commatucci began his lecture. "You have to supply your own balls. When the time is right, you push this switch to inflate the implant."

Joe started to work the switch to the whoops of the women who were witnessing the scene.

"I've had enough. I am too old for this crap." Joe handed the device back to the doctor. "Let's eat."

It was just another night out with the guys.

Two days later, I read about the episode in the "Page Six" column of the *New York Post*. Fortunately, the piece just covered the "Viagra discussion group" at Campagna's. The inflating toy was not mentioned, to Joe's great relief.

I VISITED AN old-timer who was dying of cancer in a Brooklyn tenement, at the request of a good friend. I wanted to drop by to see how he was doing before Joe and I had dinner. Joe was at my office, and I told him I wanted to visit a sick, homebound person in Borough Park.

"I want to make a house call," I told Joe.

"You make house calls, Doc?" he asked.

"Usually not, but this is a special case and a favor for a dear friend. The man is dying, and he also has problems with his feet," I explained.

"Okay, Doc." Joe was far from enthusiastic.

I packed up some materials, and we left. I could tell Joe was uncomfortable.

"I grew up in this neighborhood we're driving to," I explained. "I want to do the right thing by them."

Joe turned his head to me and asked, "You say he's an old timer, Doc?"

"Yeah, and a World War Two veteran. Joe, he has a terrible foot infection and advanced prostate cancer. It went to his bones, and they don't expect him to live much longer." I gave Joe the sad prognosis.

Joe just nodded.

"Sure, Doc, the detour is fine," he said.

"His family and friends want him to be as comfortable as possible under the circumstances." I explained my mission. "I have to take care of a nasty foot ulcer for him."

"I'll take the ride with you to keep you company. While you're checking this fella out, I'll watch the car and check on my stocks." Joe was all in. "God knows what could happen to a nice car in Brooklyn."

We drove through an hour or so of commuter traffic, then through the potholed streets of Brooklyn. It was a perfect night for a mission of mercy—rainy, bleak, bone-chilling, and cheerless. We ended up on Fort Hamilton Parkway in Brooklyn in a run-down area of Italian and Latino groceries, bodegas, and shuttered, vacant stores covered with graffiti. The dying man lived in a walk-up over a candy store, which had seen better days.

"I grew up near here," I said, "It looks familiar and unfamiliar at the same time. I knew a lot of kids who hung out at this corner. Tony Danza, the boxer turned actor, used to hang out there. The candy store was the mall of its day."

The rain fell in sheets.

"Bought my Yoo-Hoos here, like Yogi wanted," I added with a grin.

Joe nodded. I think he was ill at ease to find himself in the marginal neighborhood. I expected him to be busy locking all the doors and windows. But he just rolled up the windows and took out his *Wall Street Journal* to read.

"I'm going up now," I said. "Parking is a problem, and I don't need a ticket. Thanks for minding the car, Joe. See you later."

Avoiding potholes and cracks, I bounded out of the car and splashed across the street. I went in the doorway, which had no lock, and probably hadn't had one in years.

Each floorboard squeaked as I mounted the stairs. From one of the apartments, I heard WINS radio playing. The odor of greasy food filled the stairway. When I reached the top of the steps, I knocked on a broken door. An old woman answered.

"Thank you, Doctor, for coming all the way here." She smiled in gratitude. "He's inside. The foot is bad, but the cancer is worse. My husband is very grateful for you to come and take care of him. God bless you."

She had an undeniable dignity.

When I entered the apartment, the old woman stopped to say, "He is so depressed, Doctor. He knows that he is going to die." Her voice dropped to a whisper. "When you see him, he is just skin and bones. No one comes here. Nobody wants to visit a dying man."

She looked down in sorrow.

"I keep mirrors away from him. We are just waiting for death to come to us one night," she finished her heartbreaking story.

There was nothing I could say to make her feel better, but I gave her a hug and told her how sorry I was.

The dying man's room was very dark with shades drawn as if attempting to keep death out. There was a small altar consisting of two lit candles and a picture of the Infant Jesus.

When Anthony, the dying man, saw me, his eyes brightened.

"Doctor, you coming here means more to me than anything. I remember your grandfather, Danny, the *becchino*, the gravedigger. We worked together at St. John's and Calvary cemetery. He used to talk all the time about your piano playing and your brother's singing—two good boys. We must have put thousands of people into their final resting places. Now, all I can think about is the grave someone is going to be digging for me."

The old man's memories and thoughts unnerved me. I looked around the room and my eyes lit on a photograph of Joe DiMaggio in his Yankee uniform with his mother. I pointed to the picture.

"Hey, that's a great picture of Joe DiMaggio. Where did you get it?"

"He was always my hero, Doctor. Before Joe DiMaggio came along, every Italian was a grease ball, a guinea, and a wop."

I attended to the bed ulcers, packing the sores, which were already putrefying.

"Just wait a minute, Anthony," I explained, "I'll be back with more packing. This ulcer is really bad."

Racing through the rain to my car, I opened the door suddenly and startled Joe, who was engrossed in his newspaper. He was wearing his lopsided, one-armed reading glasses.

"That was quick, Doc," Joe said, "Everything okay up there?"

I leaned into the driver's seat to get out of the rain.

"Joe, I just saw the most pathetic sight up there."

"What's going on, Doc?"

"A veteran is dying a terrible death upstairs," I responded. "He has two pictures in his room—one of the Infant Jesus and another of you with your mother near his death bed."

I watched how Joe responded to what I said.

"It would matter a lot to him if you went up to see him."

Joe looked out the fogged up window as raindrops pelted the car. I could understand why Joe would want to anchor himself in his dry seat.

But Joe, the stand-up guy, started to get out of the car without a word and tucked his *Wall Street Journal* under his arm.

"Okay, Doc, I'm coming, I'm coming," he said as the rain whipped around him.

We climbed the creaking and dark stairs and were met by Anthony's wife, who was astonished to see who was with me. I ushered Joe into the sickroom in silence.

Anthony could not believe his eyes. Tears rolled down his cheeks.

"Is it really you, Joe?" Anthony asked in a weak voice.

"Yes, it's really me." Joe was shaken. "What's your name?"

"Anthony. My name's Anthony. I can't believe that you're here in my room," he exclaimed.

"The Doc tells me that you're going through a rough time, Anthony." Joe paused. "I see that you have a photo of me with my own mother."

Anthony managed to nod.

"Mothers are so important, both our mothers." Joe was at a loss for words.

Joe reached into his pocket and removed his rubber band wallet. I had no idea what he was going to do. I watched him pull out a scapular, a religious icon of Mary made of white-and-green felt and covered in plastic. Old timers carried this sacramental garment in their wallets or tucked into their bed clothing. The belief is that if you have the scapular on when you die you will go right to heaven.

"Now here's a blessed scapular," Joe said as he handed the religious object to Anthony. "I carry them around with me."

Anthony took the scapular and kissed it.

"Thank you, I will treasure it," he said feebly and kissed Joe's gift again.

"Yeah, life can be pretty tough." Joe searched for words that would comfort the dying man. "But we never go it alone, Anthony, that much I know."

"Yes, I know what you mean . . . never alone . . . I'm not alone now." Anthony's spirits seemed lifted. "I could use a little visit from my family. You know, I visited them in better times."

"I hope things go better for you . . . you know," was Joe's awkward attempt to say good-bye to the dying stranger.

He pressed the hand that held the scapular.

"Well, Anthony, this will keep you company. Good-bye, Anthony."

"Good-bye, Joe, until we meet again someday," said Anthony.

"Yes, meet again," Joe said, pensively.

We said good-bye to Anthony's tearful wife and headed down the steps of the tenement.

Joe stopped for a second. Turning to me, he said, "Thanks, Doc, that makes me think a little."

We got into the car and drove down the deserted, dark streets of Brooklyn on that rainy night.

My friend told me that Anthony died a month or so later. There were no flowers, no gaudy wreaths at Anthony's open casket wake. His hands held a rosary and a scapular of Mother Mary. He was not known to have worn or carried one in life. They buried him with it.

ABOUT THE SAME time as the Viagra Session, Joe decided to revive his Hollywood career, much to my surprise. I never expected him to get involved with Hollywood again, but he was a card-carrying member of SAG/AFTRA. He committed to playing himself in what amounted to a walk-on role with star billing for an independent movie called *First of May*. The plot revolves around an eleven-year-old boy, an unwanted foster child named Corey, who runs away with a forgotten old woman, played by Julie Harris, to join a traveling circus, run by Mickey Rooney. Corey is redeemed when he speaks to grandfatherly Joe DiMaggio, as Joe DiMaggio, who sorts it all out for the boy.

In Joe's mind, appearing in this movie required even more preparation than giving a speech at Yankee Stadium. Joe's perfectionism required him to make sure he had it right. When he landed the part, the acting novice was compelled to over-rehearse his lines. I knew who was going to become Joe's understudy. It was my speech-writing days all over again. I was now headed for the movie set and directing.

"Doc, we gotta rehearse my lines," Joe appealed to me. "I gotta look good in this one."

Since Mickey Rooney and Julie Harris had both won Academy Awards, Joe did not want to look like an amateur. His demands to rehearse drove me to distraction.

We ran his lines in many places, including the fine restaurant Bravo Gianni in midtown near my offices. Gianni, an Italian-born raconteur and restaurateur, was thrilled when Joe and I appeared for lunch or dinner. Gianni seated us at a booth right off the entrance—the DiMaggio Booth—next to the antipasto display, which featured platters of

Italian cold-meat delicacies and plates of heaping vegetables and salads. Since Joe was too self-conscious to be overheard, I asked Gianni to keep the neighboring tables clear. He didn't know that the reason for the request was to give the DiMaggio Neighborhood Players privacy.

I would read the part of Corey, the troubled youth, and Joe would play the Great DiMaggio. Then we would reverse roles. Corey was performed in a falsetto, and Joe would respond in a deep voice. To the consternation of Gianni, a middle-aged man and an old man were taking turns speaking in high-pitched voices in the front of his restaurant. He hid behind the provolone and soppresatta trying to make something out of what was going on. The falsetto voices threw him.

Weeks passed before I explained what was going on, to Gianni's great relief.

I had often asked Joe which actors he felt would best play him one day in a movie or show. He said Frank Langella, Al Pacino, or Tom Hanks. Not bad choices.

I am sorry to say that the film opened in March 1999, just weeks after Joe's death.

When Joe came to New York in June 1998, he decided to extend his visit. I now know why. Joe was aware that his health was failing. I had noticed a real downturn in his physical condition, but we did not discuss it. He had lost weight and was always short of breath. He didn't have the stamina to follow his normal New York schedule.

I was turning forty in a few weeks, and Joe decided to make this birthday memorable. Two of my friends from California were going to be in town. They suggested that Joe and I join them at the Friars Club for a birthday celebration. Though Joe was usually withdrawn around people he didn't know well, he was comfortable with these folks. They were excited about his joining us at the club. My birthday was a week off, but it was close enough for Joe.

Joe's pending appearance was telegraphed through the Friars Club grapevine. As a result, the attendance that night was greater than usual and significantly more intense.

Joe always said that the greatest gift you could ever give someone was your time, and that receiving such a gift was equally valuable. Jewelry, cars, furs were all great gifts, but Joe believed that these things paled when you gave your time. That evening at the club, Joe told me that his time with me was more valuable than anything else.

Joe had never said anything like this to me before. He was never an expressive man, except perhaps in anger. He wasn't known for the grand gesture, or any gesture at all. I was moved to tears. It was beginning to feel like Joe's final curtain call.

When he stood, Joe silenced the room, as only Joe could get the attention of powerful and wealthy people. He began to sing "Happy Birthday" to me. This was an exceptional moment at the Club, and a rare event in the life of Joe DiMaggio. Those who saw him as a taciturn, inexpressive man would have been shocked to witness him sing to a packed room. His dusky, low rendition of "Happy Birthday, Doc" brought down the house. At the end of this extraordinary performance, Joe looked me straight in the eye and winked.

As one never at a loss for words, I just choked up. All I could manage to say was "Joe, thanks so much for singing 'Happy Birthday' to me." I was totally inarticulate.

Joe had broken his ironclad rule of not drawing attention to himself, just to honor me, and did so knowing that this celebration would be unusually public and very special to me. My California friends were flabbergasted. They knew that Joe was too private to engage so openly in such sentimentality, too difficult to arouse socially, and just plain difficult, even by Hollywood standards.

After we said our goodnights, Joe took me aside and said, "Well, Doc, I hope we can do this again. I hope that we'll have another opportunity to sing 'Happy Birthday.'"

We both knew that this was the last time we would celebrate my birthday together.

Joe could be the center of attention at the Friars Club, but I'll always consider his appearance at the New York Stock Exchange a prime example of the DiMaggio Effect. I had been impressed by Joe's daily devotion to reading the *Wall Street Journal* and *New York Times* stock news every day and thought the Wall Street–savvy baseball player would enjoy a visit. I asked Carl Frederickson, a trader/executive for the New York Stock Exchange, who is a patient, for permission to visit with my friend Joe DiMaggio.

He thought I was joking at first, but when he realized I was serious, he reached out to the president of the NYSE, Billy Johnson, to arrange a tour. The plan was for Joe, his granddaughter Paula, his great-granddaughter Vanassa, and me to visit the Stock Exchange at eleven on a Tuesday morning. We were met by Billy Johnson, Carl Frederickson, and a crowd of executives and security, who were all starstruck by the Clipper. After Joe autographed baseballs for about thirty minutes, we were escorted to the floor of the Exchange. It was a madhouse as Wall Street used to be before everything was computerized. We entered the Garage, one of the four trading rooms.

Joe's presence immediately suspended trading. Everyone on the floor, who would usually be yelling, screaming, and listing trades—and I mean every sex, color, and ethnicity—gathered around the Clipper. Though he was the tour guide, Frederickson disappeared from view in the crush around Joe.

"The love for Joe was incredible," Frederickson said to me many years after the event, "and a memory I will never forget."

According to press reports, Joe made a habit of disrupting trading. Trading on the Chicago Stock Exchange halted for fifteen minutes when he was there. He even got to ring the opening bell.

One day, during his extended trip, we were enjoying another great meal at Bravo Gianni. I asked him what TV shows he watched in Florida.

Joe didn't have to think it over long. "Doc, my favorite TV guys are that Tim Russert fellow and Charlie Rose."

The mention of Rose sparked a connection.

"Both great guys," I agreed. "Joe, Rose has been dying to get you on his program just to talk about baseball—nothing else."

I knew Joe would have reservations.

"Doc, I'm afraid I might screw up," he confessed, "I may forget what I want to say and look like a fool in front of millions of people."

"That wouldn't happen with Charlie," I started my pitch. "He tapes the show and then edits it. If there were any gaps, he would edit them out. Your baseball stories are priceless."

And then I went too far when I said, "Joe, not everyone is interested in Marilyn."

Joe glowered, and slammed his hand on the table.

"That wasn't called for, Doc. This lunch is gonna end real soon if you keep this up."

"Joe, I'm sorry." I was sincerely apologetic. "I just feel sometimes you overdo it."

By this point in our friendship Joe knew that I had his interests at heart. I was no longer the victim of his temper tantrums, and exile was not on the table.

"Why don't you let me call Charlie?" I suggested. "We'll go visit him together on his set. You can just sit and talk with him and see how you feel. You're not making a commitment."

Joe had become even more interview-phobic in his later years. He chewed on his bottom lip as he considered my suggestion. I knew him well enough to see when he had broken through his hesitation. The tension drained out of his shoulders and a small smile formed on his lips.

"Doc, do you remember that I signed a ball for Charlie?" he asked. "I wrote, 'For Charlie Rose, the best of the best.'" Joe's infallible memory was replaying his interactions with Charlie. "Charlie was touched. I was comfortable with him the day we had lunch with him here at Gianni. Not a single one of his questions was off base."

I had completely forgotten that meeting.

"Tell you what, Doc, I'll give Charlie a call and ask if we can stop by later."

Joe had decided Charlie Rose was in the positive column.

I sprang from my chair near the sausages, provolone, and vinegar eggplant and grabbed Gianni.

"Gianni, posso fare una telefonata?"

Startled by my urgency, Gianni produced the phone *pronto*.

"Charlie, it's Rock," I said when my call was put through.

"Hey, buddy, where are you?" Rose asked.

"Charlie, I'm here with Joe Di at Gianni's. Joe wants to know if we can come over and look at your set and sit with you a while?"

"He *what*?" Rose couldn't have been more enthusiastic. The prospect of having an exclusive interview with the greatest athlete of all time was a once-in-a-lifetime opportunity.

"Charlie, I mean exactly what I said. I want to see if he will sit with you at your famous interview table. Maybe if he warms up, we can roll the tape while you're talking to him."

Charlie got right on it.

"Rock, let me call up the producer and the set people. I'll be at the studio in ten minutes!"

I hurried back to the table to give Joe the news. I had to play this right.

"Doc, what did he say?"

"He said that he's very busy, Joe. He'll try to make time to sit with you on his set. He can't leave the studio, because he's taping all day. We probably will have to sit in there with him."

Though I stretched the truth a bit, I knew what would appeal to Joe.

"Doc, is he that busy?" Joe asked.

"Yeah, Joe, but he feels obligated and wants to repay your kindness after you signed that ball for him."

"C'mon, Doc, let's get over there before he gets busy interviewing another guest." Joe was actually eager to go to the studio. "You know, my granddaughters are big fans of his. Think I can take a picture with him at his interview table?"

After we finished lunch, we grabbed a cab to the studios on Park Avenue, where Rose taped his shows. Excited producers met us in the lobby and brought us up to the studio. When the elevator doors parted, Charlie Rose was there to greet us.

"Joe, it's great to see you," Rose exclaimed.

"You too, Charlie. I know how busy you are today. I hope you don't mind us dropping by to say hello." I could see that Joe was uneasy, but he could not have had a warmer welcome.

"Charlie, why don't we go onto your set and sit down there," I suggested. "That way we won't interfere with your work."

"That's a great idea, Doc!" Rose concurred.

As we followed Rose to the set, he introduced us to his colleagues along the way, each excited to meet Joe, which made him buoyant. On the set, Joe took his seat at the interview table next to me. Rose sat opposite us.

The TV host swung into action.

"Joe, what have you been doing with your spare time?" he asked to warm Joe up.

"I've got a lot going on," Joe replied with a grin. "My great-grandkids keep me pretty busy when I'm out in San Francisco."

Rose grinned.

"Have you seen Ted Williams lately?" Rose got right to a sore spot.

"Ted and I talk every once in a while. He is closer to my brother

Dominic, who was his teammate." Joe tried to sidestep the question. "I like Ted, but we really don't have very much in common any more."

Rose was ready to pounce, in a nice way, at that opening.

"Was that always the way with you and Ted?" Rose pressed.

I could feel Joe drawing back.

"Charlie, we were fierce competitors back in our playing days. He was obsessed with me during my hitting streak in 1941. He used to have a kid stay behind the scoreboard at Fenway Park to give him updates about my streak. He wanted to know if I got a hit at my last at-bat. People would see him kicking the grass for what appeared to be no reason at all when he was in the outfield. He was just reacting when he learned that I had another hit to keep the streak going."

Rose was greatly amused by Joe's answer, so he followed up and asked, "Did you ever talk to each other off the field that year?"

"I made it a point not to fraternize with the opponent," Joe explained. "Taking a picture with them in uniform for the league was one thing. Having a beer with them after the game was another. It would have taken away my edge a bit."

Rose nodded.

"If you like someone, you feel sorry for them," Joe continued. "The last thing I wanted to do was to feel sorry for an opponent. It could make a big difference if you had to break up a double play by sliding into second and take out the shortstop or second baseman."

Encouraging Joe to go on, Rose nodded again.

"It was no different for my brother Dominic," Joe went on. "He played with Ted. When we played those big Yankee–Red Sox series games, I wouldn't even say hello to him on the field. I didn't care that my mother and father were in the stands watching their two sons playing against each other. He was no brother of mine when he put on his uniform," Joe finished up.

"How is life today for Joe DiMaggio?" Rose then asked.

"Charlie, the last ten years of my life have been my happiest," Joe said without hesitation. "I have great-granddaughters I adore. I have great friends like the Doc, who are loyal, and we have fun. I've put to rest other issues that may have been bothersome to me in the past. I come and go as I please, and I answer to no one."

Joe's words made me beam with pride. I took a leap and asked, "Joe, why don't you let Charlie roll the tape? You're having a good time, aren't you?"

Charlie could not mask how much he wanted to get Joe on tape.

Joe gave a shy but aware smile. He knew what was going on. I interpreted that smile to mean that no interview would be taped that day.

"Oh, come on, Doc, I really don't have anything interesting to say." His response was not falsely humble. He meant what he said.

"Now that I've been up here, I will seriously consider it," he softened his refusal.

Charlie and I both smiled.

"Charlie, you would be the guy I'd sit down with a talk to about baseball. My granddaughters watch your show every night. They would be thrilled to see me talk at this table with you." Then he asked, "Would you mind taking a picture with me that I can send to them?"

"Sure, Joe," Rose replied.

The network photographer took pictures of Rose and Joe grinning at the table.

"Doc will call you with a date when I'm coming in," Joe promised.

"That would be great. I'll look forward to it." Rose was pleased with the outcome. "Let me walk you guys down."

We went down to the street, where Rose hailed a cab for the Yankee Clipper and me.

"Take him to Sixty-eight and Fifth. Take care of my good buddy!" Rose instructed the cabbie.

Joe gave Rose a big smile and waved through the cab window. Shaking his head in disbelief about what had transpired that afternoon, Rose stuck around to see our cab drive off.

There never was a formal interview. No cameras rolled that day or any other, because this was Joe's last trip to New York. The greatest sports interview would never air. I consider it a great loss.

JOE FELT AT home on Broadway. The bright lights and the lines of people waiting to see shows always cheered him up. He liked to drive through Times Square to relive his golden years. He remembered Toots Shor's place, dancing girls, openings he'd attended with his good friend, legendary ticket-master George Solotaire, and the lyrics to Broadway tunes. Joe entertained me with Broadway's greatest hits, from *The King and I* to *Annie Get Your Gun*. He knew the lyrics to everything and had a decent voice. Seeing a billboard for a revival would prompt him to break into song. One night, husky-voiced Joe piped up with his own rendition of "Old Man River."

"What's so special about that song to you?" I asked.

"That song is all about life, Doc, it sums it all up. That Old Man River keeps on rollin' no matter what happens. Life goes on, no matter what. It goes on without you, and you can't change things."

As we drove east on West 44th Street toward the central hub of Times Square, I glanced up and saw a huge billboard featuring Marilyn Monroe in really tight jeans. I panicked that he would get a glimpse of his lost love spotlighted for the world to see in his Times Square. When he didn't say a word, I thought he hadn't noticed.

Joe remained quiet for a time and then said, "Yeah, let me tell you something, Doc. They've got Marilyn up there wearing those tight jeans, but I've got to tell you she looked a helluva lot better with the jeans off than she did with the jeans on."

I was touched. Joe didn't make many goddess tributes to Marilyn.

"Let's go down 44th Street again," Joe said with a sly smile. He wanted to have another look at Marilyn's derriere.

CHAPTER 14

Swinging in Coney Island

Saturday, Nov, 7, 1992

It was a refreshing afternoon for me, to talk to somebody who shared those years with me and memories of our dear friends. (George Solitere stood Shot etc. to many to name.

J oe was in good form one bright summer day and wanted to get out of Manhattan.

We decided to go for a ride in the late afternoon. I had mentioned to Joe weeks earlier that I was asked to play in the Artists and Writers celebrity softball game in the Hamptons. It had been a long time since I played ball. I didn't tell Joe that I needed to brush up on the finer points of the game, especially hitting, but I knew my friend and his memory well.

I picked him up in front of 860 Fifth Avenue with my assistant Marco Solis, a loyal friend for years, who came from Guatemala to make a better life for his family. Marco helped Joe in New York City as Joe was having more difficulty walking and managing the city. Joe trusted Marco's driving and liked him as a person.

After he was in the car, I made a suggestion.

"Joe, let's go slide by Coney Island. I loved that place when I was a kid." I did have an ulterior motive.

"Coney Island—haven't been there for a while, either. Okay, let's get there in one piece," Joe, the inveterate backseat driver, warned.

As we drove through lower Manhattan, the sun was just beginning to set.

"Doc, I know you've got that big celebrity softball game out on Long Island next month in the Hamptons," he remarked. Just as I expected, he hadn't forgotten my offhand comment from weeks earlier.

"I don't want you to make a fool of yourself, and I don't want to get a bad name."

My confusion must have shown on my face. I wondered what embarrassing myself by bombing out had to do with him.

"Doc," he went on to explain, "those fancy people all know that you and I are close pals. If you screw up, it's a bad reflection on me."

"Thanks, Joe, that is very reassuring" was all I could say.

Oblivious to my sarcasm, he continued, "Ya know, Doc, I always said that a little coaching helps no matter how good you are. McCarthy, the manager of the Yankees, who won seven World Series, always reviewed the finer points of the game with me."

Then Joe delivered an insight that made me look at sports differently—all sports, not just baseball.

"Did you know, Doc, that most games are won or lost because of mental errors—the wrong cut-off guy, not thinking before throwing the ball, forgetting how many outs there were?"

"Yeah, Joe?" I wanted to hear more.

Joe gazed out the car window and continued, "I may or may not have been the most physically gifted athlete, like Ted Williams or Hank Greenberg, but one thing I had over everybody else was my brains. I was a thinking ballplayer, and that's what made me stand out. I made very few mental errors," Joe finished enlightening me.

What he said seemed profound to me. Of course, sports were at least as much mental as physical. Joe DiMaggio, the greatest athlete of the last century and maybe all time, was squarely placing his vote for mental agility

We hit some traffic on Surf Avenue in Brooklyn. As Marco took a small detour, Joe studied the neighborhood and saw the sign for Nathan's Famous approaching.

"Hey, Doc, look over there. It's Nathan's. It hasn't changed a bit since I was here over fifty years ago. Let's stop for a hot dog and some of those great French fries."

I started to envision Joe's swollen ankles from the high salt content.

I loved Nathan's and was happy to stop. We ordered several hot dogs each and a serving of fries. We stood at the stainless steel tables devouring the Coney Island delicacies. Joe made sure we brought Marco some hot dogs, too. He doted on him and appreciated him. He took pictures with Marco and signed baseballs and pictures without hesitation.

I was ready to put my plan into action. There was a nearby batting cage concession, which was down the garish strip of fading amusement rides and honky-tonk tourist traps.

"I have an idea," I said to my unsuspecting friend. "How about some batting practice?" I had often dreamed about getting hitting instruction from one of the best players who every played the game.

"I'm sure you could use it," Joe said. "I'll give you some pointers."

I brought Joe to the cages where an attendant met us. The kid was clueless as to the identity of this old man.

"Thanks, young man," Joe responded. "We have some work to do here tonight. I don't want the Doc to make a fool of himself next month at a big celebrity charity game. He'll never hear the end of it, and neither will I."

Sunset bathed the boardwalk in a golden light, the perfect illumination for what was about to happen. The smell of cotton candy being spun in ancient, dinky vats, the greasy smell of fries and grilled hot dogs, and the laughter of kids and grownups created the perfect atmosphere for Joe's last time at bat in New York. I was still pinching myself. Wake up!

I looked at the forlorn, rusting tower of the parachute ride in weed-riddled Steeplechase Park and remembered better days. Judging from the way Joe was looking around, I'm sure he did, too.

Disco music blared from the batting-cage speakers. One look at Joe's face was enough for me to return to the car for Joe's favorite Glenn Miller CD. Marco pulled it out of the CD holder. I slapped the kid attendant a twenty to put on the Glenn Miller CD. Joe smiled, mellow again.

I entered the batting cage feeling extremely self-conscious. Though I had been a good ballplayer, hitting under the scrutiny of the greatest mental and physical athlete of all time made me more than a little uncomfortable. All I could think about was my mother telling Joe Di in my waiting room what a great baseball player I was. I took the stance at the mechanical home plate expecting to humiliate myself.

Joe was watching with a big grin on his face. He was having a great time. "Doc, let me see you hit a few before I tell you how lousy you are," he called out to me.

Now, that was encouraging.

"Jesus Christ, I feel like an altar boy reciting the Latin Mass in front of the Pope," I said to Joe's further amusement.

The pitches started coming, and to my surprise, I hit the ball with power and confidence. I didn't think I'd do so well. I beamed proudly with every hit.

Joe was not impressed. Twenty pitches from the robot arm, and I had hit most, if not all, of them.

Nope, Joe was not impressed, and he had to say so. "Ya think you're doing good, huh, Doc? It's easy to hit a pitch when you know where and when it's coming from every time," he began his lecture. "In the big leagues, the pitcher has the advantage, because he knows where the ball is going but you, the batter, do not."

I could feel myself deflating.

"Hitting in batting cages is nothing like hitting a great pitcher like Bobby Feller or Warren Spahn. That's the problem with these cages. The public comes here and thinks that they can hit a first-class pitcher, because they can hit a pitching machine. Pitching machines don't have brains. Some pitchers do, though, but most are stupid."

Joe continued his batting seminar. "Doc, let me tell you something: Hitting is one of the most difficult things to do. It requires coordination, timing, physical ability, concentration, and most important, smarts. Becoming a good guesser is just as important as trying to put the fat of the bat on the ball."

I was listening to the ultimate authority on hitting, second only to Ted Williams.

"The best skill I developed for baseball was my memory. I would memorize the pitch, speed, approach of every thrown ball, and order of the pitches.

"Williams and I would study a pitcher and remember the combinations of pitches the guy was throwing. I could remember a pitcher's attack not just from the game he was playing but also from the same pitcher last week, last month, last season. Williams and I would study a pitcher's motions and his delivery, then we would step up to the plate and put it all together," the professor finished.

I was moved that he wanted to instruct me. I remembered being at a gala at which Joe and Ted Williams were asked why they were such great hitters. They blamed the pitchers. Both men agreed, an unusual occurrence to begin with, that pitchers were "stupid."

As I recall, Williams said, "Pitchers are just plain stupid."

Both icons believed that pitchers forgot what they threw you. What made DiMaggio and Williams great batters was the fact that they would remember pitcher combinations through the years well before computers could track these things and the gathering of statistics. They knew what the next pitch would be and positioned themselves in the batter's box accordingly. This was mental acuity writ large. We mortals would call it guessing, but it was so much more than that. For them, it was about educated prediction.

"Listening to you, Joe, is a real education. Few people realize just how mental hitting that ball is," I said that day at Coney Island.

"Doc, flattery will get you nowhere with me." Joe laughed. "This is my operating room, and this is where I call the shots. Now, move that right foot a little more and bring your left foot a little farther up. You want your feet to be on a parallel line. It will give you better leverage on a pitch that's coming in at over a hundred miles per hour."

I tried to comply with Joe's instructions. "Jesus Christ!" I muttered through clenched teeth as I began missing all the robot balls.

"What are you calling Him for, Doc?" asked Joe. "He ain't gonna help you in the batter's box."

I continued to miss what seemed like jinxed balls with a glowering sports icon observing.

"You see, Doc, you're not watching the ball. Your eyes should be on that ball from the second it leaves the pitcher's hand until you see it popping off the sweet part of the bat," Joe advised.

More balls eluded my bat.

"Doc, you're still not watching the ball." Joe was stern. "And . . . now . . . there goes your foot again. Move it back a little."

I was twisting like a pretzel as I followed Joe's barked commands. The batting cage attendant, who remained clueless to the identity of my batting coach, was watching from a very safe distance. He found my batting practice cheap entertainment. He probably thought I was with my grandfather.

Joe got hypercritical as I kept missing the robot balls. "Doc! Doc, you just struck out again," Joe scolded me. "You're going to embarrass me next month at that charity softball game. Do I have to get into the cage myself to show you how it's done?"

Of course, I had this in mind when I drove us to Coney Island in the first place.

More missed balls.

"This is serious business! Baseball is not a game!" Oblivious to the small and unknowing audience gathering at the fence of the batting cage, Joe yelled at me. Nobody recognized the coach who was relaying all these instructions to me from outside the cages, which was a relief.

I had always considered baseball a game, but wasn't about to contradict him. I felt as if steam was coming out of my ears.

I turned and handed the bat to the Yankee Clipper when he entered the cage. "Joe, here's the bat . . . why don't you take a few swings to show me what the hell you're talking about?" I was a little worried about Joe swinging the bat, because Joe had a pacemaker in his left chest wall, which could limit his mobility, as well as severe neck and shoulder arthritis. Swinging could disrupt the wiring.

Joe was game. He was in the box again, nostalgic and fierce at the same time. He took the bat and choked up on the handle to get better leverage and speed as the small and clueless audience began to congregate to watch a baseball miracle—the octogenarian baseball legend swinging at robot balls to the gaudy music of the Boardwalk in the light of the setting sun. As if on cue, Glenn Miller's "American Patrol" blasted through the speakers for the last at-bat for the greatest all-around athlete in history.

Joe shrank in concentration, his facial expression changed. He was back in 1941. He looked over his shoulder and said, "Okay, Doc, watch carefully, and learn how it's done!"

The motley crowd looked on with me in amazement as the Yankee Clipper hit ball after ball in a batting cage on the Boardwalk in Coney Island. This is what I had wanted to see—Joe Di back in the batter's box, slugging them out, and dropping fifty years while he was at it. Joe's swings were disciplined, beautiful, and flowing as he hit ball after ball without fail. His timing was impeccable.

As "American Patrol" blared, Joe was there in the music and in the cleanly bashed robot balls, a perfect symmetry of man, music, and machinery. I could almost see Lefty, and Ty, and Babe, and all the other Yankees there. The hushed crowd, their fingers gripping the chain link fence, witnessed the great DiMaggio's last time at bat without knowing it or having a clue of who this eighty-plus-year-old phenom really was. He only hit ten balls, but it seemed that time stood still for a while that evening.

Joe was pleased with his performance, and I suspect he was surprised as well.

"Yes, Doc, that's how it's done, and that's how you have to hit 'em next month." He was tired, winded, and visibly sore, but he was supremely happy.

I was beaming.

"Joe, that was really beautiful. Your swing is still choreographed like a dancer's move. This was a real treat."

Joe, as usual, was unimpressed by an amateur's praise. "Okay, Doc, enough of the bullshit," he said, trying to catch his breath as he handed the bat to me. "Get back in there and let's see what you've learned."

I got back into the batting cage and hit more robot balls as dusk turned to night. Marco was watching this spectacle and was grinning from ear to ear. He was moved by the scene.

This is an account of Joe's last at-bat, a part of New York history, not known to anyone except for those lucky fans who happened to be strolling on the Boardwalk that night. It was just the way he wanted it.

CHAPTER 15

Last Dinner with DiMaggio

Thursday, April 7, 1994

He raved about the Childrens hospital (J.D.M.) as his mother had a slight heart attack in the middle of the night — and he witnessed the way they take care of people in the emergency rooms.

Tuesday Dec 7, 1993

At lunch with Barry, Mario and old friend. Bernie Kamber — was one relating to past memories with Bernie and people we knew of past years. One of reasons I have not entertained doing a book.

B*efore his return to Florida,* Joe wanted to have one last dinner at Bravo Gianni's. We had just come back from Joe DiMaggio Day at Yankee Stadium. It was a difficult day for him. He was dragging, and his energy was nowhere to be found. I dropped him off at Burke's place to freshen up and rest. When I picked him up later for dinner, he seemed weaker than he had been when he was at the stadium earlier in the day. Something was terribly wrong. He slowly got into the car. This was a different Joe DiMaggio from the slugger I had seen in the Coney Island batting cage in the past. He had become an old man in a matter of weeks. I kept my observations to myself.

"Let's go, Doc," was the extent of Joe's greeting.

As I made a beeline for the restaurant, we barely talked along the way.

This was to be Joe's last dinner in New York. Joe knew he wasn't coming back. I also surmised, with more medical precision, that we might never have dinner again. We had Joe's favorite, the farfalle di Maggio, bowtie pasta in a light tomato sauce with thin-linked sweet Italian sausage, personally named by Joe and lovingly made by Gianni, as his Last Supper in New York. When Joe finished eating, he began to talk.

"You know, I've been getting a little moodier lately. I'm really thinking things over—my son, my faith," he said. "I've gotten more philosophical. I thought much less when I was younger."

Joe had been reflecting on his life. I hoped he would talk to me about what he was thinking.

"In a way, I'm more aware of my mistakes every day. I guess that's part of growing old." He looked down. "I should have been closer to my son, but I didn't have the nerve to show up at his garage one morning and tell him I loved him, whether he hated me or not."

I was glad he could talk to me about what was on his mind.

"Life is sure funny," Joe went on. "Here I am, one of the most famous men in the world, but I still feel lonely."

"I lived for the game," he went on. "The game treated me well. But where I got to, the high spot, was lonely," Joe said, lost in thought.

I had never seen him so contemplative, nor had he revealed his deepest feelings so sadly.

"Why were you lonely?" I asked him.

"Doc, I was never sure of myself in the way my father was. He knew where he came from. He knew his place in the world and where he was going."

Joe went on to explain why he felt this way. "I mean, Marilyn, Frank, and me were all working-class kids. No one taught us this fame-and-fortune racket. In our own ways, it wounded us all. But I can say that I regret nothing. Well, almost nothing."

Listening to Joe reflect on Marilyn and Sinatra reminded me that I had failed on one of my DiMaggio bucket-list items. I wanted to orchestrate a reconciliation between Joe and Frank before one of them checked out.

Frank Sinatra died in May 1998, before my last dinner with DiMaggio. I was saddened by his passing, but devastated that I failed in reuniting the two legends.

I was so moved that he cared enough about me to confide his regrets to me.

"I miss Marilyn more than I did before. I miss my son. I don't know if they missed me, but I love them anyway." He looked so sad.

"Over the years I've believed that we're not here to be loved—just respected. I had plenty of respect, but I realize that respect often isn't enough."

There was nothing I could say or do to fill the gap he felt. Anything I said wouldn't have mattered.

"Doc, we should have reached out to help each other. Marilyn, Frank, and I tried to stand on our own. We didn't do too well. . . ."

I wanted to pull him out of his remorseful state, so I reminded him how much he had done for his family.

"But, Joe, look at the difference you made for your son's two daughters. What kind of life would they have had if you and your son didn't come along? Give Joe Jr. some credit for being brave enough to want to take care of them in the first place. He had more balls than he was ever given credit. This hardly qualifies him as a failure in my eyes. They are living rich, full lives. Their own kids, your great-grandchildren, go to the best schools, travel everywhere, want for nothing. It all started with Joe Jr.'s decision to be their parent." I was being protective of Joe's son, who always seemed to get the bad rap.

"You're right, Doc. I've worked hard to give my family a better life. I work as hard as I do now so that they will be secure for the rest of their lives. I've succeeded. I feel as if I'm done here."

Joe still seemed to be wrestling with some sort of lack in his life.

"Not much left to do," he added, but he didn't seem convinced.

Something was missing, and it was the bottom of the ninth inning, full count and two outs, and no more batters up. It was too late in the ballgame to fill the gap.

"Look, Doc, I want to talk to you about something."

"Okay," I said. I did not know what to expect.

"I want to have a really big send-off."

"What are you talking about?" I did not want to have this conversation.

"You know what I'm talking about, Doc," Joe said sadly. "I want something in St. Patrick's Cathedral—a big good-bye in New York, not in Florida or California."

I looked down and said, "Whatever you want, Joe. Whatever you want."

We left the restaurant in a somber state. We had nearly reached my parked car when Joe turned to me and asked, "Do you mind if we drive around town for a while before you drop me off at Burke's place?"

It hurt to see him so vulnerable.

"Sure, Joe, no problem." I'd do anything he asked.

Once inside, Joe rifled through the car and found Ella Fitzgerald's CD *Embraceable You*. He popped it into the player and was soon lost in the past, just as he had been in the Coney Island batting cage.

When *Embraceable You* began to play, Joe said, "That was our song—Marilyn and me."

I didn't say a word.

When the song ended, Joe straightened up in his seat and gave me my orders. "Let's go over to the West Side, my old stomping grounds. Go through the park at Sixty-sixth Street."

I took him where he wanted to go.

"Make a left here," Joe directed me. "Now go three blocks."

Joe pointed out a building to me. "That's the Mayflower Hotel. I used to live there when things were simple. Lefty Gomez stayed there, too. New York was a different place then. I spent many nights here before a big game, worrying about the next day and how I was going to help the team. I got an ulcer because of all of the stress, coffee, and cigarettes."

I gazed up at the hotel.

"It was simple, but comfortable, and home for me," Joe remarked as we passed. "Now, make a right turn. Head toward West End Avenue."

As I drove, I noticed that Joe was weakening. His voice was strained, and he held his stomach.

"Doc, I'm starting to feel funny," Joe complained. "I have this pain in my stomach. Maybe it's gas."

"Do you want me to get you a drink?" I was concerned. I knew it wasn't gas.

"No thanks, Doc, it will probably pass. Now make a right on West End Avenue and go ten blocks."

Joe sat up more firmly, his eyes staring straight ahead.

"There it is. I lived here with Marilyn for a while, right here in that building. I had so many good times here—leaving to go to the stadium, meeting Lefty Gomez on that corner. We would either hail a cab here or take the subway to the stadium," Joe reminisced.

I tried to imagine a time when star ballplayers went to the stadium by subway.

"No one could make me laugh more than Lefty."

Joe's smile turned to a grimace. His frame grew rigid.

"Doc, can you stop here? Please," Joe asked in a genuine panic.

I pulled over on the southwest corner of West 90th Street and Co-lumbus Avenue. Joe bailed out very slowly from the passenger side.

"Doc, I don't know what's wrong." Joe staggered to lean on the hood. "The pain is terrible."

I got out of the car and ran to steady Joe. He seemed light and frail. I had never seen him this way. Joe was old and sick, and it happened really fast.

"Doc, can you hold me up a minute while I catch my breath?" Joe was very rattled.

"Joe, don't move," I pleaded with him.

I didn't have to ask. Joe wasn't going anywhere. He was in really bad shape.

"Doc, in all my life I never felt so much pain, never like this."

Joe was in agony. He was like a frightened, little boy.

"Joe, I'm taking you to the hospital," I insisted. "We have the best hospital . . ."

Joe cut me off.

"No. No, you're not. Get me back to Burke's, so I can rest," Joe commanded. His eyes were rolling in his head.

"C'mon, you stubborn son of a bitch," I thought, "Pass out, so I can take you to the hospital."

Joe rallied. He would not pass out and would not be saved.

"Doc, take me back to the apartment," he repeated. "I am not going to a New York hospital."

I knew he would not budge from what he wanted. Against my better judgment, I helped Joe back into the car. I was hoping he would pass out in the car, but that wasn't going to happen. After I bundled him upstairs at the apartment, I removed all of his clothes except his socks, shoes, and a robe, and sat him down in a reclining chair.

I tried to sell Joe on the world-class care at New York Hospital, but Joe would die as he lived—stubbornly.

"No New York Hospital," Joe continued to insist. "Get me back to my Florida guys—my Florida hospital."

The Florida hospital, as good as it was, was a children's hospital.

"I want to check you into the best hospital in New York," I protested.

Joe pretended to be strong, but he wasn't fooling me.

"Doc, I was always the toughest out when I was playing ball. Do you think I'm going to give in to pain?" Joe asked.

"Yeah, Doc, I'm going home to Florida tomorrow, so don't even think of getting me into one of your fancy friends' hospitals!"

I hoped I could change his mind, but that wasn't going to happen. Joe was determined to head to Florida and seal his fate. I didn't have to see medical charts or discuss what was wrong with him. I knew it was the end.

I was shaken to the core and spent a fretful night. The following morning, I showed up to take Joe to La Guardia.

We slowly made our way into the terminal. He was in so much pain that it took great effort for Joe to walk. His crisp, professional gait was gone. I noticed the entire world racing past us and grew anxious about the approaching departure time.

"Joe, I'm going to get you a wheelchair," I said.

"Oh, no, you're not. I never want to be seen in public using a wheelchair," Joe stated as he grimaced in pain. "I don't care if it takes me half an hour to get to the plane."

I didn't have the heart to argue with him.

Joe was taking twenty steps, then stopping to rest. He looked around for an excuse to stop longer. Surrounded by the fast-moving crowd that parted around us, Joe pointed off to the side.

"There's a coffee shop, Doc. Let's stop for a quick cup of coffee."

As we found a booth, five or six octogenarians camped out at a nearby table noticed us. Two of the women recognized Joe and did not hesitate to head our way. At this point, Joe was straining even to sit, but his instinct was keen enough to sense trouble coming.

"Doc, don't leave . . . I'm going to have company," Joe said through gritted teeth.

One of the cheerful senior travelers piped up, "Mr. DiMaggio, you were my hero and my father's hero as well."

Joe scowled. "You are invading my privacy. Can't you see that I am having a quiet bite to eat?" He practically barked, "Leave me alone!"

At that, the women vanished, embarrassed and ashamed that they had disturbed the great Joe DiMaggio.

"Joe, weren't you a little rough on that lady?" I asked in shock. He was in pain, but he never behaved this way with fans.

He simmered down and decided to try to make amends for his beastly behavior.

"Doc, I feel so bad. Maybe I was a little tough on them," the Clipper admitted.

As I went to get Joe a glass of orange juice, Joe staggered to his feet and hobbled over to the table of shocked elderly women. I turned back before getting the juice to oversee the situation. Joe produced a box of his favorite treasures—his World Series rings.

"Ladies, see this box of rings?" he asked. "These are replicas of my World Series rings. Mr. Steinbrenner gave them to me at Joe DiMaggio Day at the stadium. My originals were all stolen."

The women regarded the rings with awe.

Joe went on, pointing to his left hand, "This ring is my rookie year 1936 World Series ring. It didn't get stolen, because I never took it off." Joe spoke with warmth and pride.

"All the writing is worn off now, but every time I look down at my finger I know what it says anyway . . . World Series Champions!" Joe beamed.

"Phil Rizzuto," Joe continued, "he played shortstop on my team, presented these rings to me at the stadium. I'm not going to keep them, though. They are for my great-granddaughter Vanassa."

Then Joe turned to me.

"Doc, mind taking a picture of me with these fine people?"

The women seemed stunned by the reversal of Joe's humor.

"It was really nice meeting you ladies. . . . Have a safe flight." Joe paused, then went on, "I apologize for being—abrupt."

After the ladies left, Joe said in a quiet voice, "Doc, you gotta steady me, because I'm having a hard time walking and standing."

We practically crept to the departure gate. Sam McCrann, the airline's VIP attendant, who knew Joe well, was waiting. She looked concerned as she watched our approach.

"Sam, can we board before anyone else?" I asked.

By this point, Joe's endurance was down to ten feet. Sam let me breach airport security to help Joe from the gate to the plane.

As we hobbled down the ramp, Joe draped himself on me.

"Well, Doc," Joe said, "I don't know if there will be a next time I am back in New York."

The crew allowed me to board with him, get him settled into his first-class seat, and have a quiet last moment alone with Joe.

When I snapped his seatbelt, Joe pleaded, "Doc, don't leave. Please stay a little longer."

General boarding had begun, and I was blocking the aisle.

Joe looked up at me, and said, "Doc, I just wanna let you know that I'm always going to remember the good times we had here. I hope to make it back," he said with forced optimism.

I nodded.

"Doc, you've always been one of my best friends. You never asked for anything. I want you to know how much I appreciate all the time you've spent with me over the years in New York. You have helped bring back some of the good feelings I have for this town and some great memories."

Joe was sinking in his seat. At a loss for words, I saluted. Joe grinned and returned his trademark salute from his seat. That said it all. Nothing else was needed.

Joe's next few months were spent in Florida. Morris Engelberg put Joe under quarantine in his final months. He wanted to protect Joe's privacy and to keep the media away.

I honored Joe's privacy in his dying days, even after his granddaughter Paula asked me to visit him at his home overlooking the Intracoastal Waterway. I could not bring myself to see my friend clinging to life, no longer the vibrant person I had grown to love and respect. I did break the quarantine once.

About three weeks before he died, I called Joe. I heard the voice of a cancer-ravaged man speaking through damaged lungs.

The conversation was almost one-sided, because I was awkward speaking to my dying friend.

"Doc, I love you," Joe said in a frail, raspy voice that did not resemble the voice I knew.

He caught me off guard, and I couldn't respond.

"I love you," Joe repeated.

Still too overcome to respond, I felt that Joe knew the affection was mutual. All of those memories of going places with Joe, the restaurants, the Yankee games, the cups of coffee, walking around the city, flashed before my eyes.

"I love you, too, Joe," was all that I managed to say. But that was enough and the end of a chapter in both of our lives. No better words could have been exchanged between two people as the sun began to set on this relationship.

———

I NEEDED TO drive around the city on the rainy night of March 7th. I knew Joe was clinging to life and felt his presence. My thoughts told him to let go and transition into his next world. It was comforting to me in a strange way. We were both at peace with each other, and nothing else could be done.

I went to sleep that night knowing that Joe would be gone when I woke up. I learned about Joe's death on 1010 WINS. I turned off the radio and went directly to the office at the Hospital for Special Surgery. It was going to be like any other Tuesday morning, the way Joe would have wanted it.

Afterword:
A Simple Memorial for an
Unpretentious Man

I remembered Joe's words to me about the sendoff he wanted in New York. A small family funeral took place in San Francisco, where he grew up. Joe always said that the fifteen years he spent with the New York Yankees were the best, and he loved being in New York City during the last ten years of his life. He had come full circle. I was contemplating how to proceed, when Morris Engelberg called. He asked me to plan the New York memorial service with Mario Faustini. Had I not promised Joe that I was going to give him the big sendoff he wanted, I would have flat out said no to organizing his memorial service.

Cardinal O'Connor requested that I meet with him to discuss the memorial service and lay out the rules of the day being planned. All I could remember at that moment was Joe's meeting with Archbishop Fulton Sheen in the same room to receive his judgment for Marilyn. There was no way I was going to storm out. O'Connor was gracious and impressive. During Joe's last six months, he would call me in the office for updates on Joe's condition. The man cared.

I asked Rudy Giuliani to give a eulogy at Joe's memorial service.

Joe had tremendous respect and affection for Rudy. He would have been thrilled to know that Rudy was going to be there. I had also proposed Henry Kissinger as a speaker, but Cardinal O'Connor felt Dr. Kissinger was too controversial. Though Henry would have been at the top of Joe's list, I couldn't fight with the Cardinal. It was his cathedral.

I wanted to give Joe the kind of sendoff he would have wanted— first class for a first-class guy. It had to be at St. Patrick's Cathedral with John Cardinal O'Connor officiating. I wanted it to be a lovefest, a gathering of the famous, the wealthy, the powerful, and most important, his devoted fans. Phil Rizzuto, Yogi Berra, George Steinbrenner, Bobby Brown, Dr. Henry Kissinger, Woody Allen, Ken Auletta, Richard Reeves, Dom DiMaggio, Brian Cashman, Jean Doumanian, Mayor Rudolph Giuliani, Paul Simon, Michael Bolton, Tim McCarver, E. L. Doctorow, Joe Piscopo, Tim Russert, Bryant Gumbel, Bob Costas, and a couple hundred grateful Brooklyn kids from Xaverian High School were among the people there to celebrate Joe's life.

Dr. Bobby Brown, a third baseman for the Yankees who played with Joe, spoke at the service. In describing Joe DiMaggio, he said to the overflow crowd, "I would suggest that rarely was there ever seen such consummate skill, grace, power, speed, and dignity in one person.

"I know Joe is in heaven," Brown continued. "I suspect there's a committee up there right now trying to determine when to retire his number."

At the end of the service, at Cardinal O'Connor's request, the audience stood in a sustained ovation to Joe's memory.

The service started a weekend that culminated with the unveiling of a plaque to the Yankee Clipper at Yankee Stadium. George Steinbrenner did not get his statue.

Acknowledgments

Our *thanks to:*
Diane Reverand for her excellent executive skills and insights, which helped to bring bring the New York DiMaggio to life and to keep my brother and me in line.

Bob Bender, our editor, for his stewardship, patience, and recognition of the merit and importance of this book.

Johanna Li for her constant attention to detail and keeping the progress of the book on track.

Cat Boyd, our publicist at Simon & Schuster, for helping us get the word out.

Our publisher at Simon & Schuster, Jonathan Karp, who has established and maintained Simon & Schuster as the "Joe DiMaggio" of publishing houses.

The Simon & Schuster art director, Jackie Seow, who selected a fabulous picture of Joe DiMaggio, which captures his intensity and integrity, for the cover of this book.

David Vigliano, our agent, for understanding the complexity of such a project and connecting us with the absolute best people to work with.

"Super" Steve Carlis and Hank Norman from 2Market Media for their relentless energy in bringing the DiMaggio project to the pinnacle.

Brad Hess, always a pro, for his work on the diary facsimiles and the photo insert.

Janine Bruno, Alicia Milano, Nick Luke, Liz Peraj, Javier Solis, Lucia Borgognone, Chris "Fiiyah" Lallman, Juan Romero, Kidus (KB) Gebrekidan, Danny Vera, and Kevin Harrison for keeping me on focus and at the same time managing the Joe DiMaggio Foot and Ankle Center at the Hospital for Special Surgery. They made sure that we didn't miss a beat or a deadline by keeping me on time.

Leila Logan for organizing, managing, and cataloging the volumes of DiMaggio papers over the course of the project.

Benita Somerfield for her support, assistance, interest, tenacity, and superb advice about how to best bring DiMaggio's New York to life.

Marco Solis Sr. for being there the whole time during Joe's magnificent last nine years in New York City and helping us get around from place to place where all the best *Dinner with DiMaggio* adventures happened.

Rupert Murdoch and Mort Zuckerman for giving me the opportunity to become a health columnist at both the *New York Post* and the *New York Daily News*.

Arianna Huffington for showing the empowered women of the country to really "Thrive" and make a difference and not take any nonsense from anyone.

Charlie Finch for his friendship, loyalty, and sterling advice over the years.

Dr. Keith Ablow for his endless spot-on advice, mental support, and "Berlin Wall" friendship.

Dr. Salvatore "The Hammer" Ferrera, my first coach and mentor, who stuck it out with me through thick and thin and urged me to start and finish this project.

Richard Ben Cramer, Pulitzer Prize–winning journalist, who had strongly suggested that we write a memoir about Joe's life in New York, the fun we had, and how important the dinner table was to him.

Sincere thanks to Robert Zerilli at Veniero's pastry shop in Manhattan for providing cookies to Joe Di and me during his many stays in New York.

Douglas Durst; Hamilton "Tony" James; Henry Kravis; Rupert Murdoch; Fay Vincent; William Rudin; Matthew Mallow, Esq.; Paul Tanico; Peter Sloane; Ed Ricci; Mary Lupo; Barbara Chait; Joel Ehrenkranz; Vincent Tese, Esq.; Sanford Ehrenkranz; Jonathan "Jody" Durst; Henry Kissinger; Rudolph Giuliani; Les Goodstein; Jean Doumanian; Terry O'Toole; Mark Filipski; Ivan Seidenberg; Declan Kelly; Bradford Evans; Douglas and Judi Krupp; James and Linda Robinson; Sidney and Carol Kimmel; and Richard Harriton for supporting the research and clinical programs dedicated to non-surgical treatment education at Yale School of Public Health and the Non-surgical Foot and Ankle Service at Hospital for Special Surgery.

David Spivak, Esq; William Kahn, Esq.; and Arthur Leder, CPA for their sterling advice and guidance over the years.

All the kids from the "stoop" growing up: Hope Glaser; Steven Sutera; Frank Iati; Robert Iati; Frankie Gentile; Vincent Campisi; Donnie Clementi; Jane Franco; Paul Fontana; Francis Apicella; Michael Mattia; Anthony Sclafani; Vincent Balzano; Patty Bartiromo; Jerry Ferris; Arthur Fusco, MD; Sal Cigna, DDS; John Carli, DDS; Fran Dorsa; and the many more kids from the hood and St. Athanasius Elementary School in Brooklyn.

Joan and Sanford Weill and Jessica and Natan Bibliowicz for all they have done for the Weill Cornell Medical College.

My colleagues at the Hospital for Special Surgery: Dr. Andrew Weiland, surgeon-in chief emeritus, and Dr. Steven O'Brien for sponsoring and endorsing my acceptance into the Hospital for Special Surgery.

Marc Neikrug for his unwavering support, friendship, and love over the past twenty-one years.

Francis Ford Coppola for his ultimate class, elegance, and brilliance, and the numerous contributions he has made to the cultural fabric of the world.

Charlie Rose for always and continuing to be "the best of the best."

Jack Kennedy Schlossberg who represents the great future of America.

Joanna Hess for helping the authors enlist the sanction and support of Mr. Coppola.

Paul Simon for helping me to find where Joe DiMaggio went.

Jason Binn for connecting me with so many good people.

Dr. Thomas Sculco and Dr. David Helfet for supporting the development of the Non-surgical Foot and Ankle Service and the Joe DiMaggio Sports Medicine Foot and Ankle Center at the Hospital for Special Surgery.

The love, support, and friendship of Jim Ryan and Richard Kearns—my "big brothers" in this crazy world.

The loving memory of friendship and support of Phil Ramone, Dr. Horace "Duke" DeCotiis, Warner LeRoy, Dr. Dominick DiMaio, Norman Brokaw, Dr. L Jay Oliva, Dr. Arthur Upton, Dr. Eric Mood, Dr. Bruce Frankel, Dr. Nathaniel Shafer, Dr. Louis Shure, Dr. Nick Melucci, and Pat Auletta.

Drs. Brian Halpern and Doug Seckendorf for their loyalty, friendship, collegiality, and dedication to excellent nonsurgical musculoskeletal patient care at the Hospital for Special Surgery.

Neil Young, Steven Tyler, Charles Goldstuck, Don Ienner, Sir Howard Stringer, Brian Dubin, Marsha Vlasic, and Elliot Roberts for their friendship, support, and creative brilliance.

Tony Robbins for his dedication to excellence and never settling for second best and inspiring an army of winners around the world.

All my colleagues at the Hospital for Special Surgery, Weill Cornell Medical Center, the New York College of Podiatric Medicine, Memorial Sloan Kettering, The Rockefeller University and Lenox Hill Hospital, with special thanks to those listed here: David Blumenthal,

MD; Jeffrey Borer, MD; Paul Greengard, PhD; Frank Cammisa, MD; Irwin Redlener, MD; Lawrence Yannuzzi, MD; Daniel Goldin, MD; Gil Weitzman, MD; Mark Pasmantier, MD; Marcus Loo, MD; Eugenie Tartell, DC; Steven Lamm, MD; Max Scheer, MD; Stuart Orsher, MD; Josh Dines, MD; David Dines, MD; Bryan Kelly, MD; David Altchek, MD; Todd Albert, MD; Greg Lutz, MD; Chris Lutz, MD; David Silverman, MD; Paul Kligfield, MD; Larry Rosenthal, DDS; Douglas Seckendorf, DC; Lawrence Inra, MD; Hooman Yaghoobzadeh, MD; Catherine Hart, MD; Phyllis August, MD; Robert Klein, MD; Thomas Caputo, MD; Federico Girardi, MD; Wayne Isom, MD; Karl Krieger, MD; Len Girardi, MD; Harvey Klein, MD; Sergio Schwartzman, MD; Steve Corwin, MD; Richard Bockman, MD, PhD; Dexter Sun, MD, PhD; Dean Lorich, MD; Louis Shapiro; Stacey Malakoff; Louis Levine; Michael Trepal, DPM; Kevin Jules, DPM; Jonathan Haber, DPM; Keith Springer, DPM (deceased); Ronald Soave, DPM; Ron Guberman, DPM; Jeffrey Borer, MD; Christopher DiGiovanni, MD; Robert Marx, MD; Vijay Vad, MD; James Kinderknecht, MD; Struan Coleman, MD; Russell Warren, MD; Chit Ranawat, MD; Anil Ranawat, MD; Amar Ranawat, MD; Helene Pavlov, MD; Thomas DeLauro, DPM; Martha Cortes, DDS; Richard Crowley; Jason Deblinger, DMD; Mike Apa, DDS; Gideon Panter, MD; Gary Goldman, MD; Steven Comite, MD; Richard Granstein, MD; Keith Ablow, MD; Mehmet Oz, MD; Michael DeBakey, MD (deceased); Bruce Moskowitz, MD; David Agus, MD; Glenn Gastwirth, DPM; Ralph Gibson, MD; Elizabeth Hynes, RN; John Doolan, DPM; Michael Brunetti, DPM; Philip Lupo, DPM; Salvatore Barone, DPM; Ron Safko, DC; Richard Ash, MD; Allan Gibofsky, MD, JD; Howard Hillstrom, PhD; Rache Simmons, MD; Tim Dutta, MD; Ted Tyberg, MD; Alberto Acosta, MD, PhD; Julianne Imperato-McGinley, MD; Pasquale Scotti, MD; Raymond Pastore, MD; Keith Gurnick, DPM; Raymond Mollica, DPM; Ross Taubman, DPM; John Pace, DPM; Frank Spinosa, DPM; Ron Adler, MD, PhD; Andrew Sciarrino, DPM; Christopher Murphy,

DPM; Mary Chapman Kline, DPM; Paul Pellicci, MD; Jonathan Deland, MD; Joseph Feinberg, MD; John Hunter, MD; Jon Turk, MD; David Hidalgo, MD; Anthony LaBruna, MD; William Kuhel, MD; Frank Petito, MD; Jay Adlersberg, MD; Paul Miskovitz, MD; Angie Eng, MD; David Wolf, MD; George Ellis, MD; Mazen Kamen, MD; Jason Kendler, MD; Henry Jarecki, MD; Beth Shubin-Stein, MD; Daniel Greene, MD; Roger Widmann, MD; Shevaun Doyle, MD; Randi Silver, PhD; Thomas Nash, MD; Riley Williams, MD; Daniel Libby, MD; Joseph Cooke, MD; Paul Cooke, MD; Bruce Lerman, MD; Nancy Rosen, DDS; Kevin Holcomb, MD; Fabrizio Michelassi, MD; Frank Chervenak, MD; Rahul Sharma, MD; Jordan Josephson, MD; Bassem Masri, MD; Zev Rosenwaks, MD; Orli Etingin, MD; Holly Andersen, MD; Jose Baselga, MD; Peter Scardino, MD; Peter Moley, MD; Stephen Fealy, MD; S. Robert Rozbruch, MD; Austin Fragomen, MD; John Carrino, MD; Robert Hotchkiss, MD; Michelle Carlson, MD; Steven Greenstein, MD; Oz Garcia; Lloyd Hoffman, MD; Marc Lemchen, DDS; Dan Giordano, PT; Robin Reiter, DPT; Keith Pyne; John Sitaras, Andrew Sama, MD; Nicholas Sama, MD; Matthew Pode, R-PA; Keith Williamson, R-PA; Jeremy Rinzler, R-PA; Richard Lazzaro, MD; Sandra Belmont, MD; Douglas Lazzaro, MD; E. Clifford Lazzaro, MD; Michael M. Martuscello, MD; Michael Acocella, RPT; Dan Girodano, DPT; Sherry Backus, DPT; Elliott Hershman, MD; Gregory Harmon, MD; Bruce Blau, DDS; Erin Zobel; Lawrence Gulotta, MD; Geoffrey Westrich, MD; Joan Kent, MD; Kenan Ordu; Antonio Gotto, MD; Lois Horovitz, RN; and last but not least, Louis Aronne, MD.

Ken Auletta, Dick Auletta, and Amanda "Binky" Urban for their guidance and support over the years.

David and Michael Lewittes, my Jewish brothers.

Bonnie Fuller for her wisdom and strength.

Index